CW01019545

UNDERSTANDING HUMAN GOODS

UNDERSTANDING HUMAN GOODS

A Theory of Ethics

T. D. J. Chappell

TEACHING UNIT
ST. ANN'S HOSPICE

What a piece of work is a man! How noble in reason! how infinite in faculty! in form, in moving, how express and admirable! in action, how like an angel! in apprehension, how like a god! the beauty of the world! the paragon of animals!

I had noticed once again how all thought among us is frozen into 'something other than human life'.

Edinburgh University Press

© T. D. J. Chappell, 1998

Edinburgh University Press
22 George Square, Edinburgh

Typeset in Monotype Ehrhardt
by Intype London Ltd, and
printed and bound in Great Britain by
the University Press, Cambridge

A CIP record for this book is available from the British Library

ISBN 0 7486 1029 4 (hardback)
ISBN 0 7486 1028 6 (paperback)

The right of T. D. J. Chappell
to be identified as author of this work
has been asserted in accordance with
the Copyright Designs and Patents Act 1988.

CONTENTS

PREFACE AND ACKNOWLEDGEMENTS

I began writing this book in earnest in 1995, but many of the ideas in it originated much earlier than that – some of them five or more years earlier. I am grateful to a long line of teachers, students and colleagues, in Edinburgh, Oxford, Norwich and Manchester, who have criticised and commented on my explorations. For their help and encouragement, I wish to thank Graham Bird, Rüdiger Bittner, David Charles, Willie Charlton, Stephen Clark, Christopher Coope, John Cottingham, Roger Crisp, Barry Dainton, Nicholas Denyer, Nick Everitt, John Finnis, Jerry Goodenough, Edward Harcourt, John Harris, Paul Helm, Martin Hollis, Brad Hooker, David Houghton, Michael Inwood, Jennifer Jackson, John Lucas, Cynthia and Graham Macdonald, Geoffrey Madell, Christopher Martin, Hugh Mellor, Tim Mulgan, David Oderberg, Eric Olson, Timothy O'Hagan, Derek Parfit, Stephen Priest, Hayden Ramsay, Rupert Read, Angus Ross, Dory Scaltsas, Roger Squires, Roger Teichmann, Sam Wells, David Wiggins, and Jo Wolff. Many of the ideas I advance here have been tried out, in more or less prototype versions, on the following unsuspecting audiences, for whose patience, interest and obstinate good sense I am also grateful: The Moral Sciences Club, Cambridge; The Staff/Postgraduate Discussion Group, Edinburgh; The Stapledon Society, Liverpool; The Philosophy of Religion Seminar, King's College, London; The Wheatsheaf Philosophical Society, Oxford; The Wolfson Philosophical Society, Oxford; the Graduate Seminar of the Centre for Social Ethics and Policy, Manchester University; and The Philosophy Club, Reading University. I thank the Editors of *The Philosophical Quarterly*, *The Proceedings of the Aristotelian Society*, and *Religious Studies*, for permission to reproduce (in a slightly altered form) material originally published in those journals.

I've enjoyed the latter stages (at any rate) of writing this book so much that it seems a pity now to stop. Perhaps the reader thinks I shouldn't have stopped yet. I certainly admit I haven't been able to correct every fault I have found, and no doubt there are plenty I haven't found.

The second epigraph on the title page comes from Yeats's notes, in his *Collected Poems*, on his own poem 'The Dolls'.

I thank my daughters Miriam and Imogen, and my wife Claudia, for the narrative we share. This book is dedicated, with love and admiration, to Claudia.

TDJC
Ramsbottom, Lancashire
February 1998

A SUMMARY OF THE ARGUMENT

Chapter 1 identifies three foundational questions for ethics, and attempts to answer them: (1.1) about *motivation* (what is the point(s) of acting?); (1.2) about *the good* (what is the good(s)?); and (1.3) about our *dispositions* (what are the virtues?). In each case I argue against monism and nihilism, and in favour of pluralism. I indicate some connections between these three kinds of pluralism (1.4), and argue for the 'Working Hypothesis' that there is a deep connection between the theories of motivation and of justification.

In chapter 2, I apply this Working Hypothesis by suggesting that we can arrive at a taxonomy of the goods by analysis of the different motivation-types that agents display in action (2.1). Such a taxonomy is offered (2.2), and applied to solve problems about egoism (2.3), objectivity (2.4), and the existential status of goods (2.5).

The plurality of goods poses the Problem of Reconciliation (1.1, 2.6) – the problem of how, if the goods are plural, they can be reconciled within a single life. This could even be called the problem for first-order moral theory. Once set up, it is central to the rest of the book.

There are two parts to my answer to the Problem of Reconciliation. In chapter 3, I give the first part: the Threefold Schema. This is the schema of possible practical attitudes to goods which says that, for any good, it is possible (1) to promote or (2) to respect or (3) to violate that good; and that to promote or respect a good is always *per se* at least permissible, while to violate any good is always *per se* impermissible. Hence I defend two controversial claims. First, at least some actions must be permissible and good but not obligatory, so that there is supererogation. Second, at least some non-evaluatively defined action-types must be impermissible no matter what, so that there are material moral absolutes.

The Threefold Schema gives the outline of a deontological framework such that we can see how it might be filled in. Nonetheless, as it stands, it underdetermines any agent's practical decisions. One could live all sorts of lives that would accord with any given substantive interpretation of the Threefold Schema. Yet not all of them would be equally rational. Is there no more to say about what makes an agent's choices rational or otherwise? I argue that there is. The more that I say is the second part of my response to the Problem of Reconciliation.

I approach this by considering the issue of personal identity. In chapter 4 I argue for a twin-track approach to that topic: beside the sense of 'personal identity' in which personal identity is a traditional problem in the philosophy of mind, there is a sense of the phrase (more often employed outside than within technical philosophy) in which one's (personal) identity means roughly one's sense of who one is. I argue that both senses of personal identity yield crucial notions for ethics. The ethical importance of personal identity strictly so called correlates with the deontological requirements of the Threefold Schema, inasmuch as it is strict biological human identity that determines the bounds of the ethically basic notions of agency, responsibility, and moral significance. Personal identity in the sense of integrity correlates with the superstructure of ethics – the part of the subject that has to do with what goes on *within* the constraints of the Threefold Schema. The considerations that can make it rational for an agent to choose one way rather than another, even when the Schema itself places no rational constraints upon choice, concern the agent's continuing project of seeking *narrative integrity over time* – their project of finding or creating their own personal identity in the second sense identified above. (To put it another way: where agent-neutral practical reasons run out, agent-relative practical reasons come in.) I defend these views from Parfitian reductionism, and argue against the personist view that persons (in the sense that matters for ethics) are not the same thing as human individuals.

In chapter 5 I argue that the narrative conceptions of persons, of the good, and of ethical rationality have major advantages over maximising ethical rationality. The view that rationality always requires us to maximise the good (maximalism), together with the view of the self which is natural for the maximalist, entails a List Conception of the good. Criticism shows that this List Conception is false, and that we should replace it with a Narrative Conception of the good which goes closely with our two other Narrative Conceptions, of rationality and of personhood. This facilitates an answer to the Problem of Reconciliation.

In chapter 6 these three Narrative Conceptions are further developed by exposing each to objections. These lead me to consider the problem of free will, and to two Conclusions.

The things we might say are good in themselves are those which are sought in their own right even when they are found alone, such as thought and sight and certain pleasures and honours. Even though we sometimes pursue these things for the sake of something else, nonetheless we would say that they are good in themselves. Or is nothing good in itself, except for the Platonic Universal of the Good? That claim makes the Form pointless [since the Form was posited to explain why other things *were* good in themselves]. If on the other hand such things [as thought and sight and the others listed above] are among the things that are good in themselves, then [if Platonism is right] one and the same sense of 'good' ought to be clearly applicable to all of them – just as the same sense of 'whiteness' applies both to snow and to face-powder. But the senses of 'good' in which, e.g., honour and wisdom and pleasure can be considered good are all different. So there is no single Platonic Universal to which a sense of 'good' common to all such cases could correspond.

Aristotle, Nicomachean Ethics 1096b21–25

In truth, however, instrumental accounts of rationality are not silent about the rationality of goals . . . they pretend silence, where they in fact assume some variant of the Psychological Unity of Mankind. By relying, for instance, on some vacuous universal desire to attain happiness or maximise utility, they can credit the agent with a rational goal, without actually saying so. A presumption is thus created that mere desire for an end counts as a reason for pursuing the end.

Martin Hollis, Models of Man, p. 99

1

———— • ————

THREE FOUNDATIONAL QUESTIONS FOR ETHICS

1.1 WHAT IS THE POINT OF ACTING?

One way of beginning ethics is to ask:[1] 'What is the point of acting?'

One sort of diehard optimist – call him the Hedonist – replies that the point of acting is pleasure. Another sort of diehard optimist – call him the Calvinist – replies that the point of acting is (to borrow from the *Westminster Shorter Catechism*) 'to praise God and glorify him for ever'.

One sort of diehard pessimist – call him the Existentialist – replies that there is no answer to the question, because there isn't any point in acting. Since we all die in the end (or perhaps for some other reason), everything we do is vain in the end. In Sartre's famous phrase, 'Man is a useless passion'.[2]

Perhaps we are repelled by both alternatives – by what I'll call *monism about motivation* (Calvinist or Hedonist or otherwise), and by what I'll call *nihilism* about motivation (Existentialist or otherwise). If so, a third sort of reply to our question is possible: neither monism nor nihilism about motivation, but *pluralism*.

The pluralist says that both the monist and the nihilist are missing something. Their answers to our question share with the question itself a dubious presupposition: that what we ought to be looking for is something called *the* point of acting which, if we fail to find, we must conclude that there is *no* point in acting. But why shouldn't there be lots of different actions with lots of different points?

If there are, then obviously the denial of monism about motivation need not entail nihilism about motivation. We can agree with the nihilist about motivation that we should deny monism. That won't commit us to being nihilists. We can be pluralists instead.

After all (the pluralist continues), it's obvious that there are lots of different points of action. When I brush my teeth I have dental hygiene in mind. When I comb my hair I have spruceness of appearance in mind. Spruceness of appearance and dental hygiene are genuine points of action. So nihilism about motivation is false, and either monism or pluralism is true. But spruceness of appearance is a different point of action from dental hygiene. So monism about motivation is false, and pluralism true.

If this simple argument were all we needed to settle the issue between monism, pluralism and nihilism about motivation, the issue would be rather minor and uninteresting. But there is more to the question than this. As monists and nihilists will insist, we need to know why such things as spruceness and dental hygiene should themselves be worth pursuit. Even if these things are 'genuine points of action', it doesn't follow that there is no interesting question about why they are points of action. Aren't there any further or deeper ends which are served by doing actions with such boring and banal points as these? If pluralists answer Yes, monists will suggest that the kind of further or deeper points which the pluralists have in mind will be ones which display a clear tendency to converge upon – ultimately – a single point. If on the other hand the pluralist answers No, that answer will bring a sardonic smile to the face of the nihilist, who may then rhetorically ask what price the pointfulness of action comes at in a world where there is no *deeper* point to any action than the dowdy and trivial sort of point that cleaning one's teeth or brushing one's hair has.

None of the three positions about motivation which I am considering – nihilism, monism, pluralism – can be refuted straight off. No intelligent form of motivational monism or nihilism is logically obliged absurdly to deny the obvious fact that our ordinary actions have immediate points which differ from case to case. What intelligent monism and nihilism deny is that these obvious immediate points of action correspond to a plurality of ultimate points of action. The monist denies this because he/she denies that there is more than one such ultimate point of action. The nihilist denies it because he/she denies that there is even one such ultimate point.

So when monism and nihilism are made more precise and more intelligent positions than they might at first have appeared to be, we still need to ask what good reasons there might be for preferring any one of our three positions – nihilism, monism, pluralism – over the other two.

Nihilism can be dismissed from consideration first. This isn't because nihilism is quickly or easily refutable. It is because we do not need even to try to refute nihilism unless we have already tried the other two options, and found both unworkable. Nihilism is a defeatist position, a position for those who have given up trying to find any plausible positive account of the point or points of action.[3] That isn't our predicament (not yet, anyway). Before settling for nihilism, we ought to give the other two options about motivation a run for their money. So how are we to choose between monism and pluralism?

Two thoroughly bad arguments for monism and against pluralism are often attributed to Aristotle.[4] Consider first the opening lines of Aristotle's *Nicomachean Ethics* (1094a 1–2):[5]

'Every sort of technical skill and systematic inquiry, and likewise every action and every deliberate choice, appears to aim at some good. This is why people have fittingly described the good as that at which everything aims.'

Here, apparently, Aristotle moves from the premiss that everything we undertake must have *some* point, to the conclusion that everything we undertake must have *one* point. As his commentators routinely point out,[6] this move is a *non sequitur*, depending on the fallacy of quantificational shift. (Compare the move from 'Everyone has some mother' to 'Someone is everyone's mother'.)

Second, consider another passage from the early pages of the *Nicomachean Ethics* (1094a19ff.):

> Suppose that, in our actions, there is some objective which we want for its own sake, while everything else we want only because of that objective; and suppose that it is false that everything is chosen for the sake of something else. (If that were true, then X would be wanted only for the sake of Y, and Y only for the sake of Z, and Z for the sake of something else again: we would face an infinite regress, and our wishes would be empty and vain.) On these conditions it is clear that the good and the best will be that objective which is chosen in its own right.

It is tempting to read this passage as saying that the only alternatives in the theory of motivation are monism and nihilism. Aristotle seems to argue that unless every non–ultimate motivation we have can be traced back to a foundational grounding in one ultimate motivation, then every motivation we have will be somehow 'empty and vain'. But there is no good reason for us to think this, unless we are already convinced that monism about motivation is true. This argument begs the question against pluralism.

However, the passage does suggest also a third and more plausible line of support for monism about motivation. It draws our attention to

an important idea that deeply interests Aristotle: that of attempting
to systematise our motivations or ends of action. If we're not prepared
tamely to accept the nihilist view that this attempt is either hopeless
or meaningless or both, then mustn't we be led, as soon as we engage
in it, straight towards monism about motivation?

The great strength of monism seems to be its ability to help us to
organise our thinking about our motivations, and how they interrelate,
into one coherent system. If monism is true and there really is one
ultimate point to everything that we do, then it seems reasonable to
hope that understanding what that point is will enable us to clarify our
reflections on our own motivations and their interrelations to the point
where it is possible to systematise those relations into a theory of our
motivations and our practical rationality. This monistic theory of practical rationality will be simple and complete. It will be simple because
there will be in it only one concept that functions as a reference point
for all the other concepts – that of the one ultimate point at which all
motivations aim. It will be complete once we understand the relation
of every non-ultimate point of action to whatever the ultimate point of
action is – as it seems we might eventually hope to if monism is true.

The fact that monism about motivation offers us this beguiling
prospect is a very strong argument in favour of monism. Because
monism and pluralism are logically inconsistent, this argument also
counts against pluralism unless pluralism too can offer a coherent and
convincing theory of practical rationality. So can it?

Two arguments suggest not. First, it's fairly obvious what a monistic
theory of practical rationality would look like (see the sketch in the
second paragraph of this page), and much less obvious what a pluralistic
theory would be like. By definition, a pluralistic account of motivation
claims that there is more than one ultimate point at which our actions
may aim. But here there is a dilemma for the pluralist. If such points
are all ultimate, how can they be systematised? Whereas if they can be
systematised, how can they all be ultimate? Moreover, second, even if
both monistic and pluralistic theories of practical rationality are possible
in principle and can be developed in detail, considerations of simplicity
and theoretical economy always seem likely to tell in favour of
monism and against pluralism.

These two arguments in favour of monism and against pluralism are,
I believe, the strongest arguments going. They are certainly the most
influential. The dilemma posed by the first argument is one of the
deepest questions which pluralism has to face: I shall spend most of
this book addressing it. For the moment I shall simply give this dilemma

a name – *the Problem of Reconciliation* – and point out that, although the problem which it poses for the pluralist is at this stage a puzzling one, it is not immediately obvious that the problem is insoluble.

As for the second point, about the alleged theoretical economy of monism about motivation, this can be more summarily dealt with. Monism about motivation stands no chance at all of succeeding as a theory if it cannot say *what* the one ultimate point of all actions is. Yet what could that one point possibly be?

Take the most detailed answer to this question which has yet been provided, that of the classical utilitarians, which I alluded to briefly at the very beginning of the chapter. This was that the single point of all action was pleasure. More fully, their view was that the point of acting is given either by the pleasure inherent in desirable things themselves, or by the fact that a given action is a 'means to the promotion of pleasure and the prevention of pain'.

> The theory of life on which [the utilitarian] theory of morality is grounded [says that] pleasure, and freedom from pain, are the only things desirable as ends; and that all desirable things (which are as numerous in the utilitarian as in any other scheme) are desirable either for the pleasure inherent in themselves, or as means to the promotion of pleasure and the prevention of pain. (J. S. Mill, *Utilitarianism*, Ch. 2)

This simple[7] answer is not much favoured by most modern utilitarians, who often respond, in effect, that they would rather concede the truth of pluralism about motivation than accept any such monism about motivation as hedonism, but then deny that this concession regarding pluralism about motivation has any implications for their monism about the good. (On these matters see 1.2, 1.4.) It is still worth noting briefly, however, what is wrong with Mill's thesis that the ultimate point of acting is pleasure. The obvious problem is that, although Mill's sort of utilitarian answers our question about the ultimate point of all action with the single word 'pleasure', it is very difficult to form any idea of what the utilitarian means by this answer.

> Notoriously, the term 'pleasure' suffers from multiple ambiguity.
> (1) In one sense, it denotes purely physiological sensation – or better sensations, because even the purely physiological sense of 'pleasure' does not denote any single sensation.
> (2) In another sense, it means something close to 'delight' or

'happiness'. In this sense (senses?), pleasure can be either a mood or an emotion.

(3) In a third sense – a sense on which Ryle tried, heroically, to build a whole theory of pleasure – the term refers to no particular phenomenological data, physiological or psychological, but just to one way of doing things among others.[8]

(4) In a fourth sense, pleasure-talk forms incomplete phrases. We talk of being pleased with so-and-so or being pleased that so-and-so, and generally such talk has no clear meaning until we fill in what the 'so-and-so's' are, or at least can see how they might be filled in.

(5) In a fifth sense, pleasure means the opposite of business, or duty, or possibly even virtue.

(6) In a sixth, we use '(At) your pleasure' to mean no more than 'Whatever you want'.

(7) Connectedly, it is always pleasant (in itself, at any rate) just to choose to do something and succeed in doing it.

Et cetera. No doubt there are plenty of other variations in the uses of our pleasure-vocabulary. The question is, which of these senses (1–6) of pleasure does the classical utilitarian have in mind when he tells us that the point – the single and supreme point – of acting is 'pleasure'? Or if none of these, what other suggestion about the meaning of 'pleasure' has he to offer?

Here the classical utilitarian faces a further dilemma. The longer he refuses to commit himself to any particular sense, the longer we'll remain in the dark about what exactly his thesis that 'The point of acting is pleasure' is supposed to mean. But the sooner he homes in on any one or other of senses (1–6), the sooner his thesis that 'The point of acting is pleasure' will turn out to be either false or vacuous.

Suppose, for example, that the classical utilitarian claims, like Bentham,[9] that the kind of pleasure he means is simply pleasure in sense (1) – purely physiological sensations. This is a very specific answer to 'What is the point of acting?'; unfortunately, there's no chance at all that this answer is true. For a start, what about all the actions which people do in pursuit of pleasures of types (2–7)?

Suppose, on the other hand, that the utilitarian goes for sense (7) of 'pleasure' listed above, and claims that the kind of pleasure he means is just that sort of pleasure which we can intelligibly say is involved in any case at all of doing what we want. The pleasure which gives the point to all our actions is then just the pleasure caused by succeeding in doing anything that we choose to do. (One name for this sort of pleasure might perhaps be the pleasure of 'preference satisfaction'.)

This account is bizarre. First: on this account, every conceivable action – even if it's one of those we would pretheoretically like to describe as pointless – has its point (indeed, has exactly the same point as every other conceivable action). But then not only is the claim that 'the point of action is pleasure' a uselessly vacuous one, it's also hard to see how this sort of utilitarianism can possibly come up with an account of what we mean by calling actions pointless – an account, that is, of practical rationality's normative or critical dimension. This is something that we need to have in ethics.[10]

Second: the point of acting, properly speaking, couldn't be the pleasure which comes as a by-product of acting successfully, precisely because that pleasure is a by-product. In all such actions I will, at least normally, be aiming not at that pleasure but at some other objective(s). But if there are other objective(s) in my actions, why don't these provide the point(s) of my acting instead? If they do, then what is the point of pretending that there is one thing, called the 'satisfaction' of all such 'preferences', which stands to all actions as their ultimate objective or point?

These objections to possible versions of the motivational monist thesis that 'The point of acting is pleasure' which employ senses (1) and (7) of 'pleasure' can be shown to apply also, *mutatis mutandis*, to versions featuring each of senses (2–6). Variants of the objection presented here to sense (1) of 'pleasure' will also apply to senses (2) and (5); and variants of the objection presented here to sense (7) will also apply to senses (3), (4) and (6).

This result may prompt the utilitarian to see if the other horn of the dilemma is any more comfortable, by refusing to commit to any particular sense of 'pleasure'. There are two stylish and popular ways for him to refuse to commit himself. The first is to sign up for a conjunctive thesis, according to which any of senses (1–7) of 'pleasure' will do as a filling for 'The purpose of acting is pleasure'.[11] It is hard to see such a view about motivation as strictly speaking a monistic view at all. Second, he may coin a term of art, like 'Utility' or 'Well-Being' or 'Welfare', which is supposed to avoid the inadequacies of the notion of pleasure.[12] But then we should ask how the mere invention of such terms averts those inadequacies. Such terms are commonly used in modern utilitarianism as place-holders for 'whatever it is that is the single ultimate objective of all action'. But then it's obvious that the question of what that single ultimate objective might be has not

been answered. It has merely been assumed that there is some answer
to it. It is often also assumed that it doesn't much matter what the
answer is. This assumption seems quite mistaken, given that the coherence of motivational monism depends on what kind of answer is given.
(Compare chapter 5, 1 on the Thesis of the Indifference of Ends.)

The familiar moral of this often-told story is that basing monism
about motivation on the notion of pleasure tends to lead us either into
a clearly implausible position, or into a position that can be kept
plausible only by keeping it unclear. Or else it leads us into a position
that, insofar as it is clear at all, is clearly no sort of monism about
motivation. (If this is true of monism based on pleasure, *a fortiori* it is
true of monisms based on other concepts.) By now this well-worn story
is likely to seem barely worth retelling. Yet philosophers continually
forget its moral. For all their protestations to the contrary, there are
still many writers on ethics who evidently think that, or talk as if, some
form of motivational monism were not only possible but necessary. It
therefore bears repetition that motivational monism's attempts to lump
together all the disparate elements of pleasure into one supposed unity,
whatever we may call it, which explains every case of action, is best
given up as a bad job. Only the appearance of an answer to the question
'What is the point of acting?' can be achieved by such methods. There
simply is no such thing as 'utility' or 'pleasure' or 'happiness' or
'welfare' or even 'preference satisfaction' in any unitary sense of the
required sort. Such things exist only in the fevered imaginations of
theorists.

This conclusion seems (even to some utilitarians) to spell the end of
the road for monism about motivation. If so, and if we are not yet
prepared to admit defeat in the theory of motivation and become
nihilists, presumably we should become pluralists about motivation
instead.

Consider one well-known answer to our question about the ultimate
ends of action which abandons the classical utilitarians' insistence on
monism about motivation. Namely Hume's:

> It appears evident that the ultimate ends of human actions can
> never, in any case, be accounted for by *reason*, but recommend
> themselves entirely to the sentiments and affections of mankind,
> without any dependence on the intellectual faculties. Ask a man
> *why he uses exercise*; he will answer, *because he desires to keep his
> health*. If you then enquire, why he desires health, he will readily
> reply, *because sickness is painful*. If you push your enquiries farther,

and desire a reason *why he hates pain*, it is impossible he can ever give you any. This is an ultimate end, and is never referred to any other object . . . It is impossible there can be a progress *in infinitum*; and that one thing can always be a reason why another one is desired. Something must be desirable on its own account, and because of its immediate accord or agreement with human sentiment or affection. (David Hume, *Enquiry Concerning the Principles of Morals*, Appendix 1)

Hume's answer to 'What is the point of acting?' would begin with the pluralist qualification that 'It depends which acting you mean'. For Hume is a pluralist about motivation – he firmly believes that different actions have different points. Thus, in our quotation, he speaks of the ultimate ends of human actions.[13]

Indeed, our passage shows that Hume is not only a pluralist about motivation. He would also reject all attempts to rationalise the plurality of points or ends of action in which he believes. For Hume, not only is there no one point of acting, but a plurality of points to acting. There is no inherent or necessary order in that plurality either. This makes Hume not merely a pluralist about motivation, but (as I shall call him) an anarchistic pluralist.

From what I have already said about nihilistic and monistic answers to 'What is the point of acting?', it will be clear that I think we should endorse Hume's pluralism about motivation. Should we be anarchists as well as pluralists? I think not, for three reasons.

The first concerns anarchistic pluralism's resistance to attempts to give unity or rational cohesion to the different sorts of points of different sorts of actions. This resistance is, practically speaking, rather unhelpful. No matter how diverse and uncohesive are the points of the actions that are available to me, it remains true that I am one person trying to live one life. So, even if anarchistic pluralism is true, it is – like nihilism – unliveable. To live a life at all is to try to realise some sort of unity or cohesion in that life, and this I can't do if I simply accept anarchistic pluralism. If anarchistic pluralism about motivation is the truth, then to achieve cohesion I must fly in the face of its truth – just as I can achieve cohesion only by flying in the face of outright nihilism about motivation if that position is true.

Here Hume might wonder what was meant by the claim that 'I am one person'. He might also question the claim that 'to live a life at all is to try to realise some sort of unity or cohesion in that life'. (That this claim is one that I take to be of critical importance will become

clear in chapters 4 to 6.) Hume himself cheerfully admitted that his
own philosophy wasn't liveably true. As he rightly said, that alone is
no reason to deny that his view is true. If the fact is that there is no
genuine unity and cohesion to be had in our moral lives, that fact may
be depressing. But depressingness, depressingly enough, is no mark of
falsity. A better reason for us not to adopt Hume's view of the matter
is, rather, the reason we saw for not being a nihilist: namely that Hume's
view is a form of defeatism, and our inquiry hasn't (yet) been defeated.

A second criticism of anarchistic pluralism goes a bit deeper. This
criticism is that anarchistic pluralism suffers from the same defect as
one of the forms of monism about the good based on hedonism which
I discussed above. It too seems unable to provide any account of
pointlessness. If every kind of motivation is not only admitted (making
us pluralists), but admitted on an equal footing with every other kind
of motivation (making us anarchistic pluralists), then no clear sense is
left in the claim that some actions have more point or less point than
others. It ought to be possible for the theory of motivation to have a
critical dimension. But it can't if every point of action or reason for
acting is as good as every other. Hume's anarchistic pluralism isn't in
good order as an account of this critical dimension.

The first and the second criticisms suggest that anarchistic pluralism
about motivation, like nihilism, is a *pis aller*. If we can find an account
of the point of action which is pluralist and yet does justice to the
ideal of a unified and coherent life, that account will start at a much
better price than anarchistic pluralism. Likewise, if we can find an
account of the point of action which is pluralist and yet gives us a
workable account of the critical dimension of the theory of motivation,
that theory too will be preferable to anarchistic pluralism.

The same is suggested by the third criticism of anarchistic
pluralism about motivation. The third criticism observes that it is after
all possible to draw up some sort of a taxonomy of the points of action.
It isn't as if every action had, or even could have, an utterly different
point from every other action. Motivations do come in real types: a
fact to which even Hume pays implicit homage. That's why it isn't
useless, but a vital part of explaining any particular motivation, to say
what type of motivation it is, and to say how near or far this token of
the type in question is from being a typical token of that type. So
pluralism about the points of action should not – if at all possible – be
anarchistic. Instead it should be tempered by a taxonomy of types of
possible answer to the question 'What is the point of (this case of)
acting?'.

Then, which types of motivation should go in this taxonomy? Indeed, how is such a taxonomy even to be constructed? I consider those questions in chapter 2. First, in 1.2 to 2.3, I turn to two other questions, also foundational for ethics, which we might see as parallel to the question 'What is the point of acting?'. In 1.4, I'll conclude this chapter by exploring briefly the connections between these three questions.

1.2   WHAT IS THE GOOD?

We might begin our inquiries into ethics by asking, not 'What is the point of acting?', but 'What is the good?'. If we did, the consequent argument would have something like the structure of argument displayed in 1.1. Inquiring about motivations led us to consider the alternatives monism, nihilism and pluralism (anarchistic or otherwise) about motivation. Similarly, in the theory of value our alternatives are these three:

1 *Monism* about the good: the assertion that there is, at bottom, *only one* form of value in the world, so that if, for example, friendship and knowledge are both goods, then there must be some meaningful sense in which they are instances of *the same* good.
2 *Nihilism* about the good: the assertion that there are, at bottom, *no* forms of value in the world.
3 *Pluralism* about the good: the assertion that there is, at bottom, *more than one* form of value in the world, so that, e.g., friendship and knowledge need not be instances of the same good, but may well be fundamentally different forms of value.

Like nihilism about motivation, nihilism about the good is not an option which we need take seriously until it has proved impossible to take seriously either monism or pluralism about the good. At any rate I am not going to take much notice of nihilism about the good in this book (except tangentially in 2.4). Nihilism about the good is anyway harder to take seriously than many of its proponents have made out.[14]

This leaves us with two alternatives: monism or pluralism about the good. But here are four good reasons why monism about the good is to be rejected too, so that we may conclude that we ought to be pluralists about the good.

1 If monism about the good is true, then there are two alternatives. Either (a) there must be exactly one answer to the old Socratic question 'How should I/we live?'.[15] That is: there must be exactly one best way

of living for virtuous agents now, which is specified by its being the
one course of life which most instantiates the single value recognised
by monism.[16] (For example: perhaps the best way of life, in our world
as presently organised, is the charitable one. If monism of this sort is
true, the good society will be one vast famine-relief organisation.) Or
(b) there must be a precisely defined set of alternative answers to 'How
should I/we live?', which are picked out by the fact that they all
instantiate exactly the same, maximal, amount of value. (For example:
perhaps the two best ways of life, in our world as presently organised,
are the charitable one and the nuclear-disarming one. If monism of
this sort is true, the good society will be composed of two vast organis-
ations, one dedicated to famine relief and the other to nuclear
disarmament.)[17]

Now, on the monist view, if (b) is true, then that ought at the very
least to seem puzzling. If, at bottom, there is only one (sort of) value,
how can there possibly be more than one ideal life – if it is an ideal
life we are talking about, not just a jolly good life? How remarkable it
would be if, for example, the lives of famine relief and of nuclear
disarmament had exactly the same value! What a coincidence of
numbers!

More importantly, compare the remarks of James Griffin – one
utilitarian writer who wants to defend pluralism about the good,[18] and
who seems more alive than most to the problem I am discussing: 'There
seems to be no place for an account of a certain number of different
ideal forms of human life, made ideal by being the flourishing of a
certain number of different kinds of human nature. What we lack is
a rationale for the division of human nature into . . . different kinds'.
Even if we had such a rationale, it would commit us to saying things
like: 'You are a person of type X; therefore you must live a type-A best
life'. As Plato's *Republic* shows, this is an implausibly coercive view of
ethics.

The coerciveness is lessened but not got rid of by saying, as perhaps
the monist might, that we are free to choose between the various
different best lives. Only them? Why not some of the nearly best lives
as well? The more we try to make specific the idea of a variety of
alternative best lives, the more it seems, on any plausible version of the
story, to be a variety of alternative good lives that we're talking about,
not best lives. But if it is good lives that we are choosing between, then
that last question ('Why not some of the nearly best lives as well?') is
unanswerable.

Suggestion (a), that there is exactly one best life, is even more coercive than (b), and has even more absurd consequences. If there is exactly one best life, then we might expect all those whom we call good or virtuous people at least to aspire to live that one best life. Of course, their actual behaviour may still vary. But the limits on such variation in their behaviour must, on this view, be set only by such things as the need for co-ordination, and their varying capacities and understandings. In fact, however, good people do no such thing as to try to live the same best life. Moreover the variations in what they do are vastly wider than could possibly be explained on the supposition that there was exactly one ideal way of living which they were all at least trying to realise. (Or, to return to (b), exactly two ideal lives, or three, or any small and exact number.)

To see this, take another example: the relationship between aesthetic goods and (what are commonly called) the moral goods. Compare a life dedicated to artistic beauty (Oscar Wilde's?) with a life dedicated to strenuous Tolstoyan altruism, or the furthering of a political ideology like Marxism. The justifications for calling all the lives which pursue these goods 'good lives' are real – but they're different. Why? Because the appeal, the 'motivational pull', of art – that is, the good of art – is fundamentally different from the good(s) which may be sought or realised in political or religious idealism. The monist about the good must deny (or somehow qualify) this kind of claim. Because for him only one fundamental good exists, he must say that these different goods are in some way all instances of the same good. This seems implausible.

Again, if there's exactly one best life, then such diversity as we have just pointed out will be blameworthy, because so-called virtuous people, in their diversity, will be failing to meet an overriding moral obligation to live that best life. But *pace* Jonathan Glover,[19] Shelly Kagan[20] and others, there's no non-question-begging reason to think such people blameworthy. Typical intelligent pretheoretical uses of words like 'virtuous' aren't obviously – perhaps: obviously aren't – systematically mistaken. So there is no good prima-facie reason to suppose that good people are blameworthy for living such different good lives as they do.

Indeed, we might add, the more varieties of goodness the merrier. It's high time for ethicists to question the persisting tendency of moral theories to narrow down human agents' options, often to the point where they have only one. Why should this be the only or even the primary job of moral theory? Why shouldn't there be a moral theory that shows us that there are more ways of living well than we'd ever imagined?[21]

Notice, connectedly, that (a) and (b) share a further difficulty. They are overspecific: they lay claim to an implausible degree of precision. I have already asked how it could be possible to demarcate in any precise way the best life or lives from all the almost-best lives. But even supposing we can make this demarcation, the likelihood of being able to follow through on the project of actually specifying the monist's one best life or set of lives – in detail – seems to be approximately nil. This alone is sufficient to make monism about the good hugely implausible.

2 For if the monist about the good wants to be taken seriously, he has to provide more than a rough and ready account of what the best life is like – just as the monist about motivation has to give more than a vague account of what he means by talking of one single ultimate point for all actions. He shouldn't try talking his hearers into accepting a promissory note – a blank spot in the theory, to be coloured in at some later stage of theorising, which doesn't matter for the moment. There are too many such blank spots in monistic theories of the good. And they have an unnerving tendency to appear at all the vital points. If monism about the good were right there would be *no* such blank spots. At least in principle, and preferably in practice too, it would be possible to replace them with a precise account of what the good is like. So we can't take monism seriously unless the research programme of providing such a precise account is pursued by monists with all possible energy – not, as usual, nonchalantly postponed.

In fact there isn't, never has been, and (so far as I can see) never will be a coherent and substantive monistic account of the good. Typically, for intelligent monists, 'the (overall) good' of which they characteristically speak is not discovered but invented. It isn't that intelligent monists come across their 'good' in ordinary life. It is rather that they stipulate that some such thing must exist – otherwise monism would fall apart. Indeed it would. But unless you're already a monist, this can hardly be a reason for accepting the stipulation. So typically, intelligent monistic accounts of the good are coherent, but not substantive. This makes them implausible.

By contrast, for less than intelligent monists, 'the good' of which they speak is – typically – discovered, not invented. The problem is that anything which we might discover in this way is not a good candidate for the role of 'the good'. Typically, then, less-than-intelligent monistic accounts of the good are substantive, but not coherent, and therefore not plausible either. (To illustrate this point, consider again the argument in 1.1 about pleasure and other supposed bases for monism about motivation.)

The third and fourth arguments for rejecting monism about the good are 'reversible' arguments: arguments which appear to tell in favour of monism about the good, but turn out on reflection to be arguments which point in the opposite direction, towards pluralism.

3 The first of these apparent reasons to be a monist is that, if we are (or try to be) pluralists about the good, then we need an answer to what was identified in 1.1 as the Problem of Reconciliation – the question 'If there is a plurality of goods, how are the different goods to be reconciled with one another within a single human life?' How can the pluralist answer that without sneaking in some principles for telling us which of his plurality of goods count for how much when? And how can the pluralist sneak in these principles without turning into a covert monist about the good?[22]

Well, recall objection (1) to monism about the good above – the 'many good lives' objection. If that objection to monism is right, then there can be lots of different good lives. But if there can be many good lives (and it seems obvious that there can), then there must be *lots* of pluralist answers to the Problem of Reconciliation – lots of ways of reconciling the goods within a human life, none of which forces the pluralist into a collapse back into monism about the good. So – although we don't yet have the details of the pluralist answer to the Problem of Reconciliation; cp. chapters 3 to 6 – it already looks as if pluralism can turn this objection back upon the monist. The present line of argument lends no support to monism about the good unless no pluralist answer to the Problem of Reconciliation can be made out. If such an answer is possible, then this objection reverses: it tells against monism about the good, not pluralism.

4 The second reversible objection to pluralism is this. If you're a monist about the good, then you may reasonably hope to eliminate moral dilemmas: situations in which whatever you do your action will be wrong. So monists about the good tend to argue like this:

(a) only by monism about the good can we hope to eliminate moral dilemmas (because if monism is true, there'll never be a real clash of values: such clashes can't occur if there is only one value);

(b) but (given the demands of action) we must eliminate moral dilemmas;

(c) so we must be monists about the good – even if we can get to be monists only by sheer stipulation.

As Bernard Williams has pointed out, if you think (as many people do think, and perhaps most of those who are not defending some theory at all costs) that moral dilemmas are an ineliminable datum, you can simply stand this argument on its head:[23]

(a′) monism about the good eliminates moral dilemmas (see (a) above);

(b′) but (given the demands of truth) we mustn't eliminate moral dilemmas;

(c′) so we mustn't be monists about the good, either by stipulation or in any other way.

So this argument for monism about the good backfires too. Not only does the argument not count for monism about the good: it actually counts rather strongly against that view.

One further line of thought in defence of (what I would regard as) an attenuated monism about the good has recently been pursued by James Griffin, in his magisterial book *Well-Being*. Griffin's line of thought is this. Monism as I have presented it consists, it might be said, in a more or less loose alliance between these three separate claims:

1 Any particular good is an instance of the overall good.
2 Any particular good is reducible to the overall good.
3 Any particular good is commensurable with any other particular good.

Suppose the monist about the good separated out these three claims, and embraced only 3. Unlike Griffin I regard 3 as *the* key monist doctrine – the defining feature of monism, and the thesis that we must reject if we are to establish a genuine pluralism about the good. But so far I have apparently based my rejection of 3 on arguments against 1 and 2. So wouldn't the position which accepts only 3, and agrees with me in denying 1 and 2, be a form of monism about the good which evades my criticisms so far?

This is Griffin's position.[24] Although Griffin would not call himself a monist (because he denies 1 and 2), nonetheless he accepts 3:

If . . . the denial of reduction is the denial that there is a single substantive value running through all the things that we rank (the denial of substantive monism), then it seems to me entirely correct. There is no single substantive super-value. But we do not need a super-value to have a scale. It is enough to have the quantitative attribute 'value'.

If the denial of reduction is the denial of . . . complete, strong cardinality, then again it seems to me right. Even if we abandon appeal to a super-value and use the concept of 'value' itself as our quantitative attribute, we do not get such a scale. But that does not show much. It does not show, for instance, that there is no single scale of well-being, nor that not everything can be ranked on it. And it certainly does not show that our powers of measurement are not up to the policy of maximising . . .

All that we need for the all-encompassing scale [for measuring well-being] is the possibility of ranking items on the basis of their nature. And we can, in fact, rank them in that way. We can work out trade-offs between different dimensions of pleasure or happiness. And when we do, we rank in a strong sense: not just choose one rather than the other, but regard it as worth more. That is the ultimate scale here: worth to one's life. (Griffin, *Well-Being*, pp. 89–90)

Griffin begins by denying the claim 'that there is a single substantive value running through all the things that we rank', a claim which he calls 'substantive monism'. He then goes on to claim that there is nonetheless some (presumably) *non-substantive* value, which does 'run through all the things that we rank'. This he calls, first baldly 'value', and then later 'worth to one's life'. So what is his distinction between 'substantive' and 'non-substantive' forms of value? We might perhaps think that he means to claim that the value he calls 'non-substantive' is not any particular sort of value, as for example pleasure or friendship is. Rather, it is some way of evaluating or adjudicating between the different particular sorts of value, which is itself a value not identical with any of those particular sorts.

But if so, then Griffin faces a dilemma. For all Griffin's denials, this non-substantive value of 'worth to one's life' begins to sound suspiciously like a super-value after all, and the question whether or not it is 'substantive' in Griffin's sense begins to look like a distraction. (Note these words particularly: ' . . . we rank in a strong sense: not just choose one rather than the other, but regard it as <u>worth more</u>'.) If 'worth to one's life' is a super-value, then Griffin doesn't really avoid a (disguised) commitment to (1) and (2). In that case, he's not only a monist about the good in my terms; he is a monist about the good even in his own terms.

If on the other hand 'worth to one's life' isn't a super-value, then it is hard to see what else the phrase could denote – unless judgements of 'worth to one's life' are in fact just basic preferences, ungrounded in any further value, which we form when deciding between different sorts of goods.[25] If this is how we should see such judgements, then certainly Griffin's account has obtained a genuinely pluralistic theory of the good. But in the same process it has also lost its grip on any worthwhile notion of commensurability. Suppose that these basic preferences are indeed ungrounded in any further value. Then precisely for that reason, there can be no sense in saying that any one possible way of weighing or trading off the goods against each other is rational, or any more rational than any other possible way of weighing them or trading them off. For what else but a different way of comparing values could make one method of trade-off more rational than another?

So I reject Griffin's claim that 'all that we need for the all-encompassing scale [for measuring well-being] is the possibility of ranking items on the basis of their nature' [my emphasis]. For the thesis that the goods are commensurable with each other to be interesting, it needs to say more than that such rankings as Griffin means are possible. We don't just need to know – what anyway we know already – that 'we can work out trade-offs between different dimensions of pleasure or happiness'. We need to know also that at least some of these rankings which we can devise are not arbitrary but rational rankings. Any (suitably equipped) laboratory rat can devise a ranking of goods of some sort; for that matter, a few tosses of a coin can devise such a ranking. The real question about the thesis of commensurability is 'What makes any ranking of goods a good or rational or *objective* ranking?' To this question I see no answer in Griffin's discussion which doesn't depend upon a reintroduction, however well-disguised, of the notion of a super-value.

So any theory which tries to keep 3, commensurability, while dropping claims like 1 and 2 about the existence of super-values, only evades my criticisms of monism about the good insofar as it fails to retain 3 at all. Unless something underwrites the rationality of commensurating judgements, there's no interest in the claim that such judgements are possible. But the rationality involved in rational commensuration seems necessarily to reintroduce the idea of a super-value. Hence the logical instability of the attempt to keep 3 but reject 1 and 2.

I have one final comment on Griffin's argument. Griffin is keen to find a way of retaining commensurability and pluralism about the good for an excellent reason: because he recognises that there's a deep problem for the pluralist about saying anything about how we choose between a plurality of goods. I have just argued that commensuration, or indeed any sort of measurement technique, isn't the way to deal with that problem. Such techniques lead us either to the uninteresting thesis that these choices are cases of commensurability without rationality – or else, if we try to retain the crucial element of rationality in our descriptions of such choices, they collapse our pluralism back into monism. This of course leaves quite untouched the problem of how to choose rationally between a plurality of goods – although it does corroborate my idea that that problem is not the problem of commensuration, but, as I have called it, the Problem of Reconciliation. The question remains:[26] how can there be a practical rationality which isn't a weighing and measuring rationality? We won't be in a position to answer that question fully until chapter 5.

1.3   WHAT IS HUMAN EXCELLENCE?

In the third part of this chapter I turn to virtue. I might have begun these inquiries by asking not 'What is the point of acting?' or 'What is the good?', but 'What is human virtue or excellence?' If I had done so then again the consequent argument would have had something like the structure of argument displayed in 1.1–1.2. As in the theories of motivation and value, so in the theory of virtue, our alternatives are these three:

1   *Monism* about virtue: the assertion that there is, at bottom, *only one* form of virtue or human excellence in the world, so that if, for example, justice and wisdom and courage are all virtues, then there must be some meaningful sense in which they are instances of the *same* virtue.

2   *Nihilism* about virtue: the assertion that there are, at bottom, *no* forms of virtue or human excellence in the world.

3   *Pluralism* about virtue: the assertion that there is, at bottom, *more than one* form of virtue in the world, so that, for example, justice and wisdom and courage need not be instances of the same virtue, but may well be fundamentally different forms of virtue.

Nihilism about virtue is, once more, not a live option, or at any rate not an option I'll spend much time on here. It isn't very plausible to claim that no one knows what they are talking about if they try to talk about virtue or the virtues – about human excellence overall, or about the more specific dispositions of character which instantiate or promote human excellence overall. But then we are quickly left with no good alternative to pluralism. For monism about virtue is not tenable either.

Anyone who tries to argue that all the virtues are (or 'are at bottom') one and the same virtue faces a dilemma. If it is the identity of the virtues as ordinarily understood that they are trying to prove, their claim that these are identical with each other will be implausible. If, on the other hand, their claim that the virtues of which they speak are all identical with each other does turn out to be plausible, it will also turn out that it is not the identity of the virtues as ordinarily understood that they have proved, if they have proved anything.

To illustrate this, consider a brief case study: the monism about the virtues which was famously espoused by the Socrates of Plato's earlier dialogues.[27] Socrates held that all the different virtues that contemporary Greek discussion recognised were really just applications of one and the same virtue – knowledge (or wisdom). So, for example, courage is knowledge about which causes of fear to run away from and which to stand up to. Self-restraint or temperance is knowledge about which causes of desire to respond to and which to ignore or resist. Justice is knowledge about how to distribute benefits and harms. All these 'different' virtues are just different applications of the same virtue – that of knowledge or wisdom.

If this Socratic claim were true, it would establish the identity of the virtues. It would not be apposite to object, for example, that these redefined virtues are still different from one another just because they involve different *applications* of knowledge or wisdom. If a mere difference of application were sufficient for a difference of virtue, the list of virtues would be rather a long one.

But the Socratic claim is not true. There is more to my having courage than my knowing what I oughtn't to run away from. Rather obviously, it is also necessary that I should not run away from it. Also rather obviously, my not running away is not guaranteed by my knowledge that I shouldn't run away.

When we try to remedy this flaw in the Socratic definition of courage, or the parallel flaws in the definitions of the other three cardinal virtues which Socrates identifies with knowledge or wisdom, we find ourselves moving back towards more intuitively acceptable accounts of what courage or temperance or justice is. Spelling out these better accounts turns out to mean giving an account of each virtue which builds into the description of the agent who has it, not merely a knowledge of what it requires, but also the kinds of disposition, emotional responsiveness, and willpower that make it possible to put that knowledge into practice, even in the teeth of opposing emotional forces like terror or lust or a thirst for vengeance.

But as we move back towards the common usage of the names 'courage', 'temperance', and 'justice', we are at the same time getting further away from any usage of those names which could make it look plausible to say that they were all names for one and the same virtue. It is obvious that each of these virtues involves quite different non-cognitive elements from the others.

For example, contrast someone who is displaying a disposition of justice in this filled-out sense with someone who is displaying a disposition of courage in a similarly amplified sense. Considered as a virtue of an agent, full-blooded justice typically involves such more-than-merely-cognitive dispositions as compassion, fair-mindedness or impartiality, a feel for what sorts of equality are relevant to a given case and why, a scrupulously disinterested regard for and attention to any accepted rules that may apply to this particular case, and the imaginative ability to see what it is like to be in someone else's shoes; perhaps, also, a sense of discomfort or even outrage at the perception of wrongs.

By contrast full-blooded courage, considered as a virtue of an agent, typically involves dispositions like defiance of enemies, a fixity of purpose approaching obstinacy, persistence, and a deliberately slight regard for potential dangers or harms even where these are undeniably present. It may also involve other elements like positive pleasure and excitement at the prospect of a hazard or challenge, and a kind of exulting in the struggle – though perhaps it doesn't have to.

This is a more plausible way to describe the virtues of justice and courage than can be offered by treating them both merely cognitively, as cases of knowledge.[28] But if these descriptions are correct, the virtues of justice and courage are wholly different from each other. They can't possibly be said to be two different applications of one and the same virtue, as the monist about virtue wanted to say. That claim could be made even apparently plausible only by distorting the definitions of those virtues.

This is enough to see off monism about virtue. It's clear that the apparently different virtues which our society and others rightly recognise are not even at bottom just different forms of the same virtue. The dispositions generally and correctly recognised as virtues – courage, justice, wisdom, temperance etc. – are fundamentally different from one another. In some cases (such as courage and justice) they are about as different as they could be from each other, while still remaining similar in being virtues.

1.4 THE THREE QUESTIONS CONNECTED; AND A WORKING HYPOTHESIS

I have asked three different questions in 1.1–1.3: 'What is the point of acting?', 'What is the good?', and 'What is virtue?' Each of these questions, I have suggested, is (or can be made) foundational for ethics. Asking them has led me to explore three different areas in which we might apply monism, pluralism or nihilism: the areas of motivation, values, and the virtues. In each area I have concluded that pluralism is correct, and that monism and nihilism are wrong.[29] We may now ask: How are these different pluralisms connected?

Let's start with the connection between monism or pluralism about virtue, and monism or pluralism about the good. Monism about virtue clearly entails monism about the good. If there were, at bottom, just one kind of disposition that it was good for humans to have, that could only be because there was, at bottom, just one kind of good for humans.

The converse implication evidently doesn't hold. Monism about the good seems consistent with either pluralism or monism about virtue. Still, some sorts of value monists, such as utilitarians and Socratics, have naturally been led towards monism about the virtues too. It is natural for utilitarians to think that the traits of character which are themselves good are all and only those traits which tend to promote the good. If cases can then be produced in which a plurality of virtues apparently fails to promote the one good, this (the utilitarian will be inclined to say) just goes to show that the alleged plurality needs streamlining a bit. (Cp. the familiar tactics of act utilitarians against rule utilitarianism.) Overall, their line of thought suggests the virtue monist's conclusion that there is really only one sort of individuable trait of character which is really worth having (and so really a virtue) – namely, the trait of promoting the good. It only suggests that conclusion, however; it doesn't entail it.

So monism about virtue entails monism about the good, but monism about the good does not straightforwardly entail, though it may naturally suggest, monism about the virtues. Again pluralism about the virtues doesn't straightforwardly entail pluralism about the good. In a complex world there could be lots of different dispositions which, in their various ways, helped to bring about or instantiate one and the same sort of good. Consider the various different virtues that might be needed in a typical day's work by a famine-relief worker. She may have to show wisdom in the allocation of her scant resources, courage in the face of hungry mobs or looters, justice in refusing to accept bribes, and temperance in suppressing her desire to run away for a holiday from the horrors she faces. None of this implies that there's more than one overriding aim or good which motivates her. The only good she aims at may well be famine relief.

The converse entailment does hold, however. If there is a plurality of virtues then there may or may not be a plurality of goods. But if there is a plurality of goods then there must be a plurality of virtues. For a virtue can be defined as a disposition of responsiveness to a good or goods. But if there is a plurality of different goods then there must be different ways of responding to those different goods.[30] And if there is a plurality of ways of responding to the various goods then there is a plurality of dispositions embodying such responsivenesses; which means a plurality of virtues.

What about the connection between monism or pluralism about the good, and monism or pluralism about motivation? Here I offer a Working Hypothesis: properly understood, pluralism about motivation *is* pluralism about the good; properly understood, monism about motivation *is* monism about the good. The inquiry into what motivates human agents, and the inquiry into what human agents recognise as goods, are (two aspects of) one and the same inquiry. Very roughly and provisionally, these two inquiries are related as inquiries into what we might call, using a gravitational analogy, 'ethical pull' and 'ethical push'.[31] (Here the pull is the attractiveness of goods conceived as possible ends of action, and the push is the demandingness of goods conceived as possible standards for action.)

I don't mean that, for any action, its motivation and its justification are simply identical. Clearly that would be a silly thesis. One of its absurd consequences would be that every action was justified just insofar as it was motivated, which would mean once more that our theories of motivation and justification could have no normative dimension. Certainly sometimes the motivation of an action is identical with its justification – as when the reason why I do something is because I think correctly that it is right to do it. Some Kantians make this form of motivation the only acceptable form of motivation for any action which is to count as morally valuable.[32] *Pace* these Kantians, such cases aren't and don't have to be the norm.[33] My Working Hypothesis, then, is not the over-strong thesis that justification and motivation are (virtually) identical, but the more moderate thesis that the two are always deeply connected, even when not obviously connected. Hence, to understand what kinds of considerations could justify actions, we need to understand what kinds of considerations could motivate them; and vice versa.

The Working Hypothesis's usefulness, if any, will become evident as it is put to work and further clarified in chapter 2. It's not a thesis that I propose to prove (not, at any rate, directly); the onus of proof is on the other side. The positing of connections between the theories of motivation and of value is only natural. It is the positing of separations between these two areas of theory that needs to be argued for.

Many modern utilitarians deny that there is any intimate relation at all between the justification of an action and its motivation; for them, nothing essential is revealed about the nature of the good by considering the nature of actual motivations. Hence, they deny the Working Hypothesis. To conclude this chapter, it may be helpful to dispose of some possible objections to the Working Hypothesis by considering this popular utilitarian view.

Notice first that Mill feels no such qualms as the modern utilitarians: '[Utility] being, according to the utilitarian opinion, the sole end of human action, is <u>necessarily also</u> the standard of morality' (Warnock p. 263; underlining added). Mill believes that what is good is revealed by our motivations (cp. his 'proof' of utilitarianism), and that our motivations are directed towards pleasure and freedom from pain, which therefore are what is good.

It's true that Mill also writes (Warnock p. 270) that 'the motive has nothing to do with the morality of the action, though much with the worth of the agent'. But this does nothing to dilute his rejection of the motivation/justification distinction. Mill isn't here claiming – what would be, for him, of questionable coherence – that the moral justification of actions is one thing (and is to be assessed by their tendency to produce pleasure) and the worth of agents and their motivations is another (and is to be assessed in some other way: what?). His point is rather that the justification of actions as well as the worth of motivations are to be assessed by their tendency to produce pleasure. The only qualification to this hedonism which he admits is the obvious point that the assessment of the felicific tendencies of actions and the assessment of the felicific tendencies of motivations are two different matters, because actions and motivations, being different sorts of things, have different sorts of causal properties. Hence, if both tend to produce pleasure, they do so in virtue of different sorts of causal features. To say this isn't to abandon the hedonism which Mill applies to actions. It is to widen its scope of application.

It is also, of course, to make it a possibility that motivation-type M should be preferable, even though M typically leads to action-type not-A, which is not preferable. Conversely it is possible on this view that action-type A should be preferable, even though action-type A typically arises from motivation-type not-M, which is not preferable. Whether or not this is a serious problem for Mill, my claim is not merely that Mill would have rejected the modern utilitarian distinction between justification and motivation. It's also that he would be right to do so, and that modern utilitarianism would (at least at this point) be less implausible if it went along with him in this. The separation of justification from motivation has at least two bad effects. First: the wider that separation, the more it becomes opaque where our moral notions do come from, if they really have nothing to do with our motivations. Second: the wider that separation, the less clear it becomes what the answer is supposed to be to the question 'Why should I be moral?' In other words, the separation has two standard consequences of a anti-naturalistic move. (Unsurprisingly, because that in effect is what it is.)

This suffices, for the moment, to show that there is at least a good deal of plausibility to the Working Hypothesis. It is a consequence of that Hypothesis that the two pluralist theses about motivation and justification, and the two monist theses about the same, stand or fall together. As I have argued, in the case of the monisms they fall, and in the case of the pluralisms they stand.

In chapter 2, I propose to test out further the Working Hypothesis, and to explore its implications further, by putting it to work. Considerations about motivation will be used to provide not only the taxonomy of points of acting promised at the end of 1.1, but also, simultaneously, the makings of a taxonomy of the varieties of good.

NOTES

1. Two other questions with which to begin ethics are discussed in 1.2 and 1.3. A fourth traditionally foundational question, 'How should we live?' (Plato, *Republic* 352d), is not so much addressed by one section of my first chapter as by the whole book.
2. Sartre, *Being and Nothingness*, p. 615. Cp. Conclusion, p. 627: 'All human activities are equivalent (for they all tend to sacrifice man in order that the self-cause may arise) and . . . all are on principle doomed to failure. Thus it amounts to the same thing whether one gets drunk alone or becomes a leader of nations.'
3. It is also a self-defeating position. If nihilism about motivation were correct, there would be no point to any of our actions or projects. So, in particular, there would be no point in trying to establish or defend the truth of nihilism, or in living so as to register the truth of nihilism. If the nihilist replies that this argument shows only that there is no *ultimate* point to anything he does, but that he can get by with a less-than-ultimate pointfulness, we should ask what he means by that distinction. I suspect it will turn out that his rejection of 'ultimate pointfulness' is either just a rejection of monism – in which case we should urge him to become a pluralist – or else that his rejection of ultimate pointfulness is really a rejection of any kind of pointfulness – in which case his claim that he can do without *this* sounds like whistling in the dark.
4. I think unfairly, though I shall not try to argue the point here: cp. the epigraph to this

chapter, where Aristotle clearly states a pluralist position, both about the ends of motivation (1.1) and about the good (1.2).

5. Throughout this book, translations from Plato and Aristotle are my own unless I indicate otherwise.

6. V., for example, Anscombe, *Intention*, S.21.

7. Mill's distinction between higher and lower pleasures (*Utilitarianism* Ch. 2) complicates my picture of him as a monist about motivation. So do his criticisms of Bentham for failing to see the complexities of motivation (Warnock p. 101): 'Honour, beauty, order, power, action . . . None of these powerful constituents of human nature is thought worthy of a place among the "Springs of Action" . . . Man, that most complex being, is a very simple one in [Bentham's] eyes'. What these passages show is not that Mill isn't a monist about motivation. It's that he distinguishes primary and secondary ends. He admits the plurality of secondary ends. But he still believes that there's only one primary end, utility, however strong his inclination to obfuscate about what utility is. (Warnock p. 119: 'We think utility . . . much too complex and indefinite an end to be sought except through the medium of various secondary ends'.)

8. Of such usages as 'I did it with pleasure', 'I enjoyed doing it', Ryle's comment is apt that there aren't two items, the doing of the thing *plus* an experience of pleasure/ enjoyment; rather there is one item, the thing done, plus (so to speak) an adverbial quality which that item of doing has. Why Ryle should think it plausible or worthwhile to extend this adverbial analysis to every case of pleasure, I do not know. (With 'I did it with pleasure', contrast 'I did it for pleasure'.) For Ryle's discussion v. his (1954). Similar remarks to Ryle's about pleasure have often been attributed to Aristotle himself; although here Anscombe's remark that the subject reduced Aristotle 'to sheer babble' may be relevant.

9. Bentham, *Introduction to the Principles of Morals and Legislation*, ch. 5 (p. 68 in Warnock): 'Pains and pleasures may be called by one [*sic*] general word, interesting perceptions'.

10. Mine (for which see 1.2 and chapter 3ff.) says simply that an action is pointless if and insofar as there is no real good at which it aims, intelligently, efficiently and coherently with other goods. (Thus, pointfulness is or can be a matter of degree.)

11. Has Mill a conjunctive thesis about pleasure in mind in the quotation on p. 5 above, when he writes that the various things which are desirable because of their relation to pleasure are 'as numerous in the utilitarian as in any other scheme'? This is unclear: Mill's remarks do still seem to suggest that pleasure is a name for one thing, even if numerous things can cause it.

12. Note that my concentration here, for purposes of brevity, upon the specific case of hedonist utilitarianism or consequentialism is not meant to restrict the generality of my attack, once the mutanda are mutated.

13. On the other hand, Hume's remark just quoted, that '*Something* must be desirable on its own account, and because of its immediate accord or agreement with human sentiment or affection', might be thought to show that he is a monist about motivation. Unless Hume thinks that humans have only one 'sentiment or affection', which he does not, this doesn't follow.

14. I argue this (against Blackburn (1983)'s ultimately nihilistic position) in my [forthcoming (a)].

15. For a slightly different connection, between pluralism about virtue (1.3) and the multiplicity of available good lives, v. Joseph Raz, *The Morality of Freedom*, p. 395: 'Moral pluralism is the view that there are various forms and styles of life which exemplify different virtues and are incompatible. Forms or styles of life are incompatible if, given reasonable assumptions about human nature, they cannot normally be exemplified in the same life.'

16. Cp. John Broome: 'Once we know what is good, or more exactly what is better than what, we shall know the right way to live and the right way to act' (Broome, *Weighing Goods* p. 2, emphases added).

17. Consider an analogue of this sort of connection between monism about the good and the claim that there is just one best way of living – and between pluralism about the good and the claim that there is not. This is the way in which Rawls's initial presupposition that there is a plurality of 'primary goods' makes it natural for him to claim later that '[Any given rational life plan] is presumably but one of many possible plans that are consistent with the principles of rational choice . . . these principles do not single out one plan as the best. We have instead a maximal class of plans: each member of this class is superior to all plans not included in it, but given any two plans in the class, neither is superior or inferior to the other' (Rawls, *Theory of Justice*, contrasting pp. 92 and 409).

18. Griffin, *Well-Being*, p. 60. For more on Griffin, see the end of this section.

19. Cp. Glover, *Causing Death and Saving Lives*, p. 109: 'Although there are substantial differences of side-effects, deliberately failing to send money to Oxfam, without being able to justify our alternative spending as more important, is in the same league as murder.' Also Singer, *Practical Ethics* ch. 8.

20. Kagan, *The Limits of Morality*, p. 1: 'Morality requires that you perform – of those acts not otherwise forbidden – that act which can reasonably be expected to lead to the best consequences overall.'

21. That's what I hope to do in this book. Cp. 2.2, on the advantages of keeping pluralism about the good both rich and open ended. Cp. also Amélie Rorty's remark that, beyond a minimal shared set of values 'required for standard-issue responsibility', 'ethical character tends to specialise': A. Rorty (1992), p. 47. Of course, one good reason why moral theory tends to be about narrowing the agent's options down rather than opening them up is the Problem of Reconciliation. But if we can solve that problem, as I hope to show we can, then the emphasis in moral theory can be dramatically switched: from eliminating options to creating them.

22. One fluent statement of the Problem of Reconciliation is John Harris's, *The Value of Life* p. 60: 'Since deciding what to do or not do is inescapable, in a way that deciding what to value or what to value most is not, those who hold that values are incommensurable will have to choose to do one thing rather than another while maintaining that this does not commit them to any judgement about the greater value . . . of what they have chosen, as compared with rejected alternatives . . . [but] unless such choices are always and deliberately made at random, a pattern of preference is likely to emerge. It would be difficult not to think of such preferences as moral preferences.' An explanation of how such choices can be better than random, and of the sense in which patterns of revealed preference can indeed be patterns of moral preference without this at all implying the denial of the thesis of incommensurability, is precisely what I hope to provide to answer the Problem of Reconciliation: chapters 5 and 6.

23. V. Williams 1965, 1966. He argues for an approach to dilemmas that 'may well allow for the possibility that one can be forced to two inconsistent moral judgements about the same situation, each of them backed by the best possible reasons, and each of them firmly demanding acceptance . . . The inconsistency does not necessarily show that something was wrong – except with the situation' (Williams 1966, p. 21). N.B. that Williams argues that this point tells against moral realism – by which he seems to mean, specifically, Kantian or utilitarian versions of moral realism. I argue, differently, that what it tells against is monism about the good.

24. A similar position called 'pluralist consequentialism' is thought possible by Kagan, *Limits of Morality* p. 7: 'Nothing prevents [the consequentialist] from adopting a *pluralist* theory of the good – i.e. [*sic*] one that gives independent weight to several factors'. But what does 'independent weight' mean here? If it means that different goods possess different measurable qualities, then these qualities (because they're different) won't be measurable against each other any more than (say) length and density are. The position we get will be pluralist all right; but, because it denies commensurability, how can it be called consequentialist? If, on the other hand, Kagan means only what I think he means, that different goods possess the same measurable quality *for different reasons*, then this position is consistent with consequentialism all right; but I can't see why such a view about the good deserves to be called pluralist. A ton of feathers weighs the same as a ton of lead, and precisely the same sense of 'weight' applies to both. Feathers and lead aren't different kinds of *weight*; they're different kinds of *thing*. Similarly, if goods such as art and friendship are measurable against each other in terms of some quantity like utility, then they aren't different kinds of *good*; they're just different kinds of *thing*.

25. Also, who are 'we'? Is the metric of 'worth to my life' the same as the metric of 'worth to your life'? Should it be? Griffin's argument is not only ambiguous between the claims that 'worth to one's life' is and isn't a super-value. It's also, and connectedly, ambiguous between taking 'worth' to be a single objective notion, and taking it to be something only subjectively assessable, and therefore assessable in indefinitely many ways. If worth is a single objective notion I find it hard not to see it as a super-value; if worth is a subjective notion it doesn't look like any one sort of value at all, but like an inchoate assortment of different views about value.

26. For a(n in my view, pessimistic) statement of the question, and of the whole Problem of Reconciliation, cp. Martha Nussbaum, *The Fragility of Goodness* p. 75: 'The statement of human triumphs through reason [found in Sophocles' *Antigone*] turns out to be also a

compressed document of reason's limitations, transgressions, and conflicts. It suggests that the richer our scheme of values, the harder it will be to effect a harmony wthin it. The more we are open to the presence of value, of divinity, in the world, the more surely conflict closes us in. The price of harmonisation seems to be impoverishment, the price of richness disharmony.'

27. Plato's Socrates argues for the identity of the virtues (with knowledge, or with each other *via* knowledge) in several dialogues, but most famously at *Protagoras* 329bff. (The relevant passages of the *Protagoras* are translated in my (1996a), readings 10–15.)

28. Note the frequent elisions in the Socratic dialogues of knowledge (*episteme*) and wisdom (*sophia*). Socrates wants to defend three different theses at once: (1) courage, justice and temperance are identical with knowledge; (2) courage, justice and temperance are identical with wisdom; and (3) knowledge is identical with wisdom. The most problematic of these is (3). Wisdom is a virtue: but just for that reason there is more to it than knowledge, which isn't a virtue. There need be no paradox, as Socrates perhaps thought there was, in saying that the virtue most directly related to knowledge itself essentially has non-cognitive components – dispositional elements such as (on the theoretical side) persistent inquisitiveness, the ability to see connections, open-mindedness about the results of inquiry and a desire for the truth just as such, and a sense of wonder; and (on the practical side) responsiveness to experience, coolness in a crisis, a quick eye for the ethically salient, and *savoir vivre*. It is precisely these non-cognitive elements that make for the differences between the virtue of wisdom and the disposition of knowledge, and between wisdom and the other cardinal virtues.

29. A standing question for my approach is how to individuate or count motivations, goods or virtues. In general, as will be seen in the discussion of motivations and goods in ch. 2, my motto regarding this is *solvitur ambulando*. If you can show that two or more items of one kind are fundamentally different, then you have established pluralism regarding that kind. But then there's no urgent need to provide an answer to the question what level such items are individuated at. The answer is often intuitively obvious anyway.

30. It's obvious however, that there isn't just one virtue for each value, nor *vice versa*. (For example courage is equally a form of responsiveness to any form of good which its possessor may recognise.) This is one reason why a taxonomy of virtues doesn't follow immediately from a taxonomy of goods/ motivations such as 2.2's.

31. With my terminology of 'ethical pushes and pulls' cp. Nozick's different contrast: *Philosophical Explanations* pp. 400ff. Nozick's use of 'ethical push and pull' contrasts what's good for me and what's owed to others. Mine contrasts what justifies with what motivates. There are of course connections to be made between these two contrasts – as I shall argue in 2.3. But if they were made in the most straightforward way, then my push (= goods as demands) would align with Nozick's pull (= the demands of others), and *vice versa*. An obvious point of disanalogy between calculations of ethical pushes or pulls and gravitational forces is that the latter are additive and deterministic, whereas the former are neither. More on that in 5.2 and 6.4.

32. For example Bob Brecher, in unpublished work which he has been kind enough to show me.

33. Here is one familiar sort of exception: if I take flowers to my wife when she is in hospital, it's simply not true that my action has no moral worth unless it is motivated by the thought that this is what I ought to do.

Autonomy and knowledge of one's situation – to go no further – are objective elements of well being or utility in their own right, and not as ingredients of happiness. Once this irreducible plurality has been grasped, it becomes much easier to understand how there can be deliberation and discussion about ends. The objective desirability of categorial ends can indeed only, on a naturalistic view, be established in Mill's way, by resting it on a reflective and experience-based agreement of dispositions . . . debate about the relative importance of categorial ends . . . requires analysis of the categories under which human beings do in fact pursue particular objects.

The objectivity of certain ends, established in this way, plays a regulative role in our mutual understanding. For example, if someone were possessed by an ultimate and persistent desire to mark himself with razor blades, . . . we should not simply put that down among his utilities. We would try to understand what he was doing by placing it under some recognisable human *telos*.

John Skorupski, *John Stuart Mill*, p. 301

It would seem that anyone can take up and bring to full precision an account which has once been sketched correctly.

Aristotle, *Nicomachean Ethics*, 1098a25

2

·

THE BASIC GOODS

2.1 HOW TO ARRIVE AT A TAXONOMY OF MOTIVATIONS AND OF GOODS

At the end of chapter 1, I promised to provide taxonomies of motivations and of goods.[1] I offered, and briefly defended, the Working Hypothesis that this task would involve giving one taxonomy, not two, because the taxonomy of motivations and the taxonomy of goods would be the same.

What is involved in giving this taxonomy of motivations/goods? The very idea of such a taxonomy may seem problematic. But the beginnings of such a taxonomy are constantly before our eyes. They are the everyday sorts of data found in brief dialogues like these:[2]

1(a) I am running for the train because I want to get to Oxford on time.

1(b) Why do you want to get to Oxford on time?

2(a) I am going to the National Gallery to see a sublimely beautiful picture.

2(b) Why do you want to see a sublimely beautiful picture?

Contrast questions 1(b) and 2(b). Question 1(b) is a perfectly ordinary and everyday inquiry, which calls for a further explanation of a kind which in general we can see how to supply. (Perhaps I am going to Oxford to meet someone, or for a job interview, or for a party, or . . .)[3]

Question 2(b) is not an ordinary or everyday question at all. If someone asks us 2(b), expecting the same sort of answer as we gave to 1(b), we may not have the first idea how to provide an answer of that sort. (The natural way to understand 2(b) is to take it as a question of a different sort – as a philosophical question.)

The reason for this contrast is that we can explain a desire to board an Oxford-bound train by referring the questioner back to something

else that the agent hopes to achieve by boarding that train. But –
typically, anyway – we can't explain a desire to see a sublimely beautiful
picture in the same way, by referring the questioner back to something
else that the agent hopes to achieve thereby. What the agent hopes to
achieve by seeing that picture is just the aesthetic experience of seeing
it. Nothing else beyond the seeing of the picture, in the way that going
to the job interview or the party is beyond the journey to Oxford. When
we get back to the desire to see the picture, this sort of explanation of
the motivation of the speaker of 2(a)'s going to the gallery can go no
further.[4]

The same sort of thing will eventually turn out to be true about the
first dialogue. Question 1(b) isn't odd as 2(b) is odd (nor otherwise).
Still, if the first dialogue continues for long enough – as in practice
such dialogues usually don't – we are likely at some point to reach a
question which *is* odd in the same way as 2(b). Perhaps, for example,
the dialogue might go on like this:

1(a) I am running for the train because I want to get to Oxford
     on time.
1(b) Why do you want to get to Oxford on time?
1(c) Because I have to meet with someone in Oxford.
1(d) Why do you want to meet with that person?
1(e) To renew my friendship with him – I haven't seen him for
     years.
1(f) Why do you want to renew your friendship with him?
1(g) Because he's a *friend*. It's good to renew friendships.
1(h) Why?

Here 1(h) is odd in the same way as 2(b) is odd. Someone who asks
me 1(h) is either doing philosophy, or else seriously confused or
deranged. (Perhaps both.) Not to see how renewing friendships is a
good thing is not to see something that is understood by every sane
adult. Once I have got to 1(g) it is hard to see what more I can say,
along the same sort of lines, to explain my actions further. I can explain
what I hope to achieve by boarding the train by explaining that I want
to renew a friendship. I can't likewise explain what I hope to achieve
by renewing a friendship. What I hope to achieve by renewing our
friendship is just that: the renewal of our friendship. Nothing else
beyond that renewal, in the way that that renewal is beyond the journey
to Oxford.[5] The desire to see the picture provides a (very quick) end to
the explanation of the agent's motivation in going to the gallery. The

desire to renew a friendship provides a (slightly less quick) end to the explanation of my motivation in getting on the Oxford train.

I say that 1(h) is odd *in the same way as* 2(b) is odd. There are other ways for questions about our motivations to be odd. One example comes in another development of the first dialogue:

1(a) I am running for the train because I want to get to Oxford on time.

1(b) Why do you want to get to Oxford on time?

1(i) Because I have a job interview in Oxford to get to.

1(j) Why do you want to get to your job interview?

Is 1(j) odd? Certainly. Is it odd in the same way as 1(h)? No. The oddness of 1(h) arises because we find it hard to say how more information of the same sort as already given in 1(c), 1(e) and 1(g) could answer it. This isn't the reason why 1(j) is odd; obviously, further information of the same sort as already given in 1(i) *could* answer 1(j). (You could explain to a toddler what you hope to achieve by not missing the job interview.) What is odd about 1(j) is not, as with 1(h), that we cannot supply further information to complete the explanation, but that usually we don't have to. Everybody knows why you shouldn't miss job interviews – or anyway, everybody in our immediate environment over a certain age who's not a Martian, mentally normal (and so on). Indeed, 'everybody' (in the same sense) finds the answer to this question so obvious that they may get stuck if they unexpectedly have to supply it. But this kind of struggle to supply an explanation is quite different from the sort engendered by a question like 'Why go in for friendships?'

Here's how these thoughts help to give us the beginnings of a taxonomy of motivations, of points of acting, or of goods.

Any complete chain of explanation of an action must end sooner or later. A chain of explanation that went on for ever, or indefinitely, would simply be unintelligible. It wouldn't be an *explanation* of the action. Moreover, any such complete chain of explanation must end in a reference to the source of the motivation of the action; which means, to a basic good. If a chain of explanation doesn't refer back at some stage to some basic good, then it isn't a chain of explanation – an intelligible account of the action's motivation – at all.[6]

The basic goods are foundational to one kind of practical rationality – the kind that explains, motivates and justifies actions (recall the Working Hypothesis), and which we may call subsumptive practical rationality (that is, practical rationality which explains by subsuming one explanation to another until a basic good is reached). If there are no basic goods there will be no subsumptive practical reasoning, because there won't be anything for it to aim at.

We need a different kind of practical rationality, not subsumptive but dialectical, for an account of why the basic goods are the particular goods they are. The nature and number of the basic goods are established by reflections that can take a variety of forms. One form is the project of looking for the first principles of subsumptive practical rationality which I engage in in 2.2. Other forms include reflection on what kind of ingredients we would need for a good life; on what kind of story would be a good story to be the subject of, what elements it would contain, how combined, and why; and on what elements are indispensably necessary for any kind of good life at all.[7] To answer questions like 1(b), 1(d) or 1(f) is to engage in practical inquiry, about what actually motivates or might motivate someone. By contrast, to answer questions like 1(h) is to engage in philosophical inquiry, about why the list of things that actually motivate is as it is. Such an inquiry doesn't succeed by finding a further source of motivation beyond the source of motivation we already know is there. It succeeds by saying something interesting about what it is for anything to be a source of motivation. Or else it connects the notion of this good with the notions of other goods, or of the good life in general. This is, as they say, a *constitutive* or *part/whole* connection, as opposed to an *instrumental* or *means/end* connection.[8]

Such basic goods are typically either evident or self-evident goods or both. (An evident good is a good such that no one would normally dream of denying its goodness. A self-evident good is a good such that it is self-defeating to deny its goodness.) For example, pleasure (at least in senses (1) and (2) of the various senses distinguished in 1.1) is an evident good – perhaps the most obvious evident good of all. It is a good so evident that the classical utilitarians based a whole moral system on its goodness. No one except a philosopher could deny that the prospect of pleasure is, in the absence of special circumstances, something that gives us a prima-facie reason to act.[9]

By contrast rationality – the ability to reason, to do logic, to see a contradiction, to frame an argument – is a self-evident good (and no doubt an evident good as well). Consider any argument that shows that rationality is not a good, and so not worth having. Any such argument is itself guaranteed to be not worth having, whether successful or not, because its failure shows that it is not worth having, while its success shows that no argument is worth having (and so neither is this one).[10]

Note also that basic goods are mutually irreducible. Nothing is a basic good if it isn't or can't intelligibly be sought in itself, for its own sake. So if there is more than one basic good (1.2), then more than one thing is sought for its own sake (1.1).

This is why the pluralist position which I am developing about goods and motivations does not collapse into monism. Nothing need explain (for example) my desire to renew a friendship *beyond* the perceived goodness of renewing that friendship. That I see renewing the friendship as a good thing is enough to motivate me, and to explain how I am motivated, without appeal to some further good like (say) utility. Not every question like 1(h) can plausibly be seen as referring us back inevitably to the same single form of good, as the monist about motivation required. So there is more than one form of good.

Nor does this pluralism about motivation and the good collapse into anarchistic pluralism. This is clear from the possibility of deriving from it an orderly and non-anarchistic taxonomy of goods (which, according to the Working Hypothesis, will also be a taxonomy of motivations). Such a taxonomy can now, tentatively and provisionally, be attempted.

2.2 A TAXONOMY OF THE BASIC GOODS

We have the makings of at least one method for locating and individuating the basic goods and distinguishing them from other sorts of goods, such as *instrumental* goods (things which are good because they help you to achieve basic goods) and *by-product* goods (goods which accompany the attainment of basic goods, yet are not intelligible objects of pursuit in themselves). The method is to examine the chains of practical reasoning that people actually engage in. Tracing such chains back to their origins always means tracing them back to the specification of some basic good(s).

I won't here follow out that method step by step, because this would be too time-consuming. (Recall this chapter's second epigraph!) Instead, I'll just suggest some likely or even inevitable members for any taxonomy of the basic goods. I leave it to the reader to use the method of deriving goods from motivations as a way of checking the results which I suggest.

Two examples of basic goods have come up already in 2.1: *friendship* and *aesthetic value*. As the short dialogues 1(a)–(j) and 2(a)–(b) aimed to show, actions directed at either of these goods need no further description to be intelligible (unlike some others: getting on a train, going for a job interview). Therefore the goods of friendship and aesthetic value are basic goods.

A third basic good emerged earlier, in 1.1: it is found in the area of 'pleasure and the avoidance of pain'. (This means pleasure in either sense (1) or (2) of pleasure as defined in 1.1, and the correlated senses of pain. Pleasure in the other senses noted in 1.1 isn't a basic good, because the other senses of 'pleasure' pick out a great variety of phenomena, none of them in itself an objective of action.) If it is said that I do something simply because I find it pleasant, my action can thereby be made fully intelligible. So, for example, I can explain fully why I walk into a delicatessen, and then straight out again without buying anything, by saying that I did it just for the pleasure of the beautiful smell of coffee which pervades the shop. The same is true – indeed more obviously true – if I do something simply to avoid pain: taking an aspirin, ducking a cricket ball, changing a pair of shoes that rub my heels. No one needs to know any more about these actions than that they are calculated to prevent pain to understand them as well as they can or need be understood.

What else might be a basic good? Here are some suggestions from various philosophers.

> Personal affections and aesthetic enjoyments include *all* the greatest, and *by far* the greatest, goods we can imagine . . . (G. E. Moore, *Principia Ethica*, VI, para.113)

Moore thinks that nothing else is a (basic) good, or at least not one of much importance, besides the categories he mentions, friendship and aesthetic value. Perhaps not even our third category, pleasure and the avoidance of pain, counts as a basic good for him, except insofar as that is captured within, or can be subordinated to, the first two categories.

Moore's suggestion about what the basic goods are is patently inadequate – as much for Moore's own philosophical purposes as for anyone else's. It is possible to imagine a world where humans (want to) do nothing but contemplate *objets d'art* in the company of their friends. But that isn't our world. In our world, even members of the Apostles have more sorts of wants than that. Even they do actions with points that are not limited to these two categories. If this is Moore's theory of value it obviously fails to capture how things are.

> Riches, honours, fame or glory, power, bodily goods, pleasure,

goods of the soul, different kinds of created goods . . . (St Thomas Aquinas, *Summa Theologiae* 1a 2ae. 2, article titles)

These items constitute a list of candidates for the role of 'that in which human happiness consists', each of which in turn Aquinas rejects. His preferred candidate for that role is 'the contemplation of the divine Essence' (*Summa Theologiae* 1a 2ae. 3.8). It follows that Aquinas thinks that at least 'the contemplation of the divine Essence' is a basic good. In this we can safely agree with him. If there is a Divine Essence to contemplate – of the kind in which Aquinas believes as a Catholic – then certainly contemplating that essence is a basic good. Actions aimed at realising such contemplation are fully intelligible given the possibility of such contemplation.

Accepting this theological move does not mean that none of the other items in Aquinas's list could also be basic human goods – even if they are not also 'the utmost fulfilment of human happiness', as Aquinas thinks the contemplation of the Divine Essence is. Let us consider the items in his list in turn.

Pleasure is already in the list. So I will take bodily goods and goods of the soul next. By 'bodily goods' Aquinas means such things as life and health. By 'goods of the soul' he presumably means things like mental and psychical health and harmony – that is, everything from being sane to having a well-ordered, integrated and virtuous character. Because it is a full explanation of someone's actions to know that what they are aiming at is life (staying alive, or saving or preserving life/ lives) or physical health (being well, getting better), or mental/ psychical health or harmony, all of these items seem fairly clearly to be basic goods.

One thing related to 'goods of the soul' that also seems a basic good, although Aquinas passes over it in this context, has already been mentioned as a self-evident good in 2.1. This is rationality or reason – being clear and logically consistent in that part of one's thinking which is directed towards truth. Another is practical reasonableness – the analogue of logical consistency in that part of one's thinking which is directed towards action. Thirdly there is practical hope. This means the rejection of fatalism, and the belief that I have real opportunities to act to some purpose, and need not view all endeavours as doomed from the start. It can be argued that practical hope in this sense is both an essential presupposition in all projects of action, and also a good worth pursuing and cultivating in its own right.[11] Then there is truth itself; and also knowledge.[12] These too are basic goods, because they

are goods which we can or do pursue in their own right. The point of
research is to find the truth. One of our most basic urges is the urge
to know, to understand, to find out.[13] Nietzsche and Freud notwith-
standing, this urge is not necessarily and always some sinister and
disguised kind of sublimated pursuit of power. Though of course it
can, contingently and sometimes, be warped that way, still the urge to
know *can* be a sincere urge for truth just for the sake of truth, seen as
a good in its own right.[14]

Which of the different kinds of created goods should go in the list
of basic goods? There are some obvious examples of 'created goods'
which are basic. One such basic good is the object of concern for the
environment, for the natural world in general, or for some particular
environment, some particular section of that world. Another is simply
people: individual human beings. Concern for any particular human
being is an intelligible source of motivation in its own right; therefore
any particular human being is an instance of a type of basic good.[15]

Clearly neither wealth nor power is in itself a form of basic good
(although at least a minimal level of both is usually necessary if we are
to achieve the basic good of practical hope). These are merely instru-
ments to the achievement of other goods – sometimes not even that.
No action A is properly speaking intelligible just insofar as A is done
for the sake of money or power. Wealth and power are only good
because of the other goods they enable us to achieve: they are not basic
but merely instrumental goods. Indeed someone who saw these things
as basic goods would be making both a moral mistake, and a mistake
about causality too.[16]

Notice incidentally the interesting phenomenon that we have a name
for the mistake of thinking wealth a basic good, not merely an instrumental one. The disposition that embodies that mistake is called avarice
or materialism or possessiveness, and we regard it as a vice. Similarly,
the name for the disposition (or better one of the dispositions) that
embodies the mistake of thinking that power is a basic good and not
merely an instrumental one is 'ambition'. This too is a vice.[17]

'Honours' and 'fame or glory' are similar cases to wealth and power.[18]
It is a mistake (and a kind of vice) to think that wealth and power are
basic goods; the explanation of the mistake lies partly in the fact there
is something adjacent to wealth and power which is a basic good, namely
the freedom of opportunity required for practical hope. Similarly, there
is a mistake, and a vice, consisting in treating honour as a basic good;
this vice and its various subspecies and offspring have names like
'pride', 'snobbery', 'sycophancy', etc. There are also in the vicinity of

honour, however, at least two goods that are not merely instrumental but basic. The first of these seems closely connected with the type of good I picked out earlier as the good instantiated by the existence of individual human beings. This is the good of *respect* for human beings. By this I mean self-respect, and the respect of others whom one respects. Humans want and need to see themselves as valuable, or as having dignity, or as being honourable and honoured. They also want and need to see that they are so seen by others. Their desire for this respect fully explains at least some of their actions.[19] (It also explains a connection with another basic good, that of fairness or justice. Treating humans as having dignity means treating all humans as having dignity. And that means treating them as all having the same dignity.)

As an example of the explanatory power of reference to the human desire for respect as a motivating force, consider a little example. You think I have been stealing library books, and tell me I'm contemptible. So I try to explain myself to you. Why? Because I see that you despise me, and because your opinion of me matters to me. It matters not only in itself, because I respect you. It also matters because if you despise me, then because I respect you, your contempt for me (however unjustified it may be) gives me a reason to despise myself.[20] In the right circumstances this can be a complete explanation of my efforts to explain myself to you. The completeness of the explanation helps to show that we have located another basic good.

The second basic good in the vicinity of the notion of honour is the very interesting and important form of basic good which comes under the heading of achievements.[21] Besides the respect (and the fair treatment) that humans want from others and themselves, just because they are humans, they also want to do things that are worthwhile, or impressive, or in other ways admirable. As a by-product, they want to be honoured and admired for having done them: minimally by themselves, but ideally by everybody whose opinion matters to them.[22]

This raises the fascinating question of what counts as an achievement.[23] Some answers are these: success in the arts or the sciences or sport; staying happily married and raising a family well; running a successful business; climbing Everest (or Arthur's Seat); sailing round the world; collecting the number of every locomotive engine currently in service in Britain; saving the tiger (or the greater stinking cockroach) from extinction; putting on a production of *Hamlet* in the Chapter House of York Minster;[24] running a marathon, or the country well . . .

Anyone may go in for any of these practices or courses of action. Anyone who does so may be asked why they do so. It is a fair answer, and a completely explanatory one,[25] to say 'Because success in writing a novel, or discovering a new amino acid, or raising a family well, or whatever, is an *achievement*.'

There seem to be as many instances of the basic good of achievement as there are types of achievement. That might seem an anarchistic result, because it clearly breeds the possibility of thousands of basic goods (or rather instances of a type of basic good). But this profusion is fine by me. After all, I have already argued for the basic goodness of individual human beings, and so the possibility of, at the time of writing, getting on for 6000 million instances of one type of basic good. I don't think either sort of profusion leads us into anarchistic pluralism. To prevent that result of this generosity I need only make three points.

First, however diverse the possible types of achievement may be, still all have their basic intelligibility *because* we see them as (greater or lesser) achievements. To say that something is done *because* doing it is seen as an achievement is to explain it one way, when other possible ways of explaining it are available. (I might go to the top of Everest because, as they say, it's there – or I might do it to retrieve a dropped glove.)

Second, the great plurality of possible types of achievement is an asset of my theory because the good of achievement is one of the key goods around which most good lives are constructed. Hence this plurality is one of the features of my account that helps me to explain (as 1.2 showed the monist about the good couldn't) the great plurality of available good lives.

Third, in any case not just any successfully completed task is an achievement, or as much of an achievement as every other completed task. Climbing Everest is more of an achievement than collecting the number of every locomotive currently in service in Britain. Both are greater achievements than being able to balance ten peas on one's knife.

The reasons why some things are greater achievements than others make a complex and absorbing study in their own right. They have something to do with the notions of skill and difficulty[26] – but not everything: balancing 300 peas on one's knife is far more skilled, and far harder, than balancing thirty, but it is not much more of an achievement. (Why not? – Because it is not much more worthwhile?) They also have something to do with the virtues – but not everything: it is more or less obvious that one can be a good mathematician, mountaineer, doctor or parent without being a good *person* (that is, a good human being).[27] Again, what we count as achievements must have something to do with MacIntyre's concept of a 'practice'[28] – but not everything. For a start, not every achievement is, as MacIntyre apparently thinks, necessarily determined as such by its social context. (I may be the only person in my society who thinks that climbing Everest counts as an achievement. It doesn't follow, from that fact alone, that I'm wrong to think it so.) Again, no bad course of action can constitute what should seriously be regarded as an achievement, no matter what our social context suggests. (A whole society might, for all MacIntyre shows, have a MacIntyrean practice of Jew-killing, and so regard Hitler's successful programme of genocide as 'an achievement'. Their unanimity alone wouldn't make their judgement right, or prevent us from saying that to describe any genocide as an *achievement* is fantastically offensive.)

So far I have the following basic goods in my list:

Friendship; aesthetic value; pleasure and the avoidance of pain; the contemplation of God (if God exists); life; physical and mental health and harmony; reason, rationality, and reasonableness; truth, and the knowledge of the truth; the natural world; people; fairness; and achievements.

Four comments:

1 There's no hard distinction in this list of goods between the categories usually distinguished as Aesthetic, Moral, and Prudential. This is a quite deliberate part of my broadly naturalistic strategy in ethics. (For one of its consequences, see 2.3.) It's not that the distinctions between these sorts of goods are unreal; just that they aren't fundamental. The point about the members of my list of goods is that they are all goods – first principles of motivation. In comparison with that shared feature, the differences between the various goods on the list are of much less importance.

2 With my list, compare the lists offered by such proponents of the leading modern version of the theory of the basic goods as Grisez, Boyle, and Finnis.[29] According to them, there are something like the following seven basic goods:

Life, Knowledge, Play, Aesthetic Experience, Sociability, Practical Reasonableness, and Religion.[30]

Or, in another formulation, these seven: Self-Integration; Practical Reasonableness; Justice and Friendship; Religion or Holiness; Life and Health; Knowledge and Aesthetic Appreciation; and 'activities of skilful work and of play, which in their very performance enrich those who do them'.[31]

My main criticisms of such lists are two. (a) Whatever else such lists perhaps ought to include and don't, what's most patently missing from them is pleasure and the avoidance of pain.[32] (b) They are supposed, despite their suspiciously neat heptads, to be complete lists. But to try for completeness is a mistake. This brings me to my third comment on my own list.

3 The list of basic goods which I offer is long and complex – but it certainly isn't complete. Indeed, it couldn't be completed, because of a remarkable fact about humans. This is that the horizons of what they are and what they do are open in a radical way. It's not merely possible for humans to discover (or create) new instances of basic goods. They can even discover new types of basic goods. Art is an example. There was, presumably, a time when there were humans but no art. Likewise justice or fairness. There was, presumably, a time when there were humans, but no such thing as (consciously adopted) justice between them. The list of basic goods available to humans is in fact impossible to close while humans are still developing as a species – as I take it they are. Remember here my suggestion (1.2) that moral theory needn't only be about closing down the agent's options, but can also be about opening them up – about showing agents possibilities they never dreamed of. If there is really the possibility of discovering entirely new forms of good, then who knows what radical possibilities for new articulations of what it means to live a good human life are still ahead of us?

4 Two things aren't meant by this thesis of mine, that the correct account of the basic goods is dynamic, not static, and so that there may yet be entire forms of basic good waiting to be discovered. First, the Dynamic Thesis (as we may call it) doesn't mean that discoveries of new types of basic goods are two a penny. Second, it doesn't mean that it could be discovered that something now is a basic good that used to be either some other sort of good, or morally neutral, or else plain bad.

To see why the Dynamic Thesis doesn't have these implications, consider these three features of discoveries of basic goods:

1 They are irreversible. Once a basic good, always a basic good. Any new basic goods which are discovered in the future will be an *addition* to the human repertoire, not a displacement or replacement of something already in it. (This is not to say that forms of basic good cannot, once discovered, be forgotten or

neglected. Nor is it to deny that a society can repudiate a view about the basic goodness of something when it discovers that that view is mistaken, either because what it takes to be a basic good is not basic, or because it is not good.)

2 They are pioneering. They engage with areas of human possibility that have not previously been engaged in any way at all. (Perhaps we might rather say that they create new areas of human possibility.) Consider again the discovery of art as a clear example of this.

3 They are revolutionary. It is strictly unpredictable what basic goods may be discovered by humans in the future. If we could predict the emergence of a basic good, we'd already have an appreciation of it as a good – that is, we'd already have discovered it. (Consider the way in which the emergence of basic goods like art or justice was an enlarging of the dimensions of human life which was simply inconceivable in advance of its happening – precisely because to conceive it would have been to (begin to) achieve it.)

Given the Dynamic Thesis, I won't attempt to complete my treatment of the basic goods by closing my list of basic goods. Instead, in the next three sections, I do three things. First, I display one big advantage of pluralism about the good: the way in which pluralism about the good can deal with the traditional philosophical problem of egoism (2.3). Second, I expose my specific account of the basic goods and the unclosed list of basic goods that I've offered to a serious problem which arises for it, as for any attempt to do substantive and interesting moral theory: the problem of objectivity (2.4). Third, I consider an interesting question about the apparently existential status of claims like 'There is a basic good G' that arises in connection with my Working Hypothesis. This is the question whether there are any goods *simpliciter*, or whether all goods are essentially goods-for-someone.

2.3 THE BASIC GOODS AND THE PROBLEM OF EGOISM

The problem of egoism is the question 'Why should I be moral?'. It is the question why I should accept the constraints imposed by morality on my pursuit of my own advantage. The classic dilemma is that when it is to my advantage to do what is moral, I don't need a moral reason for acting morally. But when it isn't to my advantage to do what is moral, I have no reason for acting morally, moral or otherwise. So it

seems that the rational thing to do is always to ignore the promptings
of morality, whatever they may be, and just pursue my own advantage.

Typically, the problem of egoism is bungled by such familiar non-
naturalist solutions as Kant's. These insist that the very question 'Why
should I be moral?' is flawed, because an answer to it would have to
give either a prudential reason to be moral – which (being a 'natural'
reason) couldn't be an answer of the right sort. Or else it would have
to give a moral reason to be moral – but once we grasp the very idea
of such moral reasons, as it were 'from the inside', we will at once
come to be motivated by such reasons. For Kantians, to understand
moral reasons at all is to see that they are overridingly good reasons to
act, and so to be motivated to act on them. As soon as we understand
the question 'Why be moral?' from a moral point of view, the question
becomes for us a nonsense question.

But for one thing, even if Kantian moral considerations are (as is
often claimed) compelling 'from the inside', this proves nothing whatever about their rationality. All sorts of considerations about how we
ought to act might seem equally compelling 'from the inside', and yet
be irrational. One can imagine a witch-doctor or a psychedelic guru
insisting, rather like Kant, that the only reason we aren't motivated in
the ways he is is because we don't understand voodoo or LSD 'from
the inside'.

Neither, typically, is the problem of egoism well solved by naturalist
solutions. These insist, against Kant, that we should be able to find an
answer to the question 'Why should I be moral?' by finding a genuinely
prudential reason to be moral. The problem with such solutions is
simply that every account of why in general we have prudential reason
to be moral seems also to admit the possibility of special cases where
we have equally good prudential reason to be *im*moral.

A pluralist ethical theory like mine can, I believe, sidestep the difficulties that bog down typical naturalist and Kantian approaches to
the problem of egoism, because of its understanding of the key notion
in the problem of egoism: that of 'advantage'. Kantians and naturalists
alike tend to take this notion of something's being 'to my advantage'
for granted. They assume that it is simple and natural to think that
goods are typically privative – that what is to my advantage isn't to
yours. But why should anyone outside the economics seminar adopt
this sort of view of what 'advantage' means? In particular, why should
a pluralist about the good adopt it?

Presumably it can be agreed on all sides that the idea of 'my advantage' is to be explained by reference to the notion of 'my good'. But

then the idea of 'my good' is to be explained by reference to the notion of 'good' in general. And, according to the present theory, the notion of 'good' in general is to be explained by reference to the sort of list of basic goods given above.

So given anything like the list of basic goods offered in 2.2, we can defuse the plausibility of egoism as a general claim. Only some of the goods on our list look like they might sometimes count as privative goods – the kind of things that you and I might be in competition for. Undoubtedly some sorts of achievement, like getting to the South Pole first, are intrinsically privative; the pursuit of other sorts of good too, like pleasure or aesthetic value, can sometimes involve the division of finite resources. But compare goods like friendship, rationality, people, the natural world, and the contemplation of God if God exists. Some of these goods are naturally co-operative, not privative (friendship, rationality). Others perhaps are not naturally seen either as privative or as co-operative (practical hope; contemplation). Any enjoyment of these goods is bound to involve the consideration of others, or of what is outside any plausible definition of the individual agent's own 'interest or advantage', or both. So regarding these sorts of goods, it won't typically make any sense at all to suppose that 'my interest or advantage' is in competition with yours.

To think that the problem of egoism can even be set up as a general problem is to think that all the goods in the taxonomy can be treated as if they were privative goods. There are of course people who do treat all the goods they recognise like that. But we know what to say about such people. They're making a mistake about the nature of the goods, a mistake which they might conceivably be argued out of. Their mistake, in pursuing non-privative goods as if they were privative goods, isn't the genesis of an interesting philosophical problem about egoism. It is merely the relatively uninteresting phenomenon of such traits as graspingness, possessiveness, selfishness, or simple moral confusion. (Which of these traits depends on the particular details.)

This is game-over for the philosophical problem of egoism as a general problem about ethics. A more specific form of the problem of egoism, however, applying only to those goods that really are privative, is still in play. It's fairly unproblematic to claim that anyone who treats his friends as if they were his possessions is making a mistake about what kind of a good friends are. But what about the same person's equally acquisitive attitude to (for example) material possessions? What has a pluralist to say about that form of egoism?

To begin with, the pluralist might point out that he would be an oddly warped and distorted human who only valued the privative goods. After all, such an attitude will probably put, for example, a person's friendships in jeopardy. Then the question will be whether his acquisition of privative goods is worth its price in lost non-privative goods. Does this policy of eschewing these goods altogether lead to a good life? In practice, nearly every human answers this question in the negative – and the rest of us tend to have an extremely low opinion of the few humans who don't.

Another obvious point is that even those goods on our list that it does make sense to classify as privative goods can't as a rule be well or effectively pursued without the co-operation of others. Admittedly, our attempts to participate in a given privative good won't, as a matter of *logic*, necessarily fail if they are coupled with egoism (as they will in the case of co-operative goods like friendship). Nonetheless, our attempts to participate in a given privative good will, as a matter of *fact*, normally fail if they are coupled with egoism.[33] For example, pleasure. As many people have famously found, those pursuits of pleasure which are so self-absorbed that others are excluded from them very often turn out to have something self-defeating about them. The pleasures of my luxurious wealth would be greater if I had not, as part of the way I pursue them, excluded everyone else from those pleasures.

The third, and decisive, point is this. Even if we suppose that we can make at least prima-facie sense of the notion of the egoist – the notion of someone who acts only in pursuit 'of their own interest' – it can still be shown that such a person is irrational in their own terms. Any such person's practical reasoning recognises only self-interested reasons to act. But as we have already seen, there is a wide variety of goods, pleasure and friendship among them, which aren't best pursued, and in some cases can't be pursued at all, by someone who is motivated only by self-interested reasons to act. It follows that the egoist, the person who is motivated only by self-interested reasons to act, has self-interested reason to act so that they become a person who is *not* motivated only by self-interested reasons to act. The best egoistic policy is then the abandonment of the policy of egoism. The best way to achieve one's own self-interested ends, in distinction from anyone else's ends or any ends which aren't specifically tied to any individual's self-interest, is to stop hanging everything on that distinction. Properly understood, egoism is a self-abolishing strategy.

Is it inconsistent for egoistic considerations to dictate the abandonment of egoism? – Well, what would the inconsistency be? It can't be, for example, that in exiting his system the egoist contradicts an axiom of that system. On pain of a regress similar to that to which Achilles succumbs in Lewis Carroll's 'What the Tortoise said to Achilles' (*Mind*, 1895), it can't be an axiom of the egoist's system that he operate according to the axioms of that system, and so that he not exit the system.

It may also seem tempting to say that the egoist who, for reasons arising in egoism, ceases to be an egoist must therefore still be a egoist ever after – because he is still acting upon that last egoistical reason. So perhaps we still reach the familiar paradox that everyone is really an egoist. One might respond 'Sure – call him an egoist if you like, provided that doesn't stop you from seeing the difference between him and the sorts of people we normally apply "egoist" to'. But really calling this character an egoist seems no more reasonable than saying that a computer operator who, during his working day, obeys all his machine's instructions, including the final instruction **EXIT THE SYSTEM**, is still following the computer's instructions three hours later when he is sitting at home watching *Blind Date*. Just because all the egoist's subsequent actions happen to be consistent with a single one (the last) of egoism's instructions is not enough to show that he is still following even one of egoism's instructions.

But isn't it a problem that, as soon as the egoist has acted upon his last egoistical reason, he ceases to have reason to act upon any egoistical reason – including that reason? No: the reason gets him as far as acting upon it, and that's as far as it needs to get him. Once he has done that, he can and does acquire other sorts of reasons.

If the arguments against egoism given here are correct, then, *pace* lots of theorists,[34] the standard opposition between the supposed extremes of demandingness and egoism can barely even be set up.

2.4   ARE THE BASIC GOODS OBJECTIVE?

Objectivity is a huge problem on which many long books have been written. I have no space or inclination to add to their number here. My remarks will be deliberately summary in character, and I can only ask my readers' forbearance if they think I should have written more about this topic. Myself, I would, like Parfit (*Reasons and Persons* (= *RP*) p. 453), be nearer to the opposite view – that we have had plenty of good writing on objectivism and subjectivism in recent analytical ethics, but not enough on other, less rarefied topics. Hence the distribution of emphases in this book.)

Why should we think that what our society counts as an intelligible and complete explanation of an action either (1) really is an intelligible and complete explanation, or (2) has any conceptual priority over different accounts of the action in question that another society might offer or have offered? The best answer to this question is, briefly, to take the point. There is no *a priori* reason to believe that what our society counts as intelligibility in an action explanation is bound to be either (a) certainly right, or (b) more right than any other society's account of intelligibility in action explanations.

But then what follows? It's not noticed often enough that this point, like other parallel points that are frequently made about the differences between cultures, isn't a subjectivist point at all but an objectivist one. What follows the acceptance of this point isn't the mental paralysis of subjectivism. It is the possibility of getting a critical angle on anyone's practices of action explanation and their ethical practices at large – including our own. Such critical reflection on what human social groups count as intelligibility doesn't have to *undermine* our own notion of intelligibility. It may actually confirm it; or again it may prove a reformatory influence.

Moreover, while such critical reflection is an essential part of the objectivist's repertoire, it isn't even available within a consistent subjectivism. An objectivist can look at (say) Maori or Tibetan concepts of practical intelligibility, or Quechua concepts of child-rearing, and decide that they are either in better order than ours (so that we have something to learn from them), or again in worse order (so that we have something to teach them). Such thoughts aren't even available to the subjectivist, because for him Maori or Tibetan or Quechua concepts can't be in better or worse shape than ours: they're merely different. This not only means that we can't teach the Maori or the Tibetan anything – a possibility that the more right-on sorts of subjectivist are keen to deny. It also means that we can't learn anything from them either – a possibility which right-on subjectivists usually don't like denying at all, as their whole approach was based on the desire to avoid cultural condescension. This very desire makes no sense unless subjectivism is false.

Another question that is often asked is: if objective truths are available in ethics, how come we don't seem to get any closer to them over time, as we do seem to get closer to objective truths in science? This is the problem of (to use Bernard Williams's term: *Ethics and the Limits of Philosophy* (= *ELP*) Ch. 8) 'converging' upon agreement about ethics. Ethical convergence in Williams's sense is a rationally motivated movement towards agreement about ethical questions analogous to that which we get in the development of scientific theories. It is crucial to Williams's argument for the non-objectivity of ethics that convergence isn't possible.

But Williams's claim might be disputed by reference to some obvious examples. For instance, there seems little doubt that, worldwide, more people would accept the moral claims of the United Nations Charter of Human Rights now than was the case in 1945. Moreover, it's not obvious why we can't add that they would accept them for the right sort of reasons. (This matters given Williams's insistence that convergence is not merely any move towards consensus, but such a move that is 'guided by how things actually are' (*ELP* p. 136).) I can't see why Williams should think that the guidance of 'how things actually are' should be unavailable for a naturalistic ethics which is grounded in facts in the way I suggest in 2.4. I would agree, of course, that it's quite impossible to ground non-naturalism in any such way; but that's just another reason for not being a non-naturalist. There is every reason to think that the 'globalisation' of human culture is also leading to a globalisation of such basic views about rights as those contained in the UN Charter. This process is gradual, and of course meets setbacks, such as the Tiananmen Square massacre in Beijing in 1989. For all that there seems little doubt that it continues. (And that it's a good thing. It's hard to take seriously the idea that attempts to promulgate a declaration that torture or massacre is bad should be dismissed as cultural imperialism.) Here we seem to have empirical evidence, as clear as you like, that full-blooded ethical convergence is not only possible but is actually happening.

Not that it's necessary for the moral objectivist to produce any such evidence of convergence. The evident variations in ethical belief between societies (and individuals) to which the subjectivist points are no evidence against ethical objectivism even when the arguments to which they lead prove irresoluble in practice (as they sometimes do). Variations between ethical beliefs, and even the occurrence of irresoluble conflicts between them, can be perfectly well explained without abandoning objectivism. For a start, there is the point that people typically have no practical stake in protecting their present beliefs regarding Williams's touchstone of objectivity – science; but they nearly always have a practical stake in protecting their present ethical beliefs. It is surprising if we find we can't persuade an intelligent Nazi that, say, platypuses lay eggs. It isn't at all surprising if we find we can't persuade the same intelligent Nazi that all humans have the same basic right to fair and benevolent treatment.[35]

As it happens, I suspect that nearly all of the variations in ethical belief which we observe between societies and individuals are explicable by dividing them into three classes.

1 Variations in ethical belief may be variations in beliefs about the scope of the ethical community: for example, Greek and Roman views about slaves and barbarians, cannibals' beliefs about whom we may eat, Nazis' views about the inferiority of non-Aryans. (For my views on this, see 4.4.)
2 Variations in ethical belief may be variations in understanding of how to achieve the basic goods, and of what constitutes achievements of them.
3 Differences in ethical outlook are very commonly sharpened by differences in religious outlook.[36]

All three of these sorts of variation or disagreement are for our purposes eliminable. All of them raise issues which can in principle be settled by rational argument. Hence the existence of these sorts of variation poses no fatal objection to objectivism.

The possibility of settlement by rational argument is (I think) obvious regarding (3), the issue of truth in religion. It's also a possibility regarding (1) and (2). Thus, for example, regarding (1) we may find ourselves pointing to the fact that slaves are humans just like we are – that there are, for instance, no such differences in physical appearance between slaves and freemen as Aristotle implausibly claims to discern at *Politics* 1254b26. So there's no rational basis for the differential treatment of those who are slaves. Or regarding (2), we may find ourselves questioning whether what is supposed to instantiate or promote a given good does so at all, or at all well. This can often simply be a causal question (for example, 'Does self-denial make me a kinder person – or a shorter-tempered one?'). Such questions are clearly amenable, in principle at least, to rational argument.

Hence it's easy, and indeed customary, to overstate the difficulty of finding rational arguments to support one ethical belief over another. But still: aren't there differences between what different societies take to be the goods? In fact, isn't a society's conception of the basic goods no more than a function of its history?

Briefly, the answer is no. Of course it would be ridiculous to expect just any human society to produce any lists of goods whatever, let alone lists of goods just like mine, of which all the members are recognised as separate and irreducible goods in their own right. Again, certainly there are *some* variations over space and across time in societies', or individual philosophers', explicit or implicit conceptions of the basic goods. What is usually *most* different between societies, however, (though not necessarily between individual philosophers) is not their *theories of value*, their accounts of what is good, but their *ethical codes* – their accounts of how to respond in action to what is good. At the level of the theory of value – which is the level we are currently at: for the beginnings of an ethical code, see chapter 3 – there are necessary limits, set not by magic but by the constraints of (ideally understood) intelligibility, on the degree to which conceptions of the basic goods can vary across societies and times. There may be variations in attitudes to or the degrees of recognition of some of the more peripheral basic goods. But some central goods,[37] such as truth and pleasure, are always recognised, in practice if not in theory, in every society, even a Nazi one.[38] It could not even be intelligible for a society to hold that, say, pain or hunger or disease or death or ignorance or loneliness or terror or despair were not just good things for its members under certain special circumstances, but straightforwardly good things for its members: not good as punishment, or therapy, or religous purification, or for a while, or anything like that – but just good.

(Consequently any new types of basic goods that are discovered or invented[39] in the future are likely, though not certain, to be peripheral goods too. If they were not peripheral, we would probably have a conception of them already. On the other hand, one can imagine a solitary human, or someone from a tribe that had no conception of fairness, saying what I have just said. But surely friendship and fairness, which such a person might lack knowledge of, are not peripheral goods!)

If it is a fact that there are necessary limits on what could be an intelligible conception of the basic goods, this shows that the basic goods aren't defined in a society-relative way; they are defined in a species–relative way. There are some things which any human needs, just as a human. If that is a fact, then it is the founding fact for the theory of the basic goods.

But this brings us to my last question about the objectivity of any taxonomy of the goods or motivations such as mine. Even if some such list as I offer is correct, what's the *significance* of that fact? Why should it matter, ethically speaking, that all humans seek (say) pleasure or truth? After all, it might have been the case that all humans sought stick-insects or postage stamps – 'as an end in themselves', 'in their own right'. That would seem to prove nothing for ethics, if it were true. So why should the (alleged) fact that, for example, all humans seek pleasure and try to avoid pain, has any more ethical importance than the fact that all bees seek nectar and avoid spiders' webs? Why isn't this – as Hume and Hobbes believed – a merely contingent fact of no deep significance?

In line with my claim that the variations in the conceptions of the basic goods which people actually live by are necessarily only marginal, the first necessity here is to deny that such facts could have been otherwise. It might *not* have been the case that all humans sought stick-insects or postage stamps as an end in themselves, and instead of (rather than as well as) seeking, for example, pleasure, truth, and friendship. It's just false that we could devise another set of basic goods, which shared no members (or close equivalents) with some such set as the one proposed above. No intelligible description of a human society could even be imagined on the basis of such a radically deviant list. (Try composing one and see.)

The right list of basic motivations has then some essential members. But even if this so, still the question comes back: what does that prove in ethics? Isn't it just a commission of the 'naturalistic fallacy' to imagine that we can reason from claims, even of this last sort, about what humans are naturally motivated by, to claims about what is ethically good or bad?

No: if my Working Hypothesis is right (1.4), then it's no fallacy to move from talk about human motivation to talk about human good. (On the contrary, there is nowhere *else* to start.) But at this point in ethics we always find ourselves in the grip of a powerful picture – Hume's picture of a world of causally inert facts in stark and simple contrast with an affective domain of felt values. One of this picture's effects on us is, of course, to press the question of how any naturalistic conception of the human good could be a candidate for plain truth. At best (we will say, if Hume's picture grips us) any such conception has only the authority of the consensus of human feelings which does the real work in ethical motivation; at worst, it is an ideological weapon, a clever way of disguising our real agenda. So let me try to say something very quickly to undermine Hume's dichotomy.

I don't disagree with Hume that there are 'facts' and there are 'values', and that the two aren't the same thing. In fact, I see more variety than he does in the target area. This is partly because I reject Hume's (closely connected) views about causation and the philosophy of science. As Hume knew well, interesting causal and scientific laws are not statistical. If they were, they'd be uselessly circular: they would input data and output the same data. Thus, for example, a zoological law about swans' age of sexual maturity would have no more content or interest than the returns from the surveys of swan behaviour or anatomy that grounded it. But this isn't so: such laws have, for instance, predictive power, which the data on which they are based clearly don't have.[40]

Or again, consider an example from Professor Jean Aitchison's 1996 BBC Reith Lectures on the development of speech in children. She spoke of experimental attempts to identify *phases of development* in children's speech. What is it to look for a phase of (biological/ neurological) development? It is to find experimental data, usually of a statistical form, which evidentially support a conclusion of the general form 'Between the ages M and N *normal healthy* children develop the *capacity* to perform linguistic tricks ABC'. Such a claim as Professor Aitchison's researchers made here is plainly an inference from the statistical data. So to be interesting at all, and on pain of circularity, that conclusion must be irreducible to those data.

So what we have in such cases is a move beyond the barest and starkest level of factual discourse – the *statistical* – to a rather less bare or stark level of discourse that I shall call (not too provocatively, I hope)[41] the *teleological*. For present purposes, teleological discourse has two particularly interesting features. First it is, as just noted, irreducible to the statistical discourse in which it is grounded. To say how normal healthy children develop is not necessarily to say how most children develop, any more than saying 'what spermatozoa do' means saying what the majority of spermatozoa do. Second, as this last example shows, teleological discourse has an explanatory power which science as we do it can't do without, and which statistical discourse, taken alone, lacks. In particular, it can explain by appeal to such notions as *what a thing tends (by its nature) to do* and *what a thing (by its nature) is for*. Although most glass is not in the act of breaking under relatively light pressure, there is a lot that we can't explain about any glass if we don't know that all glass is, by disposition, fragile.[42] Although most spermatozoa don't fuse with ova to form zygotes, we miss the most important point of all about spermatozoa if we don't realise the sense in which fusing with ova to form zygotes is what spermatozoa are, by nature and by evolutionary design, *for*.

It is worthwhile to develop this point a little for at least two reasons. First, it shows a sense in which not even 'the realm of fact' is homogeneously immune from normativity. What I call teleological discourse is factual all right, and unavoidable for any decent science.[43] Yet teleological discourse, with its references to 'what a thing is for', to 'what it typically does', and so forth, is itself already weakly normative. (One might call this *should-be* normativity, having in mind the 'should be' of, for example, 'If it's a human being it *should be* possessed of thirty-two teeth'.)

Second, the point is interesting because of the odd relation of defeasible inference which seems to hold between the statistical and the teleological. No amount of statistical data documenting the sad fate of the majority of spermatozoa is going to make it true that spermatozoa aren't designed to fuse with ova to form zygotes; and yet it isn't as if the statistical evidence had no relevance to the question at all. (If no spermatozoon ever fused with ova to form zygotes, or again if arrestingly salient consequences didn't follow when spermatozoa did fuse with ova, there would be a real doubt about whether this *was* what sperm were for.) So the relevance of the statistical to the teleological is interestingly oblique.[44] The statistical clearly is not sufficient alone to determine the teleological: other factors, such as explanatory salience, have to come into play. But just the same sort of interesting obliqueness seems to hold when we consider the relation of what, as a matter of statistics, humans are found desiring to the kind of motivations which are said to be natural for humans by a theory of motivations such as I offered in 1.1. Again the empirical data seem to underdetermine the shape of such a theory: even though they are clearly relevant to its shape, they are not relevant simply for head-counting purposes, but for other and subtler reasons (such as the agent's own ability to decide for herself on what is important about such data: 2.2). It looks then as if rather the same sort of defeasible inference is in question in this second relation too. (As for a third relation, that of the theory of motivation or the good to the theory of the right, that relation is another interesting problem again; as this book aims to demonstrate.)

So there isn't just one thing called the fact/value distinction. There is a number of different distinctions in the relevant area. As we move across these distinctions from the statistical towards the strictly ethical, we find that normativity has set in much sooner than a Humean might have expected; we also find the same process of defeasible inference happening more than once. Above all, I suggest, we find ourselves moving towards the view that the kinds of claims characteristic of a theory of human motivations and goods such as I offer here go deeper, and do more work, than the Humean can allow. For they pick out what we must see as important or essential about human beings if we are to understand human beings, just as such, at all. Salience in this sort of essentially normative philosophical anthropology is not to be understood as a function of salience in any lower-order description, for instance of the sort that a head count or opinion poll might provide. What the facts which are salient for such a description do is ground (defeasibly) the kind of ethical claims that turn out to be justifiable on the basis of an essentialist consideration of human nature. If we can't see how such a philosophical anthropology might be of use to ethics – or even indispensable to ethics – that is probably because we are still, at heart, too orthodox in our Humeanism.[45]

2.5 GOODS AND GOODS-FOR[46]

I turn to a different question, about exactly what ontological commitments are entailed by my claim that 'there *are* certain basic goods'. We may ask: Can anything be simply and non-relatively good – good *simpliciter*? That is, can anything be good without being good for someone, at least potentially? The question was famously discussed by G. E. Moore in a thought experiment which he developed in criticism of Sidgwick:

> Let us imagine one world exceedingly beautiful . . . put into it whatever on this earth you most admire – mountains, rivers, the sea; trees and sunsets, stars and moon . . . And then imagine the ugliest world you can possibly conceive. Imagine it simply one heap of filth, containing whatever is most disgusting to us . . . supposing [these worlds] quite apart from any possible contemplation by human beings; still, is it irrational to hold that it is better that the beautiful world should exist, than the one which is ugly?' (G. E. Moore, *Principia Ethica*, Ch. 3, S.50)

Moore's answer to this question is, apparently, a qualified 'No' – although the qualification is far less emphasised in chapter 3 of *Principia Ethica* than in chapter 6, S.113, where it appears that the 'mere existence of what is beautiful has value, so small as to be negligible, in comparison with that which attaches to the *consciousness* of beauty' [my underlining].

Leaving aside Moore's indecisions, how should we answer the question if we believe that there are many different basic goods? Are those goods goods-for, or goods *simpliciter*? Can any goods, including what I call basic goods, exist without anyone being conscious of them? Or are they necessarily always goods for some consciousness?

First, we should disentangle these two questions:

1 Are all goods essentially goods goods-for, and not goods *simpliciter*?

2 Are all goods goods in someone's consciousness or experience?

A positive answer to (2) puts us on the way to the subjective hedonist account of goods. But that account is clearly false. By contrast a positive answer to (1), though it has often been mistakenly used as support for subjective hedonism, gives us something different, namely the view that there is an intrinsic connection between the notion of agents or subjects and the notion of goods. The claim is that there can be no clear conception of what 'good' means without a clear conception of how a given good is or might be a good for anyone – for any human agent or for any non-human agent who is sufficiently anthropomorphised to be intelligible to us.[47]

So phrased, this latter claim seems uncontestable – especially if you're an ethical naturalist, as I am, and are prepared to argue, as I have, for the Working Hypothesis that there is an intrinsic and necessary connection between the three notions of good, motivation, and justification. More clarification is still needed, however, of what we are committed to by a positive answer to (1). Contrast the following theses:

A There are humanly conceivable goods which (necessarily, in some deeper than physical sense of necessity) could not be goods for anyone (= any human/humanoid).

B There are humanly conceivable goods which as a matter of fact are not goods for anyone.

C There are humanly conceivable goods which as a matter of fact are not goods for someone.

(A) is self-contradictory. To say that something is a humanly conceivable good precisely entails holding that it could be a good for someone. Part of what seems right about answering Yes to question (1) must be that Yes to (1) rules out (A). Yes to (1) shouldn't rule out (B) or (C), however. It shouldn't rule out (B) because, as I argued in 2.2, there may yet be further goods for humans to discover, as there certainly were for humans in the past.[48] (That was my Dynamic Thesis.) Nor should Yes to (1) rule out (C), for two reasons. First, because (C) is entailed by (B). Second, because as I argued in 2.3, some people (egoists, for example) hold, confusedly, a stunted or warped conception of the human goods, which omits some goods that really are human goods.

So (A) is logically false, but (B) and (C) are true. There is also this interesting converse to (C) to consider:

> D There are goods for someone which as a matter of fact are not goods.

(D) is self-contradictory. From 'G is a good for someone' we can't infer 'G is (actually, and not *ceteris paribus*) a good for everyone'. But we can infer 'G is a good'. Given that entailment, (D) implies that there is some good such that it isn't a good. This ain't so.

Compare (E), however:

> E There are 'goods' for someone which as a matter of fact are not goods.

(E) says, slightly elliptically, that some people believe some things to be (instantiations of) goods which aren't (instantiations of) goods. Unsurprisingly, no doubt, this modest claim is true. It is shown to be true simply by the evidence of examples. Anscombe's example is the most dramatic case of this phenomenon, Milton's Satan:

> 'Evil be thou my good' is often thought to be senseless in some way. Now all that concerns us here is that 'What's the good of it?' is something that can be asked until a desirability characterisation has been reached and made intelligible. If then the answer to this question at some stage is 'The good of it is that it's bad', this need not be unintelligible; one can go on to ask 'And what is the good of its being bad?', to which the answer might be condemnation of good as impotent, slavish, and inglorious.' (G. E. M. Anscombe, *Intention* S.39)[49]

Let me now return to our original question, 'Are there any goods which are not goods for someone, but goods *simpliciter*?' I can now say that, in one way, the answer to this is No, but in another way, it is Yes.

The sense in which the answer is No is given by the denial of (A) above. To deny (A) is to say that there are no humanly conceivable goods which could not be goods for any human. But any ethical naturalist is likely to hold that what counts as a good, for humans, is to be defined by considering what counts as a good-for-humans.[50] This then is one natural way of interpreting the claim that there are no goods *simpliciter*, but only goods-for, which makes it come out true.

Even then, however, there is still an important contrast between the good-for-humans and the good-for-someone-or-other. The good-for-humans is normally explanatorily prior to the good-for-someone. We can't explain why something G is a good-for-someone by 'Because it's a good-for-him'. But we can explain it by 'Because G is a good-for-humans'.[51] Normally and for the most part, that's just what we do. Such explanations to the good-for-humans are explanations to an ethical first principle. Goods-for-humans are first principles for ethics, whereas goods-for-someone, or goods-for-some-group-of-people, aren't.

As for the sense in which the answer to the question 'Are there any (humanly conceivable) goods which are not goods for someone, but goods *simpliciter*?' is Yes, this is revealed by the claim I labelled (B) above. (B) was the claim that there are humanly conceivable goods which as a matter of fact are not goods for anyone. Given (B), we can see how to answer Moore's question 'Is it irrational to hold that it is better that the beautiful world should exist, than the one which is ugly?' Our answer should be No. *Pace* Moore, the existence of his beautiful world is not a state of affairs that couldn't conceivably be a good for anyone. After all, Moore is prepared to describe it as *beautiful*. We know what kind of good beauty is; so we know what kind of good would be available to anyone who did contemplate Moore's beautiful world. Therefore, any sense of 'impossible' in which it may be impossible to contemplate Moore's beautiful world is not relevant to assessment of whether the beautiful world's existence is a good thing, or a better thing than the ugly world's existence. And so Moore's beautiful world is only contingently, not necessarily, not a good for anyone. But if (A) and (B) are true, then the beautiful world can be both as a matter of fact not good for anyone, and yet also good in a humanly conceivable sense. The sense in question has to do with the way in which it would be good-for any human who perceived it.

This conclusion has clear implications for, for example, environmental ethics. By this sort of argument, we can explain how it can be reasonable and intelligible for us to attach value and importance for example to the existence of things that none of us is ever especially likely to see: the dramatic wildernesses of Antarctica, or the beautiful forests of some planet near Alpha Centauri. We know how such things have value by knowing what it would be like for creatures like us (or indeed, in some cases, unlike us) to enjoy their value. It doesn't follow that, for us to think that such things have value, we have to suppose that anyone actually enjoys (or even could enjoy) their value.[52] (Suppose we knew that the Alpha Centauri planet's forests always had been, and always would be, uninhabited by any animal. Would it be any less an environmental crime – as opposed to a humanitarian crime – to send off a rocket to destroy those forests?)

This point about goods doesn't only apply to the goods which are relevant in such areas of inquiry as environmental ethics and environmental aesthetics. It is of very wide application, and helps us to see in what sense, quite generally, the goodness of humanly conceivable goods both bears intimately upon the possibilities of benefiting from and being motivated by such goods, and yet also transcends the scope of those possibilities. That is, it shows us something about when and in what sense it is correct to say that such goods *exist*. In a nutshell, the basic goods don't depend upon us for their existence; but on the other hand, for humans, nothing could be a good which couldn't be a good-for-humans. Human conceptions of the good necessarily depend on what actually benefits or harms humans.

2.6 CONCLUSION

We have now seen how the pluralist, equipped with what might be a plausible (unclosed) taxonomy of the basic goods (2.2) formed on the principles suggested in 2.1, might tackle three notorious problems in moral philosophy: egoism (2.3), subjectivity (2.4), and the relative or absolute existential status of the goods (2.5). But the most important problem facing pluralism about the good is none of these, it's the Problem of Reconciliation: the question of how we are to reconcile such diverse basic goods within a single life. I commented in 1.2 that 'anarchistic pluralism' about motivation, of the kind I there attributed to Hume, was bound to be sorely pressed by that problem. The same must be true of any form of pluralism about the good, anarchistic or not, especially if it is as generous and open-ended in its conception of the goods as mine is. It's now time to begin, in chapter 3, to explain pluralism's answer to the Problem of Reconciliation.

NOTES

1. I offer no taxonomy of the virtues in ch. 2, though I make some brief remarks about how such a taxonomy might be grounded in 3.4. Any such taxonomy presupposes a taxonomy of goods or motivations, and also something like the notion of commitment to a good explored in 3.4. I don't, anyway, have much to add to standard taxonomies of the virtues like Aquinas' in the *Summa Theologiae*, which I assume are easily compatible with my taxonomy of goods and motivations.
2. Some of what follows is adapted by kind permission from my (1996b).
3. I ignore the obvious but irrelevant complications that you can have more than one motivation for a single action, and that several actions can have the same motivation.
4. Again, I might go to see the picture because my art teacher tells me to, or to recall what fruit the goddess at the bottom right holds, or ... But these are not the reasons why the speaker of 2(a) goes to see the picture – unless there's something he's not telling us.
5. What if the renewing of my friendship is not the last term in the explanatory chain? Suppose

I am renewing my friendship with Jones only to find out where he buried some treasure. Then the question arises why I want to find that out. Just because the chain does not end where we thought it did does not mean it does not end somewhere.

6. Cp. Aristotle's argument quoted in 1.1 against the view that everything is chosen for the sake of something else: 'if that were true, then X would be wanted only for the sake of Y, and Y only for the sake of Z, and Z for the sake of something else again: we would face an infinite regress, and our wishes would be empty and vain' (*Nicomachean Ethics* 1094a19ff.).

7. Hence we might infer (at least some of) the goods that must be or might be in our taxonomy of goods by asking what might or must appear in the narrative of a good human life – although I shall proceed more or less in the other direction in this book. On the relationship between goods and a life narrative, see 5.2.

8. Cp. Ackrill (1979).

9. A philosopher who denies exactly this is Grisez, discussed below in Note 32. Cp. Aristotle, *Nicomachean Ethics* 1153b27.

10. This argument alone, of course, does not show that rationality is a basic good rather than an instrumental good – merely that rationality is necessarily preferable to irrationality.

11. For an argument to this effect v. my (1996b).

12. Cp. John Skorupski, *John Stuart Mill* p. 300, for a slightly different claim: '*Knowledge of one's situation* is an end which people do pursue, not simply as a part of happiness, but as an organising category, coordinate with happiness, under which a multiplicity of desired objects fall'. Whether in fact the goodness of knowledge as a source of motivation can be separated from the goodness of truth as a source of motivation is another question I leave for the reader.

13. For a brilliant depiction of the importance of this urge to humans, v. A. S. Byatt's novel *Possession*.

14. It is no objection here to observe, as we should, that truth, knowledge and reason can also be goods instrumental to the achievement of other goods. What needs to be shown by someone who wants to argue that these or other goods are not basic is not that they are sometimes intelligibly treated instrumentally, but that they are never intelligibly treated non-instrumentally. (Cp. Aristotle, *Nicomachean Ethics* 1096b21ff., in epigraph to chapter 1: 'Even though we sometimes pursue these things for the sake of something else, nonetheless we would say that they are good in themselves'.)

15. This might prompt the question 'Why humans particularly?'. To which I answer 'Why indeed?' I am happy to entertain the thought that other animals are instances of basic goods too, though I'd deny that they are instances of the same sort of basic good. V. my remarks on speciesism in (Chappell 1996c) and (Chappell 1997).

16. *Pace* John Rawls, who includes among his 'primary goods' (= 'things which it is supposed a rational man wants whatever else he wants') 'rights and liberties, opportunities and powers, income and wealth' (Rawls, *Theory of Justice* p. 92). Rights and liberties, I'd say, aren't basic goods, but things we are owed because of the way it is with certain basic goods, for example justice and respect. Opportunities and powers are instances of basic goods, for example health, intelligence and practical hope. Income and wealth aren't basic goods at all, though their presence can as a matter of fact be needed for us to participate in the basic good of practical hope.

17. Possibly, then, the mistaking of instrumental goods for basic goods defines a whole genus of vices.

18. For one influential discussion of why honour (*timê*) is not an intrinsic good, v. Aristotle, *Nicomachean Ethics* I.5, 1095b23ff.; also Aquinas on *honores* and *fama sive gloria*, *Summa Theologiae* 1a2ae.2.2–3.

19. Cp. Rawls, *A Theory of Justice* pp. 440ff., on the importance of the 'primary good' of 'self-respect'.

20. Respecting your despiser need not always be part of the story. To be despised by anyone is unpleasant. As many schoolchildren are unlucky enough to know, it can be hard to resist the impulse to despise yourself because you're despised, even when the despisers are people whom you despise.

21. One consequence of taking achievement as a basic good is to clarify at least part of the unattractiveness of opting for Nozick's 'experience machine': 'Perhaps what we desire is to live (an active verb) ourselves, in contact with reality. (And this, machines cannot do *for* us.)' (Nozick, *Anarchy, State and Utopia*, p. 45).

22. Contrast respect for me and respect for my achievements. It is unpleasant for me to lack anyone's respect – even the respect of someone I don't respect. But if (what I take to be) my achievements aren't respected by people whose opinions about that sort of achievement I don't respect, I am unlikely to care much – provided those whom I take to be competent judges of my achievements do respect them. What makes for this contrast, I suppose, is the fact that respect for persons is something that we think anyone has a right to, completely generally and just *qua* human being. (No doubt there is a connection here with the notion of a right.) By contrast, respect for achievements is contingent upon their satisfying the criteria of some special area of endeavour.

23. A question first drawn to my attention by an early version of (Martin 1994) which Christopher Martin kindly showed me.

24. This (to lapse into irrelevance for a moment) is something I've wanted to do ever since I last visited York Minster. More relevantly, recall Aristotle's virtue of *megaloprepeia* – magnificence, putting on a good show, for example by building beautiful cathedrals or producing first-rate dramatic or social events like a good *Hamlet* or a storming College Ball. Obviously some of the reasons why magnificence really is a virtue have to do with aesthetic good; some other reasons, I think, have to do with achievement goods. One of the dispositions opposite to *megaloprepeia* is what we sometimes call the *utilitarian* mindset – the dreary and boorish attitude which can't see why the Ball Committee (or the cast and director of *Hamlet*) put so many months' effort into what is after all only one short summer night of dissipation (or of drama).

25. Provided, at least, that the inquisitor accepts the description of the activity as an achievement. If I don't think collecting every train number in some category is an achievement, I may still ask 'But why do you think that's an achievement?', and be puzzled by whatever answer I get. But I have still learnt something by learning, at any rate, that *the train-spotter thinks* what he does is an achievement – even if I disagree. I do at least know, for example, that the train-spotter doesn't think that train-spotting is worth doing because it makes his mother happy.

26. Compare Aquinas' remark that virtues are necessarily concerned with what is difficult: *Summa Theologiae* 1a2ae.63.4.

27. More obvious at the beginning of this list: less obvious towards the end of it. Some roles (especially those of parents or spouses or friends, and in professions such as nursing or counselling) are very difficult indeed to play well unless you're also a good person.

28. Meaning – and try saying this without drawing breath – a 'coherent and complex form of socially established cooperative human activity through which goods internal to that form of activity are realised in the course of trying to achieve those standards of excellence which are appropriate to, and partially definitive of, that form of activity, with the result that human powers to achieve excellence, and human conceptions of the ends and goods involved, are systematically extended' (MacIntyre, *After Virtue*, p. 187).

29. See, *inter alia*, Grisez, *Christian Moral Principles* and *Living a Christian Life*; Finnis, *Fundamentals of Ethics*, *Natural Law and Natural Rights*, and *Moral Absolutes*; and (Grisez, Boyle and Finnis 1987). My account of what a basic good is is fairly close to Grisez's, Boyle's and Finnis's. My account of which are the basic goods is very different. Since encountering their writings during the development of the present theory, however, I have gratefully learnt a great deal from them; especially Finnis, who kindly commented in detail on an early form of chapters 1 and 2 of this book.

30. Finnis's list: *Natural Law and Natural Rights* pp. 86–9.

31. Grisez's list: *Christian Moral Principles* 5D. A similar sevenfold list occurs, in reverse order, in (Grisez, Boyle and Finnis 1987), pp. 103–4. Here the main difference from the *CMP* list is that 'practical reasonableness' seems to have been replaced by a reference to 'peace of conscience and consistency between one's self and its expression'.

32. For Grisez, Finnis and Boyle, physical pleasure isn't an 'intelligible good', merely a 'sensible good' (and so not a basic good), because it doesn't necessarily contribute to 'integral human fulfilment'. This seems to entail that pain doesn't necessarily detract from such fulfilment, which is plainly false. It also takes the theory several steps away from (what seemed to be) the original simple vision of correlating everything that motivates in its own right with everything that is basically good, and several steps towards an unhelpful Cartesian dualism.

33. For the point that the exceptional cases in which egoism looks attractive are less important than they are often thought to be by those who take ethical egoism to be a serious opponent of more standard positions in ethics, cp. Raz, *Morality of Freedom* pp. 318, 321: 'Occasional

conflict between well-being and morality is endemic. But so are conflicts between different aspects of one's well-being . . . morality and personal well-being are not two independent and mutually conflicting systems of demands, and there is no essential tendency in their demands, or the reasons for action that they generate, to conflict.'

34. One classic exposition of the Kantian idea that egoism is the central problem for ethics is Sidgwick's *The Methods of Ethics*. Another is Nagel's (*The View from Nowhere*, p. 164): 'The central problem of ethics [is] how the lives, interests, and welfare of others make claims on us and how these claims, of various forms, are to be reconciled with the aim of living of our own lives'. See also more recently (Crisp 1996).

35. Here the Nazi might for instance claim that Jews (or homosexuals, or gypsies, or whoever) are not *properly speaking* humans. If he does, notice first that the Nazi's claim is, as a matter of zoology, just plain false, and second that, whether true or false, his move is patently not motivated by rational considerations, but by a desire to make an arbitrary delimitation of the moral community. The fact that such wriggles are possible – they nearly always are, as every teacher of these subjects knows from experience – has no subjectivist implications either.

36. Derek Parfit would agree – though he puts it rather differently. In the past, he says, 'belief in God, or in many gods, prevented the free development of moral reasoning' (*RP* p. 454). But now people are ceasing to believe in God (as he thinks: his perspective seems rather culture centred). As a result, he suggests, it will be easier for people to arrive at a moral consensus.

37. On the distinction between central and peripheral basic goods, v. 3.6.

38. Objection: 'This concedes too much. If even a Nazi society can recognise the basic goods, then recognising the basic goods can't cut much ice in moral argument. The interesting disagreements between Nazis and the rest of us must be finer grained than this. They must turn, not on questions about what the basic goods are – perhaps we do all agree on that, at least roughly – but rather on questions like "What counts as instantiating the basic goods?" So your theory of the goods is not much use!' – First, this objection is inconsistent with another objection with which it is nonetheless frequently seen, which says that we can't get a theory of the basic goods going at all. Second, I never said that a theory of value, an account of what the basic goods are, is sufficient on its own to cut any ice at the level of first-order ethics. If it was, there would be no need for this book to have more than two chapters. The reader won't see whether my account of the basic goods is any use until he sees how it can be put to use as the basis for an ethical code.

39. 'Discovered or invented' – which? I doubt it matters very much, provided we remember that to say that goods can be invented doesn't imply that they are 'only subjective' goods. One might as well say that the fact that the wheelbarrow was invented implies that the wheelbarrow is 'only subjectively' capable of carrying loads.

40. *Pace* Hume such claims aren't reducible to instinctive expectations, either; they are the ground for reasonable expectations.

41. My sense of 'teleological', I hasten to add, is quite independent of any views whatever about the theory of evolution; and it has nothing to do with either (1) the sense in which the teleology of any thing is simply God's will for it; or (2) the sense in which the teleology of any thing is a mysterious animistic entity inside it which pushes it in some directions and not in others. Such notions of teleology are often attacked as Aristotelian. In fact it is unlikely that any respectable medieval Aristotelian scientist could be found to defend either of these strange views. View (1) is more like a nineteenth-century view, now discredited: Bergson's vitalism. View (2), undeniably, is reminiscent of Ockham's view of teleology. But then the whole point about Ockham's view of teleology is that it isn't a standard one for the science of his time. On the contrary, it is so non-standard as barely to be a view about *teleology* at all. So Ockham can hardly be a proper target for modern attacks on <u>Aristotelian</u> science.

42. Unlike the man in Molière who made his well-known appeal to <u>*virtus dormitiva*</u>, I don't suggest that any explanation is *completed* by referring to a disposition. Wth fragility, for instance, it will be helpful to say not only that glass is fragile, but why; which means explaining glass's disposition of fragility by reference to further dispositions possessed by the chemicals that compose glass. (Will we then end up with 'dispositions all the way down'? Perhaps; but that won't show that no explanatory work has been done, merely that no more, beyond a certain possibly quite distant point, is available. Cp. Mellor (1973). Actually even Molière's doctor was not saying something *completely* useless. That laudanum induces sleep in this patient because it has a sleep-inducing virtue can be helpfully explanatory. After all, it tells

us first that laudanum would probably have put any other patient to sleep, too, and second, that this patient didn't only fall asleep after taking his laudanum because he had worked hard today, or because he had a peculiar disposition which made him get sleeping sickness on taking laudanum.

43. Can this notion of transitions from statistical *is* to teleological *should be* be used to solve the classic problem of induction? Well, the notion of such transitions usefully captures what we are trying to do in making inductions. In particular, it captures what their explanatory power is supposed to be; again, the defeasibility of such transitions reflects better than many accounts the fallibility of all inductive inferences. However, the notion of *is/should be* transitions cannot get us over the central difficulty about induction. For it is logically possible that humans' (or anything's) essential tendencies might change overnight. In which case we should either say that our notion of what humans naturally do no longer has any (even defeasible) predictive power – or else perhaps that the human species has vanished and been replaced by something else, like humanity but essentially different. This possibility can't be ruled out. The best reason not to take it seriously is that doing so makes science altogether impossible; but that argument is hardly the exclusive property of this way of dealing with the problem of induction.

44. Ruth Garrett Millikan, *White Queen Psychology* p. 286, on psychology: 'The job of psychology is to describe the biological norms and explain their mechanisms. It is irrelevant how often or how seldom these norms, these ideals, are actually attained in nature.' Well, not quite; it wouldn't be irrelevant if they were *never* attained. But I take it that Millikan's real point, like mine, is about the obliqueness of the relation between frequency and normativity.

45. For another engagement with Humeanism, making a different point, see my [forthcoming (a)]. On facts and values cp. 4.4.

46. I am grateful to Alan Hobbs for putting me on to this question.

47. For a similar claim v. Raz (1997), p. 192: '[I endorse] the humanistic principle which claims that the explanation and justification of the goodness or badness of anything derives ultimately from its contribution, actual or possible, to human life and its quality'. Another way of raising the question of whether anything could be good or bad without being good or bad for humans/humanoids would be to ask whether it was good or bad for some different kind of creature; but you couldn't intelligibly ask the question whether anything was good or bad without *any* such qualification.

48. Possible objection: 'But any such goods to be discovered in the future can't be conceivable for us now; for as argued in 2.2, if they were conceivable for us now, they would already have been discovered!'. Possible answers: (1) 'Then we need only say that it is conceivable that such goods are conceivable'; or (2) 'Just to be able to make, and accept as plausible, the claim to which the objection is raised is already to have done all the conceiving that the claim requires to be true'.

49. Note incidentally how Anscombe's example shows the difficulty of real disagreement about the basic goods, even for a Lucifer.

50. Or at the least a humanly intelligible good, as pain or fear or desire in a dog or a cat or a Vulcan is humanly intelligible.

51. Or again by 'Because he's a weight-lifter (/diabetic/toddler), and this is a good for weight-lifters (/diabetics/ toddlers)'. Such cases reveal some interesting intermediate cases between goods that are goods solely for individuals and quite general human goods. Cp. *Nicomachean Ethics* 1106b4 (on weight-lifters); and Slote, *Goods and Virtues* (on toddlers and on relative goods).

52. In this context, I will pass over the Berkeleyan point that enjoying the thought that no one is enjoying a given wilderness is itself a way of enjoying that wilderness.

There are many and various forms of dispositions, patterns of feeling and desire, which can motivate people to counter-utilitarian acts; some themselves virtues, some more particular projects, affections and commitments ... They can be variously admired or deplored, cultivated or discouraged [by the utilitarian; but] the difficulty is that ... one cannot have both the world containing these dispositions, and its actions regularly fulfilling the requirements of utilitarianism. If you are a person who whole-heartedly and genuinely possesses some of these admirable dispositions, you cannot also be someone in whose thought and action the requirements of utilitarianism are unfailingly mirrored, nor could you wish to be such a person. If you want the world to contain generous, affectionate, forceful, resolute, creative and actually happy people, you do not wish it to contain people who uniformly think in such a way that their actions will satisfy the requirements of utilitarianism.

Bernard Williams, Moral Luck, p. 51

The heart of Shakespeare's drama is not reached till the storm and tempest are over and we come to the stillness of Lear's reconciliation with Cordelia. Here at last he recognises goodness for what it is in its own right. And the play's real theme is the gratitude of the converted heart at such a revelation. To see the virtues struggling in a world where their very virtue is the cause of their undoing is to be aware of tragedy; but – and this is the touch of nature that makes the reader kin with the poet – this makes us love the virtues not less, but more.

Peter Alexander, 'Introduction' to the Alexander Text of Shakespeare

Sicut autem ens est primum quod cadit in apprehensione simpliciter, ita bonum est primum quod cadit in apprehensione practicae rationis, quae ordinatur ad opus: omne enim agens agit propter finem, qui habet rationem boni. Et ideo primum principium in ratione practica est quod fundatur supra rationem boni, quae est, *Bonum est quod omnia appetunt.* Hoc est ergo primum principium legis, quod bonum est faciendum et prosequendum, et malum vitandum.

St Thomas Aquinas, Summa Theologiae 1a2ae.94.2c

3

———— • ————

THE THREEFOLD SCHEMA

The Problem of Reconciliation (1.1, 2.6) consists in two questions. First: if there is a real plurality of human goods, how, in general, is a single human life to respond to that plurality? Second: if there is a real and irreducible plurality of basic goods, then how can any single human life possibly reconcile its responses to those goods?

The task of providing answers to these questions, thus adding an ethical code to the theory of value set up in chapters 1 and 2, will occupy me for the rest of this book. First, in chapter 3, I shall propose and defend an outline of the good life (or rather, of course, good lives: cp. 1.2). I will provide a general schema setting the parameters within which we can begin to see roughly the kind of shape or shapes that, on a pluralist conception, good lives might have. As we'll see by the end of 3.2 below, this schema recognises as crucial three attitudes to goods which an agent can adopt. I shall therefore call this schema *the Threefold Schema*. In chapters 4 to 6, I'll begin to specify some more of the form and content of the good lives which might be lived within these parameters. But I begin by arguing for the Threefold Schema.

3.1 WHY PLURALISTS CAN'T BE MAXIMISERS

If pluralism about the good is true, how can we live in a way that is fitly responsive to the different goods? The first point is that if pluralism about the good is true, then maximising is not the way, in fact is not even a possible way, to deal with the plurality of goods.

Let's give the name *maximalism* to the doctrine that one should always maximise – do what will (or can most reasonably be expected to) bring about the greatest available amount of good. The first point about maximalism so defined is not merely that pluralists can't be maximalists. (Although they can't, the reason why is the second point, not the first.) The first point about maximalism is that no one can be a maximalist,[1] because maximalism faces the *Description Problem*.[2] One of the fundamental intuitions underlying maximalism is the claim A:

> A Any situation at all can be so described that we can find something in it which can play the role of what-is-to-be-maximised in our deliberations.

A is perfectly correct so far as it goes. But it goes nowhere near far enough to establish the possibility of a substantive maximalism. What maximalism – monist or pluralist – needs to get going is claim B:

> B There is one and the same something, in any situation at all under some description, which can play the role of what-is-to-be-maximised in our deliberations.

The move from A to B commits the very same fallacy as Aristotle was accused of in 1.1 – the fallacy of quantificational shift. Moreover, as we saw in 1.2, B can be made true only by stipulating that monism is true – a stipulation that there's no reason to accept unless we think we have to accept it to save our theory. Also, the true but trivial claim A, unlike the substantive but false claim B, doesn't exclude the possibility that anything whatever might be justifed by appeal to some or other maximalist ranking of preferences.[3] We need to be shown how maximalism is to resolve the situations where different possible rankings return contradictory verdicts on the same situation, so as to prevent the possibility that maximalist pretexts might be found to rationalise doing just whatever we want. (This seems to be how maximalist thoughts are often used in practice.)

Notice also this aspect of the Description Problem. Not only does the Description Problem entail, given claim A, that any action whatever can be justified by some maximalist ranking. It is also consistent with claim A that there should be indefinitely many possible maximalist rankings of preference, and indeed that any method of choice whatever might (if you like) be redescribed as a maximalist method of choice. Even what we might intuitively think was a radically anti-maximalist method of choice could be so redescribed!

Now this last point seems to be quite commonly thought to entail that maximalism must be inescapably true. Experience of teaching philosophy suggests that people seem to feel an intuition of this sort about as often, say, as they feel an intuition that altruistic actions are psychologically impossible. But, of course, the line of thought is a *non sequitur*. The universal applicability of maximalist descriptions of actual procedures of choice doesn't show that maximalism is inescapably true.

Rather it shows that maximalism is either unavoidably vacuous, or else obviously false. The maximalist claim is that 'People always choose what they regard as best'. To say this without any interpretation of 'best' is to say either nothing at all, or else only that people always prefer to do what they prefer to do; and to say it with the maximalist interpretation of 'best' is to impose on ordinary practical decisions an implausible load of theoretical commitments.

These are the sort of problems that ought to suffice (but often don't) to stop anyone from being a maximiser. Still, it should be particularly obvious that pluralists about the good can't be maximisers. Pluralism about the good is inconsistent with maximalism. If the different basic goods for the existence of which I have argued in 1.2 and 2.2 really are basic and really are different, they can't just be aspects of some further good or super-good such as 'utility' or 'happiness'.[4] There *is* no such further good or super-good (cp. 1.2). But without such a further good or super-good, the idea of maximising doesn't even make sense for a pluralist – as I shall now argue.

A pluralist can't coherently hold that the right attitude to the various goods is the attitude which goes with attempting to maximise some one or some group of those goods. For which good or group of goods is he to maximise? And why would it be right to maximise these goods, and impermissible to maximise any others?

It's hard to see how anything we might do that might count at least as maximising one of the goods available to us could be anything but a crazy way to act or live. Suppose Ann's life is aimed exclusively at maximising instantiations of the basic good of achievement, while Barbara's is aimed exclusively at maximising the basic good of pleasure. Is Ann to forgo every opportunity for pleasure that comes to her if it conflicts (as it is often likely to) with the maximal pursuit of achievements of some sort (what sort, incidentally?)? Is Barbara to rest content with aiming at total non-achievement, provided she aims to experience maximal pleasure? And what about all the other goods? Should Ann and Barbara both simply ignore every other sort of good apart from the one they aim to maximise, so that (to mention just one problem) both ruin their physical and mental health in the process of seeking to maximise that good? No plausible answers can be given to these questions by a would-be pluralist maximiser which doesn't depend on showing that the good or group of goods favoured by Ann (or Barbara) ranks higher than other goods not similarly favoured. But for the maximiser to admit the possibility of such a ranking entails his denying pluralism, and a reversion, on his part, to monism. Hence my claim that pluralists can't be maximisers.

Again, a pluralist can't coherently hold that the right attitude to the various goods is the attitude which goes with attempting to maximise all of those goods. For one thing, the very idea of trying to maximise all the goods at once is loopy. How could I simultaneously seek as much as possible of pleasure, and friendship, and aesthetic value, and truth, and the contemplation of God, and achievement, and the well-being of the natural world, and . . .? All of these different (instantiations of) goods would be marvellous things to achieve. But it is quite absurd to think that I (or any one person) might do or even try to do them all.

It would be saner for the would-be pluralist maximiser to try to find a maximising combination of the different goods. Instead of going hell for leather for every good at once, he might try to find the optimal balance between the different goods. But how? What makes any balancing of the different goods the best one? The pluralist maximiser has no hope of answering this without reintroducing some way of ranking and commensurating all the different goods and their combinations. But then he is no longer a genuine pluralist. He doesn't believe that, at bottom, there is more than one sort of good around. His position has collapsed back into monism. Hence, again, my claim that pluralists can't be maximisers.

3.2 A FIRST ATTEMPT ON THE PROBLEM OF RECONCILIATION

If we have to be pluralists about the good (as argued in 1.2), and can't be maximisers, especially not if we are pluralists (as argued in 3.1), what can we be? If the different goods can't be reconciled within a single life by maximising strategies, then how can they be reconciled?

A determined consequentialist might insist (cp. the second 'reversible' argument of 1.2) that all that's shown by the arguments just given is not the implausibility of any serious consequentialism but, on the contrary, the implausibility of any serious pluralism about the good. The problem that has emerged is that if there are many goods, then it's impossible to pursue them all unreservedly – that is, to maximise them all. We have to pick and choose which goods to maximise when. But we don't know how – on what rational basis – this picking and choosing is to be done, if not on the basis of the monist assumption that the different goods are commensurable.

Can the pluralist admit any rational basis for the reconciliation of his plurality of goods? This crucial question (the consequentialist may argue) poses a dilemma for the pluralist. If the pluralist's answer is Yes, then what is the rational way that he proposes of choosing which basic goods to maximise when? Isn't he going to have to admit that if such decisions can be made rationally, then there must be something in terms of which all those different goods can be commensurated? That is, that something like 'utility' or 'welfare' or 'the overall good' does exist after all – and so that any rational pluralism about the good does collapse back into monism about the good as soon as we try to elaborate it?

Suppose, on the other hand, the pluralist answers 'No', and admits that there is no rational way of making decisions between the basic goods as to which we should maximise when. In this case he seems to be admitting that his theory is so indeterminate that it is virtually useless for any practical purpose. What's the use of a moral theory that identifies a variety of basic goods but can't tell you which goods to pursue when? How could such a theory help anyone, whether to resolve a deep moral dilemma or merely to make a straightforward decision (like whether to go on talking to my friends, or head for the library)?

This poses the Problem of Reconciliation as a neat dilemma. The pluralist should respond that a pluralist, non-maximalist theory can indeed provide choices between different basic goods with a genuinely rational basis. But that doesn't mean that that basis will in every case be one that the consequentialist would agree was rational.

Consider the word 'reconcile' as it occurs in the claim that 'The trouble with pluralism about the good is that it has no way of reconciling the different goods that it posits'. We may make a distinction about the meaning of 'reconcile' in that claim. To 'reconcile' any two basic goods G1 and G2 could mean any of three things:

1 to reconcile the maximising of G1 with the maximising of G2;
2 to reconcile the maximising[5] of one of the pair G1 and G2 (but not both) with a non-maximising but still sufficiently favourable attitude to the other member of the pair;

or

3 to reconcile non-maximising but still sufficiently favourable attitudes to G1 and to G2.

Type-(1) reconciliations between different basic goods are bound to be rare things – if we can imagine them occurring at all. Unlike type-(2) and type-(3) reconciliations they are the exception rather than the rule. Even when they do occur, they are as fortuitous as a conjunction of comets. It may be that over a lifetime (at any rate) my pursuits of, say, knowledge about philosophy and of the good of friendship may run neatly in parallel, because – as it happens – my wife is a first-rate philosopher. But if so, that's just my good luck. The vast majority of other sets of possible circumstances (including many sets that are far less unlikely than this one) would have made it impossible to reconcile the maximising of these two goods.

More importantly: as we've already seen, there couldn't be a type-(1) reconciliation between all the different basic goods. Even when it's possible to maximise two goods G1 and G2 at once, there is bound to be some third good G3 a non-maximising of which is entailed by the joint maximisation of G1 and G2. The very existence of any type-(1) reconciliation between any G1 and G2 will entail, for some G3, that there's no type-(1) reconciliation between G1, G2 and G3.

As I shall now illustrate, this point about type-(1) reconciliations doesn't apply to type-(2) and type-(3) reconciliations between different basic goods. Suppose, for example, we are considering a type-(2) reconciliation between pursuing the goods of friendship and of knowledge. Is it possible to go all-out for knowledge about philosophy and yet still pay (what ordinary usage would call) sufficient attention to your friendships? The answer to that question is generally thought to be 'Normally, yes'. And rightly so. As a rule, no one can manage a type-(1) reconciliation of these goods: one cannot be both a full-time Distinguished Research Professor and a full-time socialite. Yet – as a rule – a type-(2) reconciliation is perfectly possible. You can be a Distinguished Research Professor without becoming a depressive loner or a misanthropist. Again – as a rule – a type-(3) reconciliation is also perfectly possible. You can pay sufficient attention both to the good of friendship and to the good of knowledge without becoming (or trying to become) either a Distinguished Research Professor or a full-time socialite. In particular, you need not give up some other career, as (say) a polar explorer, to count as paying sufficient attention to them.

In short: unlike type-(1) reconciliations, the occurrence of a type-(2) reconciliation between any G1 and G2 doesn't entail that there is no type-(2) reconciliation between G1 and G2 and some G3. *A fortiori*, neither does it entail that there is no type-(3) reconciliation between G1 and G2 and some G3. Most people not already committed to maximalism will say that my engaging in the maximising (or near-maximising) pursuit of one good doesn't entail that there is any other good towards which my non-maximising attitude is insufficiently favourable. Nor will they think that the fact that I have a non-maximising, but still sufficiently favourable, attitude to some one good entails that there is any other good towards which my non-maximising attitude is insufficiently favourable. So the basic goods don't as a rule have to be irreconcilable with each other in our lives, provided that (a) we don't try to pursue them all as hard as we possibly can, and provided that (b) we show at least a modicum of respect for those that we are not pursuing.

My discussion has now identified two senses of 'reconciliation' – types (2) and (3) as just defined – in which reconciliations between different basic goods might normally be possible – as they normally aren't if we take 'reconciliation' in my sense (1), as meaning 'jointly maximisable'. This conclusion has dropped straight out of my exposition of pluralism about the good (the view that there are irreducibly different basic goods). It is a consequence of pluralism about the good that we can't pursue all the goods maximally. So there must be something wrong about thinking that it is always wrong to fail to maximise any particular good. Kant's Law states that Ought implies Can.[6] So by contraposition, what we don't do because we are unable to do it, like maximising all the goods all the time, can't sensibly be viewed as instantiating a moral failure on our part.[7] As I have pointed out, it certainly isn't so viewed by common opinion – or at least by common opinion that hasn't yet signed up for maximalism.

Moreover, pretheoretically we normally take it that it is up to us whether we choose to maximise given particular goods in our choices about how to conduct our lives – though sometimes of course special circumstances may occur in which it clearly isn't up to us, as when a child needs to be rescued from a burning building. Again we take it that in not maximising any given good, we aren't necessarily doing anything wrong – as we would be if, instead of merely not maximising a particular basic good, we consciously and deliberately chose to act in a way which violated that good.

Take for example the basic good of life, and saving lives as a way of instantiating or responding to that good. No one normally thinks that they have a quite general duty to maximise savings–of–life. A normal person who isn't a medic or a paramedic has a duty (as opposed to a permission) to save lives only in emergencies which immediately confront[8] him. He doesn't have a duty to go out and look for emergencies to save lives in. So a normal person does not have a duty to maximise the good of life by saving lives. On the other hand he does have a duty to show respect for that good by not killing people except in very special circumstances (such as self-defence).

Contrast the case of a medic or a paramedic. Like anyone else such a person has a duty not to kill unless he is put in very unusual circumstances – to respect the good of life by not violating it. He also has, we may agree, a duty to maximise (or as we might more accurately say, promote or pursue)[9] the good of life by saving lives. But this duty to promote that good is one which he chose to be subject to when he chose his career.[10] He would have done nothing wrong if he'd chosen not to be a doctor, but (say) a medical researcher. That would have been a choice to focus his attention on the good of (scientific) knowledge, instead of focusing it on the good of life as instantiated in saving lives, preserving or promoting health, and so on. It would, in normal circumstances,[11] have been a perfectly permissible choice.

These data of ordinary moral discourse can't easily be accommodated by a maximising moral theory. But they fit neatly with the thesis proposed here: that not all non-maximising attitudes to any given basic good are morally culpable because insufficiently favourable. Besides reconciling attitudes towards any given goods that *promote or pursue* those goods (such as the choice of a career as a life-saver), there are also reconciling attitudes towards them that merely *respect* them (such as a choice not to go around killing people). Such attitudes to given goods genuinely are reconciling attitudes. They are just as morally legitimate as the promoting attitudes. The attitudes that aren't morally legitimate are not all and only those that fail to *promote* a given basic good. They are those that not only fail to *promote* that good but also *violate* it (as for example murder violates the good of life).

So I propose a schema of attitudes towards goods that rejects the consequentialist view that there is only one alternative to morally licit maximising of the good – namely morally illicit failure to maximise the good. In the proposed schema (the Threefold Schema) there are three alternative possible attitudes to any good: *promoting* it, *respecting* it, *violating* it. The three are always distinct, except in cases where there's no way to respect a good but to promote it (as with child-in-burning-building cases). The first two are (as such) always permissible. The third is (as such) always impermissible.[12] In the next section I shall explore this Schema further.

3.3 A PARALLEL; AND ANOTHER ARGUMENT FOR THE SCHEMA

Let me recapitulate a little, by giving first a(n apparent) historical parallel to the Threefold Schema, and second, another version of the argument for adopting it.

Here's the historical parallel. It may be thought a benefit of the

Schema (or there again it may not) that it fits in nicely with, and in a new and interesting way makes good sense of, a famous principle of Aquinas's called by him 'the first precept of the natural law': ' . . . This then is the first precept of the [natural] law: that good is to be done and pursued, and evil is to be avoided.'[13]

The commonest reaction among the commentators to this doctrine of Aquinas' is the following two-step. (1) Aquinas himself describes the First Precept as a 'self-evident proposition' or 'indemonstrable first principle', and compares the law of non-contradiction in logic.[14] So (2) the First Precept must, like logical truths, be an obvious and uninteresting claim, stating nothing more controversial than a firm line against sin. What's interesting is not the (tautologous) claim expressed by the First Precept, but the ways in which Aquinas argues that such and such material actions or choices are or aren't in accordance with that formal claim.[15]

I won't attempt to settle the exegetical question of what Aquinas himself might have thought about all this, and in particular about the meaning of 'self-evident proposition'.[16] But I will point out that his First Precept doesn't have to be seen as 'self-evident', if that means as a merely formal or tautologous principle. Our discussion has put us in a position to see Aquinas' First Precept in a rather different light – and I think a more interesting one. We might see his First Precept as a way of characterising the interrelations of the three different possible attitudes to the basic goods which is very close to that offered by the Threefold Schema:

> promoting them (= *bonum prosequendum* – pursuing good),
> respecting them (= *bonum faciendum* – doing good), and
> not violating them (= *malum vitandum* – avoiding evil).

This much could not simply drop out of a merely formal principle. Thus interpreted, Aquinas's First Precept immediately entails the rejection of what is in effect the consequentialists' 'first precept': that 'good is to be pursued [where "pursued" means "maximised" – cp. Note 9] – even if that means <u>not</u> doing good, and <u>not</u> avoiding evil'. Any principle that entails the rejection of the consequentialists' first precept can hardly itself be boringly axiomatic or merely formal, as St Thomas's commentators too often assume. On the present interpretation, the First Precept of natural law is a sensationally substantive principle!

So much for the historical parallel. The second version of the argument for the Threefold Schema is this. Anyone who tries to give a formal schema specifying how pluralist non-maximisers might be oriented towards the goods they recognise will necessarily face certain constraints on what such a schema could possibly be, given that it is a pluralist and non-maximising schema. In two ways, these constraints will lead him in the direction of what I call the Threefold Schema.

First: the very idea of pluralism about the good is the idea of an attitude that recognises that there is, irreducibly, more than one sort of good or thing-to-be-pursued. This means that pluralism must either be incoherent in its attitude to the goods (for example, by trying to maximise them all at once, as above), or else must hold that agents have a certain freedom as to which good or goods they choose to promote or pursue, and which they choose merely to respect, either in any given situation, or over a life.

Naturally, to being incoherent I prefer recognising the phenomenon of supererogation – that is, the fact that not everything we can do which is 'best' in some sense is something that we must do (though of course some things are). There are actions that are 'above and beyond the call of duty'.[17] There are actions such that the moral goodness of doing them, and the strength of obligation that we have to do them, cease to be proportionate to each other. Duty makes certain demands on us (more about these in a minute); certain other demands it doesn't make.

Combine this thought about supererogation with our earlier argument from the diversity of possible good lives to pluralism about the good (1.2), and you get the following picture. Above a certain minimal level of respect, an agent's attitude towards any good is in many situations entirely up to her. Very often agents are literally and completely free to choose from the different sorts of good that they find around them, as to which they would like to pay most attention to.

Consider for example a choice between being a full-time parent or following a demanding career or trying to make childcare and work meet in the middle. Or a choice between going into business or becoming a schoolteacher or trying to make it as a musician. Or a choice between going to the cinema with friends this evening or staying in and reading some philosophy.

This sort of choice between different alternative goods is – quite often – entirely unconditioned by overriding moral *musts* such as maximisers implausibly hope to find in every situation except that of the evaluational dead heat. Regarding questions about, for example, whether I should become a schoolteacher, a musician, or an entrepreneur, there often is no truth of the matter. This isn't because there is an evaluational dead heat, an exact equilibrium of preferences, in such cases. Such cases don't presuppose evaluations or preferences of the relevant kind: they create them (6.4). Provided there aren't obvious flaws in my character that are bound to prevent me from succeeding in one or the other (tone-deafness, an instinctive dislike for children, an insuperable aversion to wearing a suit, or whatever); and provided there is no other course of action that is of necessity laid out for me (I have a sick parent who needs full-time care and ought to get it from me, or I have already signed up for the Army); it can easily be true that the only answer to the question 'Which should I do?' is 'It depends what kind of person you want to be'.[18]

Unlike the maximiser, monist or pluralist, the pluralist non-maximiser can allow without any difficulty the suitably vague statement that, though not every kind of person is a good kind of person, still there are indefinitely many good kinds of person to be, and that it makes little or no sense to regard any of these kinds as unqualifiedly the best kind of person to be. Again, she can explain the differences between the various kinds of good people that there obviously are. She can say that what makes for those differences between kinds of good people is precisely their choices about which goods to pursue in their lives, and which goods, while not being deaf and blind to their appeal, not to pursue, but merely to respect.

This contrast between pursuing a good and merely respecting it makes room within our moral theory, not only for the phenomenon of supererogation, but also for the possibility of a plurality of possible good lives (1.2). This contrast is then the first crucial point about the constraints on possible moral schemas which logically follow from the adoption of non-maximising pluralism. The second crucial point concerns the other contrast, between respecting and violating a good. This is the contrast which makes room within our moral theory for the phenomenon of material moral absolutes.

The argument for moral absolutes closely parallels that for supererogation. I've said that the very idea of pluralism about the good is the idea of an attitude which recognises that there is irreducibly more than one sort of good or thing-to-be-pursued. I've pointed out how the conception of this plurality of goods or ends of action can be combined with the plausible thought that it can't be a demand of any reasonable or sane ethics that we should try to maximise all of these goods. Together these thoughts have led us to say that there must be morally permissible ways of reconciling those goods which consist in doing considerably less, in respect of at least some of those goods, than maximising or promoting them – merely in respecting them, as I put it.

Likewise, the very idea of pluralism about the good is the idea of an attitude which recognises that there is irreducibly more than one sort of evil or thing-to-be-avoided. The conception of this plurality of things to be avoided leads us to material moral absolutism – the view that some material action-types must be simply impermissible.

First, a definition of this term. *Material* moral absolutism is distinct from *formal* moral absolutism. The distinction I make between the two positions[19] turns on whether the action-types they pick out as not to be done are materially specified (= by solely non-evaluative criteria), or just formally (= by criteria that are at least in part evaluative). Thus formal action-types are action-types picked out, evaluatively, by their formal properties, as, for example, 'not maximising the good', 'contravening the categorical imperative', or merely 'doing wrong' or 'φing wrongly'. So formal moral absolutism is the thesis that any actions that fit such formal, evaluative, descriptions are not to be done, no matter what. By contrast material action-types are picked out, non-evaluatively, by their material properties, as, for example, 'murder' or 'rape'. Material moral absolutism is then the thesis that any actions that fit some such material, non-evaluative, descriptions are not to be done, no matter what.[20]

Formal moral absolutism isn't a controversial thesis for almost anyone who has any pretensions to consistent moral thinking: any consistent moral thinking necessarily involves acceptance of some formal principle or other.[21] Material moral absolutism is a controversial thesis.[22]

To see that material moral absolutism is a consequence of the Threefold Schema, recall our contrast between monism and pluralism about the good. As we saw, accepting monism about the good means accepting that there is only one ultimate end of moral action – namely, instantiating or promoting that one good. Compared with the importance of achieving that single end, all other considerations must be as nothing for the monist. For him, in fact, moral considerations other than the instantiation or promotion of the one overall good can matter only insofar as they turn out on reflection not to be truly other than the achievement of that one good, but either tactically or strategically implicit in its achievement. It follows that accepting monism about the good means accepting at least the possibility that just anything might be a means to the one overriding end of the single good. If monism is true then it remains possible that, in some sufficiently dire situation, the overall good might be served, or served best, by doing absolutely anything at all as a means to that overall good – rape, murder, firebombing babies, or whatever.

But if monism about the good is false, as I argued in 1.2, then there is no one overriding end of the good. According to the pluralism about motivation and the good which I've developed and defended here, different actions serve different good ends. Moreover, there are fundamentally different sorts of good around, of a more specific nature than 'the overall good'.

It follows that according to pluralism there is no one good compared with which all other goods are as nothing in their importance. So it also follows for the pluralist that the goodness or badness of any action is not assessed, so to speak, in just one dimension – by just one test, the test of whether that action promotes the single overriding good. Rather, because there is for him no single overriding good but a variety of different goods none of which overrides the rest, the pluralist must say that the goodness or badness of any action is assessed in a number of different dimensions.[23] It is assessed, that is, by as many different tests as there are different goods relevant to the performance of the action in question.

Moreover, the form of each of the pluralist's several tests of the goodness or badness of any action will be quite different from the monist's form of test. As we have seen, the monist needs to know only whether the action in question promotes the single overriding good: if it does so (or does so more than any available alternative), then he should do it. What the pluralist needs to know, by contrast, is whether the action in question promotes some one (or more) particular good(s) without violating or failing to respect any other good(s) which that action in one way or another employs as a means to its end.

Now the plurality of goods which the pluralist posits are genuinely different from each other. Therefore the different goods have different attractions for, and make different demands upon, agents. What it is to respond to or to enjoy or to respect any one good differs in definition from what it is to respond to or to enjoy or to respect any other good.

Precisely for this reason there must for the pluralist be some conceivable means of achieving some particular good(s) that violate some other particular good(s). It must be at least possible that what it is to pursue or respect any one good in some circumstances could differ from what it is to pursue or respect some other good in those circumstances not only in definition, but actually in extension. Given pluralism about the good, it must sometimes be possible for an agent to respond to some good G1 by making some other good G2 a means to the achievement of G1 in a way that commits the agent to ignoring, repressing, rejecting, or insulting the goodness of G2, and his own responsiveness to it. In a word, to violating G2.

To show by giving examples that there are such possibilities is just to show what sort of actions will be subject to moral absolutes for a pluralist. What is more: to say that some conceivable means to some ends are for a pluralist absolutely impermissible is to talk about some material action types as absolutely impermissible. (Perhaps, for example, it is to say this of rape, or murder, or dropping bombs on babies, seen as means to some end or other. Or perhaps it is to say it of more fine-grained material action-types, like performing a token of some broadly defined action-type under some particular circumstances. But it is still, necessarily, to talk of material action-types.) To say this is just to endorse the thesis I set out to establish: namely material moral absolutism.

To sum up: because the pluralist takes it that there are different goods which make different demands on us, the pluralist must also hold that there are some conceivable means of achieving some particular good(s) which violate some other particular good(s). But, for the pluralist, there is no single overriding monistic good that could be pressed into service to impose on the agent the demand that, in such cases, he violate one good if by so doing he can effectively pursue another. For the pluralist that demand is simply incoherent. Because for him there is no monistic good, there is no clear sense in which it is ever better to violate any one good in pursuit of any other than not to violate it. And because for the pluralist the good that is violated in any such case is a good in its own right, there is an exceedingly clear sense in which it is always worse to violate that good in pursuit of some other good than not to violate it – even when not violating it means not being able to pursue the other good. Again, in the absence of any single overriding monistic good, there is nothing that, for the pluralist, could even make such violations permissible – on the grounds that such violations are, so to speak, a price worth paying given the other goods that they make available. Thus, violations of goods are, for the non-maximising pluralist, bound to be absolutely impermissible.

Notice that this argument is, in the terms of J. L. Mackie's useful distinction (J. L. Mackie, *Ethics* pp. 165–6), an argument for material moral absolutism about means, not about ends. What it specifically rules out is the doing of any actions of types that constitute violations of some basic good(s) as a means to (or as a constitutive part of) the pursuit of some other basic good(s). Why don't I also argue specifically for material moral absolutism about ends?

Once the Threefold Schema is accepted, it is easy enough to see how such an argument could be supplied. If it's forbidden to do any action which violates any basic good as a means to pursuing some other basic good, then *a fortiori* it must be forbidden to do any action that is expressly designed to do nothing but violate some basic good. I doubt, however, that any such argument is necessary. For I doubt whether anyone ever performs any action fitting this description. Because the basic goods are (according to the Working Hypothesis of 1.4) also the ends of all motivation, the very idea of doing an action expressly designed to do nothing but violate some basic good seems unintelligible. To see something as an action at all is to see it as aimed at some (perceived) good or other (1.1 to 1.2, 2.1). So how could one see anything as an action aimed at nothing but the violation of some or other good? How could one even conceive of an action that had as its end nothing but (perceived) evil?[24]

The point is not that there can't be malicious or fundamentally bad actions. It is that what makes any action malicious or fundamentally bad can't be its intentional directedness towards (what is at least perceived as) an evil end. The idea that actions might be so directed doesn't even make sense. To locate the badness of intelligible actions is not to discover their (actually) bad ends, but to discover the ways in which they embody mistakes (culpable or otherwise) in what they perceive as good ends, and the ways in which they use (actually) bad or inappropriate means to some (perceived) good end. So there is no pressing need to argue for material moral absolutism about ends, because no one is even capable of infringing that sort of absolutism.

The upshot of this section so far is that acceptance of the Threefold Schema has two distinct consequences: (a) that there is supererogation, and (b) that there are moral absolutes. These two consequences of non-maximising pluralism determine the first part of our answer to the Problem of Reconciliation. In 3.2, that problem was posed by the consequentialist in the form of the dilemmatic question: 'Can the pluralist admit any rational basis for the reconciliation of his plurality of goods without abandoning pluralism?' I suggested that the right answer to this was to say that a pluralist, non-maximalist theory can indeed provide choices between different basic goods with a genuinely rational basis – but that that doesn't mean that that basis will in every case be one which the consequentialist would agree was rational.

The reader may now see why the consequentialist won't agree about the rationality of the basis for choices between goods which the pluralist offers. What non-maximising pluralism provides as a basis for such choices is the Threefold Schema. One half of this Schema – the half that provides for the possibility of supererogation – boils down to the simple claim that quite often there is no determinately right or best thing to do. The other half of it – the half that stipulates the necessity of material moral absolutes – boils down to the simple claim that quite often there are before the agent conceivable choices which it would be wrong for him to take, no matter what.

On the one hand, the Schema offers the consequentialist a disquietingly underdetermined ethical freedom. On the other, it offers him an equally disquieting set of indefeasible ethical prohibitions. The consequentialist will very probably gag on both ingredients of the recipe. He will struggle with the half of the schema that offers him supererogation, because he mistakenly thinks that any rational basis for action necessarily has to give a unique answer, on every occasion except those that constitute evaluational ties, to the question 'What should I do?' He will struggle with the half of it that offers him material moral absolutes, because he mistakenly thinks that a rational basis for action, as such, cannot possibly involve agents' taking the attitude, to any materially specified action-type, of excluding the performance of any token of that type from the outset, or of refusing even to consider doing such a thing.[25]

The consequentialist may therefore doubt whether either half of the Threefold Schema does suggest any rational basis for choices between goods. Non-consequentialists needn't share this doubt, even if they concede that not everything has yet been said that is necessary to clarify the precise meaning of the Threefold Schema. In 3.4 I shall add some further clarifications, by considering further what exactly is involved in accepting the material moral absolutism that the Threefold Schema commits us to.

3.4 MATERIAL ABSOLUTES, COMMITMENTS, AND THE VIRTUES

So far I have argued for material moral absolutism only in the sense that I have argued for the claim that there are at least some material moral absolutes. To argue that much is not yet to make it clear *which* material moral absolutes there are. I offered some examples of what I believe are material moral absolutes (notably rape and murder). But these were asserted rather than argued for. So how, the reader may wonder, are we to go about arguing for *specific* moral absolutes?

Another question that arises at this point is the following. Material moral absolutism, as I have developed it, makes crucial use of the notions of *violation* of a good, *pursuit* or *promotion* of a good, and *respect* for a good. What do these notions mean? How are these metaphors – if that is what they are – to be cashed out?

I'll take these two questions together; their answers are closely related. Answering them brings us back to the taxonomy of virtues promised at 2.1 (Note 1).

We must begin by introducing the notion of a *commitment* to a good. Consider this remark of Charles Taylor's (*Sources of the Self* p. 3): 'Much contemporary moral philosophy . . . has tended to focus on what it is right to do rather than on what it is good to be, on defining the content of obligation rather than the nature of the good life; and it has no conceptual place left for a notion of the good as the object of our love or allegiance or, as Iris Murdoch portrayed it in her work, as the privileged focus of attention or will.'[26]

The idea of a commitment to a good is what Taylor refers to as the idea of some particular basic good 'as the object of our love or allegiance or . . . as the privileged focus of attention or will'. Commitment to a good in this sense means reflection or meditation on that good. A key activity of the agent who is committed to a good G is to attend to G, to ask 'What is G like?', 'What does G demand (of me)?', 'What is the place of G in my life, or any good life?', 'How can G be furthered, defended, honoured (by me)?', 'What would be a paradigm case of the pursuit (or violation) of G?' and so on. It is only by this sort of ethical reflection – by what Murdoch called just and loving attention to particular goods and their relations to us and to other goods – that the agent can become clearer in his own mind about what any particular good is like *in itself*, and also about what it means *for him* to be committed to that good.

Notice four points about this notion of commitment to a good. First, to set a purely negative point aside, it doesn't imply the obviously silly view that it's entirely up to the agent to choose which goods to be committed to – nor that an agent can at identifiable points in her life be discovered selecting commitments to goods in the same way that she selects tinned soups in the supermarket. On the contrary, any agent is necessarily 'thrown', as Heidegger would say, into very many commitments which are set up for her before she has become a self-conscious agent at all. On the other hand it doesn't imply, either, that an agent can never take on any new ethical commitments; nor that there's no distinction between an active and intelligent commitment to a good, and a passive and unreflective commitment to it.

Second, and more interestingly: being committed to a good entails, among other things, knowing or trying to find out what that good demands: what it is, in practice and in detail, to take that good as an end of action. It entails knowing which action types characteristically instantiate that good, or tend to bring it about that there are more instantiations of that good than there would otherwise be (which is to say: which action types promote it). So, in particular, being committed to a good means being able to recognise paradigm cases of action types that promote or instantiate that good. That is, it means being able to see which are the action types that are centrally and focally promotions or instantiations of that good. It is in the agent's knowledge of which these action-types are in the case of any good that the agent's knowledge of what constitutes the promotion or pursuit of that good consists.

Third: conversely, being committed to a good entails – among other things – knowing or trying to find out what it is, in practice and in detail, to act contrary to the demands of that good upon agents – that is, in a way that involves disregarding or inadequately regarding its demands. So it entails knowing which action-types characteristically instantiate rejections or denials of the demands of that good; which is to say, which action-types violate it. In particular, being committed to a good means being able to recognise paradigm cases of action-types that violate that good. It means being able to see which are the action-types that are centrally and focally violations of that good.[27]

Fourth: from these definitions of what it means to pursue or violate a good, we may also derive a definition of what it means to respect that good. Respecting a good simply means not violating it. So to know what it is to pursue a good is to know what it would be like to respond as fully as you could to that good's demands. To know what it is to respect a good is to know what it would be like to respond minimally to that good's demands – to do no more than you must in responding to it. To know what it is to violate a good is to know what it would be like to respond sub-minimally to that good's demands – to do even less than the bare minimum that you must do in responding to it.

This close connectedness between the definitions of pursuing, respecting and violating goods can be made clear by examples. In general, it should be reasonably clear why a commitment to a good must be a commitment to do good (of the relevant sorts). It should also be clear why a commitment to do good which wasn't also a commitment not to do evil wouldn't be a commitment to do good at all – no more than an alleged commitment to run the college bar honestly and competently could count as a genuine commitment to do that if it wasn't also, and indeed *ipso facto*, a commitment not to steal from the till or throw away the account books.[28]

Here it may be objected that this explanation of the meanings of pursuit of, respect for, and violation of goods is still unsatisfactory, for two reasons. First, because I've merely replaced mysterious talk about 'pursuing', 'respecting' and 'violating' goods with another kind of mysterious talk – this time about the 'demands' of goods. Second, because it's still not clear whether commitment to any good entails knowledge of formal action-types which constitute paradigm cases of the promotion or instantiation of that good, or knowledge of material action-types.

The first objection seems mistaken. There's nothing (at any rate) more mysterious about talk about the 'demands' of the various goods than there is about talk about those goods themselves. Indeed, the two sorts of talk are intimately logically related. It follows from my Working Hypothesis, and from the connections pointed out in 1.4, that to talk about a good is precisely to talk about a source of 'ethical pulls and pushes'. Talk about a good is no more and no less than talk about a source of potential causes of intentional action – of motivations – and of standards for the rational assessment or criticism of intentional action – of ethical demands. That's just what goods are: sources of reasons of the pushy and the pulling sorts: of demands, and of motivations. This is why it is on the basis of his understanding of the pushes and pulls generated by any good G that the agent who's committed to G comes to understand what it would be to promote or respect or violate G.

Hence also the answer to the second objection, which reopens the question of what *sort* of demands the person who is committed to a given good needs to become aware of. Will it be merely formal action-types, or will it be material action-types, that he will come to grasp as paradigm cases of promotion or violation of that good? The answer is, of course, quite possibly both – and quite possibly other sorts of things besides action-types of any sort – for example, disposition or emotion types. Because the goods differ from one another, exactly what a given good is going to demand of an agent who's committed to it must depend on the exact nature of that specific good.

For some goods there might be no material action-type performance of any token of which constitutes a violation of that good. For some specific goods, reflection on their demands by an agent who is committed to them may show that violations of them consist in the performance of tokens only of formal, not of material, action-types. For other goods again, such reflection may show that violations of them consist not in the performance of tokens of any sort of action-types, but only in the presence in the agent of certain sorts of emotion-type or disposition-type.

Hence there is no a priori guarantee that for each particular good there is some material action-type the performance of any token of which constitutes a violation of that good. To violate some goods may simply mean doing actions that fit some purely formal description. To violate other goods again may simply mean being a certain sort of person, or entertaining or being subject to certain sorts of emotion[29] – a possibility that the reader may recall is taken seriously by Aristotle (*Nicomachean Ethics* 1107a9–12): '[Some sorts] of action or emotion (*pathos*) . . . are no sooner named than their intrinsic connection with defective character (*phaulotes*) is apprehended; for example *Schadenfreude*, shamelessness, or envy [among the emotions], and among actions, adultery, theft and murder . . .'

To see the contrasts between the demands that different goods might make on agents, consider as examples the three goods of humour, art, and life. What kinds of things count respectively as violations of these goods?

In the case of humour, I suggest, what counts directly as a violation of it is only the lack of a disposition – namely having a sense of humour.[30] In the case of art, apparently the good which it represents is violated by the lack of a disposition (a lack which may be called philistinism). But that good is also, no doubt, violated by the performance of tokens of a certain action-type: namely that of destroying works of art when there is no very good reason to do so.

This action-type, however, is not a material but only a formal action-type. The action-type of 'destroying works of art when there is no very good reason to do so' is an action-type that is defined (partly at least) by an evaluative criterion, to do with what constitutes a very good reason to destroy works of art. Hence (cp. the definitions in 3.3) that action-type is a formal action-type. The related material action-type would presumably be expressible in the same definition minus its evaluative component. That is, it would be simply 'destroying works of art'. But it would be totally unreasonable, given the place of art in a good human life, for an agent committed to the good of art to think that that good demanded of him that he never perform any token of this action-type. Given a choice between the deaths of my children and burning the Mona Lisa, I burn the Mona Lisa every time.

Here it is crucial to see that the agent isn't ethically freed to make that choice because the demands of the other goods which are in the offing in such a case *override* the demands of the good of art, permitting its violation (though no doubt the seeming closeness of what I'm saying to that claim is part of the 'error theory' that explains consequentialism's attractions). Rather she is enabled to make that choice because in such a case there is no violation to be overridden in the first place. Here the good of art makes no demands, or at least does not make the crucial demand that she should not burn the picture; burning the picture in the envisaged circumstances is not, then, a violation of the good of art. This isn't a verdict that emerges from some consequentialist process of commensuration of different goods, the output of which is to show that human lives are 'worth more' than pictures. It is a verdict that emerges from reflection on what commitment to the good to art itself involves. Art is certainly the sort of good to demand of us openness, attentiveness, listening sympathy, emotional engagement. But it certainly isn't the sort of good to demand of us that at all costs we do not deliberately destroy its innocent exemplars; whereas humanity is. So the point isn't the relative importance (in some ranking-and-measuring sense) of the two goods of art and humanity. It is the different natures, and hence different demands, of those two goods.

Contrast, with humour and art, the good of life. There is probably at least one disposition an agent's possession of which constitutes a violation of the good of life. For example, bloodthirstiness or murderousness, or again plain callous indifference to the causing of deaths, seem in different ways to be plausible candidates for that role. There is also in a sense a formal action-type performance of any token of which constitutes a violation of the good of life. We might call that action-type 'committing murder when there is no very good reason to do so'. But this formal action-type is there only 'in a sense'; for the demands of the good of life mean that there is never very good reason, or indeed any reason at all, to commit a murder. That is to say, the absolute which applies to the formal action-type 'committing murder when there is no very good reason to do so' drops out of consideration because – in this case – it proves to be co-extensive with a material moral absolute, which applies to the material action-type 'committing murder – fullstop'.

'Committing murder' is, I suggest, a material action-type, and not merely a formal one, performance of any token of which constitutes a violation of the good of life. For 'murder' can be defined without the use of any evaluative criterion: at least roughly, it is the deliberate killing of any human who is not deliberately[31] posing any immediate lethal threat to anyone else. Properly understood, no part of this definition is evaluative.

Sideshow: But what if the person I kill (A) is deliberately posing an immediate lethal threat to someone else (B)? The answer to that depends on what B is doing. If B is deliberately posing no immediate lethal threat to someone else again (C), then I am killing to prevent a murder, which may well be a permissible act, depending on the circumstances. If B is deliberately posing an immediate lethal threat to C, then (provided C isn't deliberately posing an immediate lethal threat to someone else (D)), in deliberately killing B I am killing someone who may well be intentionally described as killing to prevent a murder. If so, and provided I realise that fact, my action of killing B is itself an act of murder. There again, if C is posing an immediate lethal threat to D, my act in killing B will be (or may be, depending again on the circumstances) an act of preventing an act which is a murder in the sense that it is an act of killing someone who is trying to prevent a murder. What all this shows, contrary perhaps to first appearances, is that the definition of murder that I have suggested not only isn't evaluatively loaded, but doesn't generate a vicious regress either. Presumably possible series of the sort just described could be stretched out to indefinite, though clearly not to infinite, lengths. But, within the limits imposed by what a non-omniscient agent can know, the length of such series doesn't matter morally. What matters is how many steps it takes for such series to get back to an act of aggression against a non-aggressor. (Aggression and non-aggression, incidentally, can be evaluative concepts; but they don't have to be. 'Aggression' can just mean, not 'unjustifiable attack', but 'attack on a non-attacker'. There is nothing evaluative here, unless it's evaluative to distinguish action from passivity. And it isn't – though I don't suggest that the distinction is always easy to draw.) Roughly speaking, if the number of such steps is an even number (for example, (1) I kill (2) an aggressor against a non-aggressor), or is zero (no aggression occurs against a non-aggressor), then my action (or in the case of zero steps, my inaction) is likely not to be murder. But if the number of steps is an odd number (for example, (1) I kill a non-aggressor; or (1) I kill (2) an aggressor against (3) an aggressor against a non-aggressor, then my action is likely to be murder).

Leaving aside these intricacies, why in any case – it may be asked – should the good of life generate a material moral absolute against murder? Why not an absolute against any killing? In fact, the answer to this difficult question runs in parallel with the intricacies just explored. The answer is that one thing that commitment to the good of life can demand is the active negation of intentions to violate that good. Someone who intends to violate the good of life is setting their will to negate that good. By that act of the will, they *ipso facto* make it the case that no violation of the good of life is involved in killing them so long as that act of the will is sustained,[32] provided the killing in question is unavoidable and is done with the intention of negating their attempted negation of the good of life.

The case is, so to speak, a case of a double negative equalling a positive. What is perhaps most noteworthy about it is that it is crucially different from the case where the killing of an *innocent* is proposed as a means of preventing violations of the good of life. The crucial difference lies in the set of the will. The would-be murderer's will is set on violating the good of life by killing innocents. It is this feature of what he does or proposes, and this feature alone, that puts the would-be murderer outside restrictions on killing so long as he remains a would-be murderer; it is precisely *his* active choice to violate or to negate the good of life which negates the good of life where *he* is concerned, and so makes it licit to kill him if there is no other way of preventing his choice to violate the good of life from becoming not just active but effectual. Nothing of the sort is true of an innocent. Because by definition an innocent has made *no* choice to violate or to negate the good of life, the good of life is *not* negated where he is concerned, and so he isn't put outside restrictions on killing.

We saw above that an alleged commitment to run the college bar honestly and competently couldn't count as a genuine commitment to do that unless it was also a commitment not to steal from the till or throw away the account books. Just likewise, we may now say that to be committed to the good of life is, and is centrally and paradigmatically, to be committed to abstaining from murder. To be uncommitted to abstaining from murder is to be uncommitted to, or at least to misunderstand, the good of life and its demands on agents altogether.

Thus my general claim that there are *some* material moral absolutes depends on the point that different goods make different demands on us, so that it is possible to describe *some* conceivable action-types that satisfy one good's demand by violating another's. By contrast, my specific claim that there is a material moral absolute against murder depends, like all such specific claims, on claims about what is demanded by a correct understanding of commitment to the good(s) in question (which, in the case of murder, is certainly the goods of life and justice, and may be other goods as well).

Here someone might object as follows. 'You say that the existence of some material moral absolutes is shown by the fact that it is possible to describe some conceivable action-types that satisfy one good's demand by violating another's. You also say that to prove the existence of any specific material moral absolute depends on a correct understanding of commitment to the good(s) violated by infringement of that absolute. Then what if we reject, in turn, every specific example of a material moral absolute you come up with? How much content will be left in your unspecific claim that there are some material moral absolutes, if you cannot make good even one of your specific claims about which the material moral absolutes are?'

I don't wish to deny that, when we get to the question of what is demanded by commitment to any particular good, we are close to the intuitive bedrock of ethics. That is, unfortunately for my argument, true; and the consequence, that at this point conclusive arguments begin to run out, can't be helped, but must be lived with. So, if someone could sustain such a refusal to admit examples of material moral absolutes, there would be little I could say to them to convince them of absolutism. The question is whether such a refusal to admit any examples of absolutes can be seriously and honestly sustained, by anyone who rejects monism about the good and is sincerely attempting to understand the difference between right and wrong, and what it is to be committed to a plurality of goods. If anyone claims to be a pluralist about the good, and committed to the plurality of goods which he recognises, and yet also claims to believe that it might be all right, sometimes, to do actions of such types as torturing babies, or raping or murdering or area-bombing, there is bound to be a question about whether he can really be seriously a pluralist, or seriously committed to those different goods and their different demands, at all. As we have seen, there is no way of being sure that torturing babies would necessarily be a violation of the monist's good. But we can be as sure as we can of anything that torturing babies is necessarily a gross and paradigmatic violation of at least some of the pluralist's goods – goods to do with fairness, the value of people and of respect for them, not causing pain, and so on. So for someone to claim that he was a pluralist and, as such, committed to such goods as are violated by torturing babies, and yet claim that torturing babies wasn't ruled out by those commitments, would be a mockery – or a misunderstanding.[33]

(Of course, if someone remains a monist, or if he isn't interested in the difference between right and wrong – if, that is, he is wicked – then it's easy enough for him to refuse to admit any proffered example of an action-type as being one which he should always steadfastly refuse to do. Against such responses, I've already argued that monism about the good is false (1.2); I don't have to offer any arguments against wickedness.)

In any case it must be obvious by this point that the notion of commitments plays a crucial role in substantiating my case that for a pluralist there are material moral absolutes, by making it possible in principle for me to be completely specific about which the absolutes are. To round off this section, I'll say a bit more about that notion.

We have seen how commitment to a good involves allegiance to it, meditation on it, attention to the question of what that good's demands on the agent may be. At the extreme, goods may demand of us the recognition of material moral absolutes; less demandingly, they may also demand that we recognise formal moral absolutes; or that we should be certain sorts of person, or feel certain sorts of emotion, or have (or lack) certain sorts of disposition. Hence it's clear that commitment to the goods necessarily involves having the virtues – the dispositions of character necessary for the promotion and instantiation of the goods. And so it also becomes clear that it is only by reflection on what is involved in commitment to the goods that we can formulate the taxonomy of virtues which was promised at 2.1.

In fact, such reflection isn't the only prerequisite for a taxonomy of the virtues. We still also need a clearer understanding than we have yet of the notion of a good human life – a notion that won't be discussed until chapter 5. We may anticipate that discussion, however, with a rather conservative proposal. Whatever the forthcoming discussion of 'the good human life' may show, it is highly unlikely that there can be any acceptable taxonomy of the virtues that doesn't at least include, in one form or another, all or nearly all of the four cardinal and three theological virtues recognised in the tradition of virtue ethics: justice, self-control, courage, and practical wisdom; and faith,[34] hope, and love. Without at least these dispositions controlling the ways in which we pursue or respect all the basic goods, we have little hope of success in pursuing or respecting any basic goods. Other virtues may well be necessary (or helpful) too. But these ones at least seem likely to be essential.

With that rather minimal and provisional taxonomy of the virtues, I conclude the main part of my discussion of the Threefold Schema, and the doctrines about supererogation and moral absolutes which (as I have argued in 3.1 to 3.4) it entails. In the last two sections of this chapter I list some of the advantages of the Schema (3.5), and answer two objections (3.6) – one of them interesting though rather minor, the other an absolutely basic objection.

3.5 SIX ATTRACTIONS OF THE THREEFOLD SCHEMA

The first attraction of the Threefold Schema is that it saves the phenomena of supererogation and moral absolutes or constraints – phenomena which maximisers of every kind can only struggle with.[35] Also, it allows us to make sense, in a quite different way from consequentialists and maximisers, of what those theorists suppose themselves to be uniquely equipped to explain – the phenomenon of trade-offs between goods – without buying into either maximalism or consequentialism.

The second is that on this picture we may offer a reasonable explanation of why good people aren't all the same, and why it is vague to a degree what good people are like – two things which (as we saw above) maximisers and monists find it surprisingly difficult to explain.

A third attraction that the proposed picture offers is the possibility of a sensible subjectivism[36] – which turns out to mean a local subjectivism. On the proposed picture we can accommodate the liberal-democratic moral subjectivist who is so much a stock character in the dramas of our society. We can simply accept his basic intuition: that what is a good way for the individual citizen to live, flourish, develop, contribute to society (etc.) is up to him. To a considerable (though not unlimited) degree, that's true. What isn't true, and what should stop us accepting any less local subjectivism than this, are the different ideas (1) that what counts as a good way to live, or (2) that what counts as a good, could be up to any individual. That is no more up to individuals than the rules of chess are up to chess players – though, of course, it is up to them how they develop their rooks.

Fourth advantage: our picture also shows us how to refute ethical determinism. Ethical determinism is the thesis that, because it is always determinate what is the best action in any case (except evaluational ties), and because everyone always desires most what they think best, no one ever voluntarily does what they don't think best. It follows that an agent's diversions from maximising (for example weakness of the will)[37] can be explained only by that agent's ignorance of what's best, or by other causes of involuntariness like compulsion or irrationality.

This counter-intuitive conclusion can be blocked by non-maximising pluralism, which shows that there is good reason to deny both the premises on which it depends. Because there's a real diversity of goods, it isn't always determinate what is the best action in any case (though it is sometimes). Because supererogation is possible, everyone doesn't always desire most what they think best (though they do sometimes).

Fifth, consider personhood. We are now in a position to suggest that one's identity as a personality (as opposed to one's strict identity as this (human) animal – a very different issue) is something which one succeeds, more or less, in constituting by one's choices about how to live. Coherence or integrity in such choices means success in effecting a reconciliation (of one of indefinitely many possible kinds) between the different goods. Coherence in such choices leads to coherence over a life, which is a necessary (but not of course sufficient) condition of well-being.

Sixth, well-being is constituted by wisdom – and good luck – in such choices between the goods.

If these principles are right, then notice a further consequence for the case that Griffin argues in *Well-Being* (cp. 1.2). Well-being, on the present account, can't possibly give any determinate measure of value by which to commensurate the different goods between which we make our choices. The value of those goods in themselves is one thing, and their value in a given life is another thing, and one that may vary very widely. It can happen very easily that a good which is a great good in your life can be a very small one in mine. (Think of different people's different attitudes to the importance for them of goods like friendship or music or the quest for knowledge.) This is why I agree with Griffin that the good life is the locus (and the only possible locus) for the reconciliation of the different goods. But I don't accept his claim that this reconciliation amounts to a commensuration between the goods. As argued in 1.2, there is no such thing as <u>the</u> best way of living – no one best way of reconciling the different goods in a life. Rather there is one indefinitely large variety of good ways of reconciling the different goods; a second equally large variety of dubious or faulty ways of reconciling them; and a third equally large variety of ways of living which fail to be reconciliations of the goods altogether.

These notions of freedom, personhood and well-being, and the way in which these notions provide further guidance to an agent about how he might act, of a sort which no one but a maximiser need insist is not rational guidance: all of these notions towards which I have just gestured will be further developed in chapters 4 to 6. Before that, and lastly in this chapter, our two objections.

3.6 TWO OBJECTIONS

First objection: Does the Threefold Schema capture everything? Isn't there more to being morally wrong (or right or permissible) than violating or not violating the basic goods?

Answer: The Threefold Schema doesn't claim to capture everything. Certainly there is more to being morally wrong (or right or permissible) than violating or not violating the basic goods. As Aquinas would put it, not everything that is wrong is intrinsically wrong. Circumstances (which doesn't just mean consequences)[38] can make a difference. Some actions that are fine in one circumstance, or done in one way, are wholly inappropriate in another circumstance, or done in another way. How so? Precisely because there are some further restrictions on what choices can count as permissible (or good) for agents that aren't directly (or at any rate not obviously) implied by the Threefold Schema.

Three important restrictions on, and two important additions to, the ethical freedom of an agent who operates within the Threefold Schema which haven't yet been mentioned, are noted in the following five points. A sixth point is added more tentatively:

1 It could not be right to respect every good but promote no good whatever. That would barely be a life at all, or at best a life of dead moralistic legalism. In a good human life you can't, by merely respecting all the goods, avoid promoting some good at some time.[39] (But then, given the connection between goods and motivation, who'd want to?)

2 You may be bound to perform certain sorts of action which would otherwise be supererogatory because you occupy some special role which you have chosen (for example, a doctor's: 3.2).

3 You may be bound to perform certain sorts of action which would otherwise be supererogatory because you occupy some special role that you haven't chosen. For example, a child has special duties to her parents just because she is their child and they are her parents. Cp. the notion of being 'thrown' into some of our commitments: 3.4.[40]

4 Conversely, chosen special roles can release you from what would otherwise be obligations, making performance of the acts in question supererogatory. (A worker for a famine-relief charity might reasonably say that he isn't obliged to give any financial donations to any famine-relief charity – even though others are.)

5 Likewise, non-chosen special roles can release you from what would otherwise be obligations, making performance of the acts in question supererogatory. (Because I am a child, with parents to pay taxes on my behalf, I don't have to pay taxes.)

6 Clearly some goods are more central[41] to the good human life than others are. So possibly there are some basic goods, or instantiations thereof, which are so minor that a life devoted exclusively to them would be an insufficiently good life to count as acceptable or choiceworthy. (A life of backgammon, say?)

I'm happy to assert (1 to 5). Point 6 is more dubious. On the one side it does seem true that some goods, or instantiations of goods, are more central than others to a good human life: backgammon matters less than love. (For this point cp. my discussion of claim (R) in 6.4(a).) This is so in virtue of facts about what good human lives in general must be like which I take to be objective facts (2.4). On the other side, a life that does not involve violations of any basic goods, and does involve promotions of at least one, surely can't be described simply as a wrong way to live if we are serious about the Threefold Schema. Although we may allow that the devoted backgammon player is no saint, the Threefold Schema makes it clear that there's nothing actually wrong with not being a saint – even if not being a saint isn't as good as being one.

My suspicion is that (6) is false, and gains an illusory plausibility from an equivocation in such phrases as 'a life of backgammon' (and, for that matter, 'no saint'). The phrase 'a life of backgammon' could mean a life such that the person living it didn't respect any goods except the good of backgammon. On any development of the Threefold Schema, such a life would clearly not be ethically minimal (even). This is for reasons that have nothing to do with the fact that it is a life devoted to backgammon. That isn't what makes it a bad life. What makes it a bad life is the neglect, and hence violation, of other goods which its form of pursuit of backgammon entails.

We could take the phrase differently, to mean a life that was devoted to backgammon and yet didn't violate any goods at all, even though it pursued no goods at all except backgammon. In certain cases such an agent might have to recognise a morally compulsory duty of one of the sorts listed above under (2) and (3) (for example, to rush away from the board when his wife is at death's door) which would override the pursuit of backgammon even for him. But it isn't true, according to the Threefold Schema, that such morally compulsory duties will override his pursuit of backgammon *everywhere*. So it needn't be true that, for example, hyper-moralistic thoughts about famine relief will make it the case that the minimally moral backgammon player in fact lives exactly the same sort of life as every other minimally moral agent of whatever sort – and spends almost his whole time down on the famine-relief project. Minimally moral agents will, according to the Threefold Schema, still have a genuine range of choice, and a very wide one too, between all sorts of distinctive lives. None of these lives will be positively wrong ways to live, just because they are less good lives than others that are available. On the other hand, the fact that they are less good may explain why many of the ethically available lives turn out, like the backgammon player's life, to be rather strange lives.

Second objection: What about the problem cases?

Answer: This objection breaks up into a number of sub-questions. The first is the familiar problem of blackmail cases. If someone threatens (for example) to blow up the world if I don't (for example) torture a baby, shouldn't I torture the baby? Despite what I suppose are most people's intuitions, the correct answer to this is the absolutist one: No, I shouldn't. This isn't because I should be less concerned about the fate of the world than about keeping my hands clean, or about preserving one baby when so many babies' lives are threatened by the destruction of the world. It is because to accept the blackmailer's bargain and torture the baby is to concur with the blackmailer in a fantasy about causation.

The fantasy lies in the blackmailer's implicit claim that it is *my* action in torturing the baby that causes the survival and prevents the destruction of the world. This claim is, when you think about it (and how carefully we are educated *not* to think about it), just plain wrong. What causes the survival and prevents the destruction of the world in a blackmail case is the *blackmailer's* decisions, not mine. The blackmailer might just as well decide not to blow up the world after all, even though I have refused to torture the baby; or else decide to blow it up anyway, even though I have tortured the baby.[42] The causal power to bring about or prevent the world's survival, and therefore the moral responsibility for the world's survival, lies squarely with him, not with me. So it's just *untrue* that, when I am blackmailed like this, 'the future of the world lies in my hands'. No: it lies in the blackmailer's. Whether he and I like it or not he can't, merely by offering me imaginary transactions, pass that responsibility on to me in the way that he can pass it on to me by handing me his weapons. My situation when thus blackmailed is already crucially misdescribed by saying, as nearly everybody does who talks about these cases, that I face the dilemma of whether to accept or reject a proposal to save the world *'by'* (?) torturing a baby. That proposal is no more put before me by the blackmailer's actions than is a proposal to turn the moon into green cheese *'by'* (?) torturing the baby.

The second sub-question is: 'Why not prevent six violations of a good G1 by committing one violation of another good G2?'. First, let's keep in mind the doubts about causal fantasies that I have just raised, that is, doubts about the role of the word 'by' in that last sentence. What would be a situation where it was truly the case that I could prevent six violations of a good G1 *by* committing one violation of another good G2? But even if such a case can be provided, which may be harder than you think,[43] still our answer to this question is already clear. The reason 'why not' is that, in the absence of a coherent conception of a monistic super-good, there is no way of measuring such a bargain as being worthwhile or otherwise. (For one thing, how big are the violations?) Because the plurality of goods places genuinely different demands on us, there is no sense in the thought that we might try to homogenise those differences. If we are really committed to those goods themselves at all, we must attend to each good's *particular* demands on us. To fail to do so is just to show that we aren't really committed to the pluralistic goods themselves, but to some conception of a monistic super-good. Because the pluralistic goods are real and the monistic super-good isn't, this is an unfortunate predicament ethically speaking. Anyone in it has replaced a practical and specific commitment to a real good by an abstract and theoretical commitment to a chimerical and non-existent good. This development seems likely to be bad for one's character.

The third sub-question is familiar too: 'Why not prevent six violations of a good G1 by committing one violation of the same good G1?'. This question too raises deep worries about the notion of causal efficacy which it blandly assumes. That aside, though this question is often thought[44] to be a harder one for the absolutist than the first question, nonetheless it can be answered in a very similar way. Just as there is no way to be committed to 'the good overall' except by being committed to the *particular goods* – to each of a plurality of values, not just one thing called 'the good', so likewise there is no way to be genuinely committed to any particular good except by being committed to the *instances* of that good which come in one's way. But the demands of those instances can't rationally be balanced by maximising strategies:

individual goods are no more numerically quantifiable than is 'the good overall'.

Someone might doubt this, and protest, for example, that it's plausible to think that one murder is a good trade-off for six murders (in a way that any number of murders may not be a good trade-off for any number, say, of rapes or acts of treachery). But as utilitarians since at least Godwin have themselves been aware, it isn't as simple as that. What if the six murder victims are alcoholic, misanthropic ne'er-do-wells, while the one murder victim is a cello-playing Olympic-standard philanthropist? As we saw in discussing the Description Problem (3.1), the problem with the proposal to maximise is that it presupposes the proposal to quantify; and the problem with the proposal to quantify is not that we can't think of *any* ways of quantifying, it is that we can think of *too many*, none of which has any more than an arbitrary and stipulative priority over all the others.

In the face of this problem in its multiple-good form (as posed by the second sub-question), we decided that it was altogether implausible to think of commitment to the good as consisting in a commitment to bring about as much good as possible of whatever type at whatever cost in evils brought about along the way. Rather, we decided, we're bound to see 'commitment to the good' as a matter of particular commitments to particular types of good of the sort suggested by the Threefold Schema, according to which commitments to do and to not do turn out to be typically central to (and definitive of) ethical commitment. The same pattern of reasoning, I suggest, emerges when we consider the same problem in its single-good form. It is implausible to think of commitment to any one particular good as consisting in a commitment to bring about as much net good as possible of that type at whatever gross cost. Instead, we should see commitment to any one good as consisting in particular commitments to particular instances of that type of good of the sort suggested by the Threefold Schema. But we know from the global version of the Threefold Schema that the commitments in question are usually both positive and negative in form: they are not only commitments to pursue, but also commitments not to violate. This then is what rules out committing one violation of a given good to prevent six other violations of that good.[45]

A fourth and last sub-question concerns the possibility of insoluble dilemmas – problem cases where whatever you do, you will do wrong. Such cases are perhaps real enough (cp. 1.2), but they provide no disproof of material moral absolutism, nor of the non-maximising pluralism which theoretically underlies it. They just provide counter-examples to Kant's Law (3.2) – rare instances where 'Cannot' does not imply '(Not) Ought'. An agent in such a situation is caught between two unavoidable demands, and will violate at least one of them whatever she does. But that doesn't show that those demands have ceased in her case to apply.

It is quite mistaken to assume, as is commonly assumed, that all that is needed to refute material moral absolutism is to point to possible situations where serious acceptance of a given moral absolute would lead its adherents into dire straits – whether these dire-straits cases have the structure of blackmail cases, of cases where one is tempted 'to do evil that good may come', of insoluble dilemmas, or some other form. To argue that serious commitment to material moral absolutism leads us, or can lead us, into dire straits, and *therefore* ought to be rejected, is (as it stands) just a *non sequitur*. All sorts of commitments that human beings constantly make do lead them, or can lead them, into dire straits which they wouldn't otherwise encounter. It doesn't follow that they are wrong to make those commitments. To enter into a friendship or a marriage, to try to get a philosophy professorship or a seat in the House of Commons, to try to write a novel, go up Everest, or put a chapter on moral absolutes into a book on ethics: to commit ourselves to any of these endeavours or forms of value is to give hostages to fortune, for each of these commitments may get us into dire straits. But that's no argument for hiding under the bed-covers. From the mere fact that we give some hostages to fortune by making or recognising any commitment – including any ethical commitment – nothing necessarily follows about the inadvisability or otherwise of making that commitment in the first place.[46]

3.7 CONCLUSION

With these remarks my defence of the Threefold Schema and its consequences is complete. What I set out to answer at the beginning of this chapter, however, was the Problem of Reconciliation – the problem of how, if there is a real plurality of basic goods, any single human life can respond to them and can rationally reconcile them. To give the Threefold Schema as an answer to that Problem is to give it an incomplete answer. We have said something about how to respond to goods; there is more to be said about how to reconcile these responses. So in chapters 4 to 6 I'll go on to say it. I'll consider further the suggestions about ethical freedom, well-being, and personal identity and integrity which I made at the end of 3.5. I'll give a further description of what it might be like to live according to the Threefold Schema, and of how the Schema, and the different goods that might be recognised by an agent who operates within it, might rationally guide and prompt an agent's choice without (as the maximising monist thinks goods must) rationally determining it.

NOTES

1. *Pace* e.g. Gauthier, *Morals by Agreement* p. 56: 'We shall only assert that the only serious candidate for an explanatory schema for human action is: choice maximises preference fulfilment given belief'. N.B. Gauthier's robust confidence not only about maximisation, but also about the instrumental view of rationality which goes with it: on this cp. 5.2, 6.3. James Griffin is more cautious: 'Maximisation, in some sense, is our prudential policy: we want to have the most valuable life we can' (*Well-Being* p. 34).

2. For the classic statement of this problem v. Anscombe (1958): 'Mill . . . fails to realise the necessity for stipulation as to relevant descriptions, if his theory is to have content . . . Pretty well any action can be so described as to make it fall under a variety of principles of utility if it falls under any . . . [Mill's] position is stupid, because it is not at all clear how an action *can* fall under just one principle of utility.'

3. Cp. the distinction between the possibilities of *some* sort of commensuration and of *rational* commensuration: 1.2.

4. Or 'my advantage'; again, the same form of argument disposes both of hyper-moralism and of amoralism or egoism. Cp. 2.3.

5. But could the sort of pursuit of a good described in (2) genuinely be a *maximising* pursuit of it? Cp. Note 9.

6. V. Kant, *Critique of Practical Reason*, (tr.) Lewis White Beck, p. 38 (Academy edition, p. 36): 'It is always in everyone's power to satisfy the demands of the categorical command of morality'.

7. Qualification: Kant's Law is generally true, but it may have counter-examples. Certainly it is usually the case that Ought implies Can, and so that Cannot implies Not (Ought). But if there can be tragic dilemmas (1.2), then it is at least possible that sometimes Cannot won't imply Not (Ought). Cp. 3.6. With or without Kant's Law, it still seems crazy to claim that we are <u>constantly</u> guilty of moral failures to maximise – even though we are unable to avoid such failures.

8. There is some interesting work to be done in determining exactly what *confront* means here.

9. One obvious reason for preferring 'promote' or 'pursue' to 'maximise' arises from the 'Description Problem' (3.1): there is a general difficulty about the sense of the claim that any sane person ever tries to maximise any (one) thing.

10. Does the duty to promote the good of life by life-saving apply to a doctor *qua* doctor? Or *qua* person who is a doctor? That is: does he still have to promote the good of life-saving when he is off duty? Presumably the answer is: Yes, but not in the same ways as when he is on duty; though neither is what is morally required of a doctor, in his attitude to life-saving at any time, the same as what is morally required of a non-doctor.

11. 'Normal circumstances' means 'circumstances where there is no special reason why someone must choose to be a doctor'. What could such a special reason be? It might arise in something like this scenario: just one qualified doctor is needed to prevent enormous harm, and there is only one person who has the intelligence to become the doctor required by the case. Such scenarios are possible, but wildly improbable. (It is already clear how special roles can generate special constraints and permissions: cp. 3.6.)

12. 'As such', because there is nothing in the description of an action A as a promoting or a respecting of a good that <u>guarantees</u> that A is impermissible. If A is impermissible, that's because of some further <u>description</u> that applies to A. (What might some such further descriptions be? Cp. 3.6 on special roles.) Contrariwise, there is something in the description of A as a violating of a good that <u>does</u> guarantee that A is impermissible, and indefeasibly so: no further description of A can override that guarantee.

13. Aquinas, *Summa Theologiae*, 1a2ae.94.2, cap.: Hoc est ergo primum praeceptum legis, quod bonum est faciendum et prosequendum, et malum vitandum.

14. Aquinas, loc. cit.: Nam illud quod primo cadit in apprehensione est ens, cuius intellectus includitur in omnibus quaecumque quis apprehendit. Et ideo primum principium indemonstrabile est quod *non est simul affirmare et negare*, quod fundatur supra rationem entis et non entis: et super hoc principio omnia alia fundantur, ut dicitur in IV *Metaphysicis* [1005b29].

15. So Luscombe (1982), pp. 709, 711: 'The foundation of Aquinas' classic formulation of the doctrine of natural law is the teleological principle that all beings have within themselves inclinations which direct them to the end which is proper to them. Good has the nature of an end and evil is its contrary ... The first and fundamental precept of natural law is "good is to be done and pursued and evil is to be avoided" and this precept is self-evident since all creatures act on account of their end, which is the good for them.'

16. *Propositio per se nota*. On the vexed issues raised by the phrase, see Finnis, *Natural Law and Natural Rights*, p. 67ff.: 'A proper discussion of self-evidence would have to be embarrassingly complex ...'. Certainly Aquinas' *propositiones per se notae* needn't be self-evident to just anyone. Some (e.g. 'God exists') are self-evident only to God: *Summa Theologiae* 1a.2.1.

17. For an intricate and ingenious account of supererogation, see (McNamara 1996). One point that McNamara makes especially well is also very important here: that there can't be a coherent conception of the supererogatory without a coherent conception of the morally minimal. Cp. my contrast between pursuing and respecting a good.

18. See 4.3, 5 and 6. In 'Moral Luck' Williams argues that a right answer to 'What should I do with my life?' can be provided by hindsight: I can now see that I was wrong to go in for business, because I've now failed in business. But some things are worth trying even if they don't work out. It isn't *per se* irrational to prefer any project in which I have less chance of success to any project in which I have more. If I'm very good at push-pin and rather bad at poetry, it can still be rational to spend my life on poetry not push-pin if poetry is worth more than push-pin. There may even be projects which are so worthwhile that there's nothing irrational about pursuing them even if I think my chances of success are *nil*: e.g. various sorts of artistic endeavour, or political or religious idealism (or romantic love: perhaps Petrarch felt this way about his love for Laura).

19. Cp. Finnis, *Moral Absolutes*. Formal moral absolutes aren't my main concern, so I shall often abbreviate 'material moral absolute' as 'moral absolute'.

20. Note the negative forms of both versions of absolutism. Could a plausible moral absolutism have a positive form – 'Actions of type X are to be done, no matter what'? Yes: e.g. consequentialism is a positive formal moral absolutism – it says that utility-maximising actions are always to be done no matter what. What about a positive material moral absolutism? Wouldn't it be crazy to insist that actions of, e.g., the type 'giving to charities' were always to be done (all day every day)? Not necessarily if we specify the action-types carefully enough: consider the action-types 'Going down with the ship if one is its captain', and 'Going to the rescue when one is confronted by situations where children are trapped in burning buildings and there is no one else to do it'.

21. Some deny that consistent moral thinking involves acceptance of any moral principles. Jonathan Dancy, in his *Moral Reasons* chapters 4 to 6, reaches this conclusion by arguing against 'generalism' – the view that if any moral reason in itself counts in a given direction (say, in favour of an action) in one case, then it must in itself count in that direction in any similar case. But there's no reason why defenders of moral principles must accept either generalism or Dancy's alternative – particularism: this being the thesis that there are no moral reasons at all such that if in themselves they count in a given direction in one case, then they must in themselves count in that direction in any similar case. Between these extremes lies the possibility that some moral reasons might be generalisable, while others aren't. This is a possibility which Dancy himself seems to need, despite his official rejection of it, by his chapter 12: consider his notion of 'silencing' considerations.

22. One reason why it's controversial is because it is thought to be a blind leap across the 'is/ought gap' to move directly from (non-evaluative) 'F is of material action type T' to (evaluative) 'F is not to be done'. This thought is muddled. The material moral absolutist need not leap, for he can syllogise. His minor premiss is the non-evaluative 'F is of material action type T'; his major premiss is the obviously evaluative 'Any action of material action type T is not to be done'. So it's just false to say that he is trying to get *directly* to an

evaluative conclusion from a non-evaluative premiss. In this context the issue of the 'is/ought gap' – whatever our views about that (cp. 2.4) – simply doesn't arise.

23. For the analogy of 'dimensions' of moral assessment cp. (Steiner 1996) p. 231: 'Utilitarianism rejects both [permissions and requirements to act sub-optimally . . . this is] attributed to its uni-dimensionality or what J. O. Urmson [(1976)] has aptly named its *mononomism*. For utilitarians, the results of performable actions possess only one morally relevant feature . . . Different instances of this feature are all held to be commensurable. And the varying amounts of it that are . . . present in different results of action fully determine the comparative moral worth of those results.'

24. I discuss this question at length in my (1995), especially chapters 4 and 8.

25. On this possibility see Bernard Williams, 'Moral Incapacity', in his *Making Sense of Humanity*.

26. For Murdoch's views, v. *The Sovereignty of Good*, especially pp. 53ff.

27. 'If a procedure *is* one of judicially punishing an innocent man for what he is clearly understood not to have done, there can be absolutely no argument about the description of this as unjust. No circumstances, and no expected consequences, which do *not* modify the description of the case as one of judicially punishing a man for what he is known not to have done can modify the description of it as unjust. Someone who attempted to dispute this would only be pretending not to know what "unjust" means: for this is a paradigm case of injustice.' (Anscombe, 'Modern Moral Philosophy'.)

28. Likewise, we may ask, what is the content of a commitment to the practice of medicine if it does not rule out deliberately acting so as to injure one's patients? Cp. Cottingham (1995).

29. I don't imply that if a given good generates a material moral absolute, then it can't also generate a formal moral absolute, or absolutes against entertaining a certain sort of emotion, or being a certain sort of person. On the contrary – a good that generates a material absolute almost certainly will generate all these other sorts of absolute; but the converse does not hold.

30. So is it *absolutely impermissible* to lack a sense of humour, or to be a boor about art? Not exactly. Dispositions aren't actions, hence aren't responsive as actions are to volition. But at any rate it's true that the kind of person who not only doesn't acknowledge, but positively denies, that they're missing something humanly important by rejecting or ignoring art or humour, is without qualification a bad sort of person to be.

31. One corollary of my definition concerns 'innocent threats'. If someone poses an immediate lethal threat to me but not deliberately, e.g. by getting stuck in a pothole through which I need to escape rising flood waters, then I can't kill him without murdering him. – But can't I kill the stuck potholer without murdering him *if he gives me permission to kill him*? Isn't such a case more like self-sacrifice on his part than murder on my part? Perhaps; but what if the potholer is my own son? Would I be prepared to kill *him*, even with his permission? If not, does that show that I care about my own son too much to do what I ought? Or does it show that I am only prepared to kill the stuck potholer who is not my own son because I don't care enough about *him*?

    A third case often discussed in this context seems different again: someone who is shooting at random at anything that moves or makes a sound in the bushes where I am concealed can (I think) be killed without murder, if killing him is the only way to stop him killing me. For even though such a person won't kill me *deliberately* if he does kill me, still he isn't an *innocent* threat: he is a culpably negligent one. He, like the murderer, has something wrong with the set of his will: his behaviour is lethal behaviour even if it is not directed at any particular lethal act.

    I find these casuistical questions very hard. This is why my definition of murder is only a rough one.

32. My definition of murder and my claim that murder is absolutely wrong together entail that capital punishment is absolutely wrong. The popular idea that executing people isn't murder because it is a *literal* defence of innocent parties is a transparent pretence. No one we're in a position to execute is at all likely to pose any *immediate* lethal threat, or to be *presently* intending someone's murder. Or if they do (if, say, the prisoner on his way to the gallows lashes out with a razor at his guard) then it may be permissible for the guard to kill the prisoner – but, of course, so killing him won't be an execution. As for the popular fall-back position that executing people is some kind of *metaphorical* defence of innocents, this may be true, but can only legitimate metaphorical executions.

33. Incidentally, I for one have never seen the point of the frequently alleged opposition between ethical sensitivity and ethical rules – or 'rigid' or 'abstract' rules as they are routinely (and

rather glibly) called when this opposition is being set up. (For this opposition see, for instance, the Preface to Martha Nussbaum's *Love's Knowledge*.) If what I say here about reflection on our ethical commitments is right, then the correct thesis about rules is rather that the existence of some ethical rules is itself one of the deliverances of ethical sensitivity at work in understanding the sensitive agent's commitments. *Pace* Nussbaum and others, this thesis was obviously held by Aristotle (*Nicomachean Ethics* 1107a8ff.).

34. For doubts about whether there will be a virtue of faith at all unless God exists cp. my (1996b).

35. For a discussion of some of their struggles regarding supererogation in particular cp. Mulgan (1993).

36. David Wiggins's phrase – though what I use it for here has more to do with Essay VI than V in his *Needs, Values, Truth*.

37. It is remarkable how often Davidson (1980)'s definition of weakness of the will as 'intentionally acting against one's *best* (or better) judgement' goes unquestioned in the literature. If 'best judgement' means (as it seems to) 'judgement as to what it is best to do', then we get the absurd conclusion (absurd even for a maximiser) that every non-maximising act displays weakness of the will.

38. So far from just meaning 'consequences', 'circumstances' could mean non-essential modifications of the description of an action, say giving money to a beggar, arising from almost any of Aristotle's nine non-substantial categories. Quantity: I give a beggar too much money. Quality: I give him Irish money, or give it grudgingly. Relation: I give him money which I owe to someone else. Place: I give him money where we are surrounded by cut-throats. Time: I give him money as a cut-throat passes. Position: I jab the money into his eye . . . And so on.

39. Quite possibly, in fact, it could be argued that this requirement is implied by the Threefold Schema, because never to promote any good would, very likely, entail violating some good to do with yourself, such as self-respect. Perhaps it would entail violating the good of achievement as well.

40. In an unpublished paper 'Making, Allowing, and the Exigence of Morality' which he has kindly shown me, J. E. J. Altham suggests that the well-known doing/allowing distinction, so often attacked by consequentialists such as Bennett and Glover, isn't an essentially morally significant distinction. Yet it can have moral significance brought to it, selectively, in particular circumstances such as those of promising. That idea may, I believe, be fruitfully connected with the idea underlying items (2 to 5) in my list of special circumstances, which is that special moral duties or permissions are typically generated by special moral relationships. For it is these relationships, I think, that are the commonest reason for variations in what we count as morally important doing or allowing.

41. Once again I must emphasise that to say that some goods are 'more central' to the good life than others is not to position any of the goods along any sort of metric. Rather it is to talk about features internal to those goods themselves which give different goods their different relations to human flourishing in general, and to the flourishing of any individual human.

42. I'm not making the (irrelevant even if true) point that the blackmailer's actions are unpredictable – a point that Williams, in *Moral Luck*, has rightly described as 'Bluntly, a cop-out'. I'm saying that the conditionals relevant to the causation of the blowing up of the world are conditionals about the blackmailer, not about me.

43. I'm not suggesting that there are no such cases; merely that finding them is not as easy as is often thought, and that often, in practice, the plea that the end justifies some means rests upon a view of what means are necessary to that end which is as much a fantasy as the blackmailer's view.

44. For example, Shelly Kagan apparently thinks that this is the hardest question for the moral absolutist: see his *The Limits of Morality* for the argument that commonsense moral constraints are self-contradictory or self-defeating because they forbid the efficient pursuit of the very goods which ground them.

45. Notice that this answer to the objection does not (at least directly) invoke the acts/ omissions distinction – although it might be said (e.g. by Kagan) that a covert appeal to that distinction is built into my argument by way of its focus on the notion of *particular agents and their particular commitments*. Perhaps this is right; because I believe in the acts/ omissions distinction, I don't mind if it is.

46. Cp. Alexander's comments on the possibility of tragedy in the second epigraph to this chapter.

A strength of hylomorphism, particularly in its more materialistic version, is that it does point to *human being* as being a basic concept in the philosophy of mind, and, consequently, in ethics . . . [The idea in some contemporary moral philosophy is] that when some (biologically) living human being lacks [certain higher capacities], it is not a person; while it is to *persons* that we owe various basic duties (such as not killing them). Such ideas are used by, for example, Tooley, who is thus encouraged to speak of humans who are not yet persons, or who have ceased to be so . . . and to claim that they fall outside moral restrictions on killing. So far as infants are concerned the application of the doctrine seems anyway arbitrary – it turns just on where the lines of *potentiality* are drawn . . . The Aristotelian approach avoids [Tooley's] slippery slope by taking the moral categories (or these fundamental ones, at least) to apply in the first instance – though they may reach also *more* widely – to a *kind*, to which the senile undoubtedly belong. (This is a thought we undoubtedly use: the possibility is to be taken very seriously that we may not know morally how to do without it.) The gross weakness of the schema now under consideration is that *person* appears as a fake natural kind, assisted by the sortal grammatical character of the term 'person'. But *person* is not a natural kind, and its grammar is misleading, rather like that of 'dwarf' or 'giant': the characteristics involved in its application are in fact *scalar* characteristics, and there is a real arbitrariness in the degree or level of mental functioning which is going to qualify for one's being a 'person'. This scalar character of the underlying considerations, together with the misleading 'on-off' grammatical character of 'person', has genuine and thoroughly undesirable consequences for its use as a central concept of moral argument.

'Human being' does not share these difficulties. It cannot be impossible to make clear how 'human being' can be the foundation of what is correctly called a 'humane' ethics . . .

Bernard Williams (1986); cp. *ELP* pp. 114ff.

The citizen should put himself in good order, and by attaining self-mastery and structure become a friend to himself. He should find a way to harmonise the three elements of his soul – the high, the middle, the low – and whatever there may be between them. He should bind all together and become, in every respect, one out of many . . .

Plato, *Republic*, 443e

It is a mark of great folly not to have ordered one's life towards some objective.

Aristotle, *Eudemian Ethics* 1,214b10

4

———— • ————

PERSONS AND IDENTITIES

Chapter 3 proposed the Threefold Schema as the first part of my answer to the Problem of Reconciliation. That proposal leaves open at least part of the question of what constitutes rationality in choices of and between a plurality of goods. To the theory of value offered in chapters 1 and 2, the Threefold Schema of chapter 3 adds no more than an outline deontological ethical code which, as it stands, still underdetermines any agent's decisions as to what to do. You could live all sorts of lives which would accord with any given substantive interpretation of the Threefold Schema. Yet surely not all of them would be equally rational. So is there no more to say about what makes an agent's choices rational (or morally justified), or otherwise? Yes – as we shall see in chapters 4 to 6.

Of course, there might *not* have been any more to say. We might, for instance, welcome the underdetermination of practical rationality just described. This might be because we think that moralists have no right to lay down the law about how private individuals live their own lives provided they keep within the rules of the Threefold Schema and don't violate any of the basic goods. We might hold that any choice within those limits is as rational and as good as any other. This *laissez-faire* approach to the Problem of Reconciliation would no doubt appeal to some of the intuitions of those who live in modern liberal societies, and can be attracted by the visions of society offered, for example, by Robert Nozick in *Anarchy, State and Utopia,* or by the Mill of *On Liberty,* or (non-philosophically) by the powerful forces of consumerism and individualism that dominate Western society.

The main problem with this approach is that it fails to register differences of preferability and rationality between ways of living which *should* be registered. There is a difference between, for example, a life that is not wicked but totally *directionless*, and a life that is neither wicked nor directionless, but good.

Alternatively, 'the more that there was to say about practical rationality' might be maximising in form. We might banish any trace of underdetermination from our answer to the Problem of Reconciliation by saying that it is a further demand of practical rationality that individuals should *maximise* (something or other) within the limits of the Schema. This would be a move that took us back in the direction of consequentialism – towards a sort of maximalism-within-limits.

Given pluralism, the obvious problem with this approach is to say *what* it might be that was thus to be maximised. For reasons we have seen in chapters 2 and 3 it could hardly be any one of the goods, nor any combination of the goods. But what does that leave to be maximised? How, if we're to maximise at all, could it possibly be more important or rational to maximise something *else* than to maximise at least some or other of the basic goods?

The second part of this book's answer to the Problem of Reconciliation will offer neither a *laissez-faire* answer, nor an answer that is maximalist-within-limits. The answer it offers will depend on a view about personal identity which comes in two parts. One of these parts we might call a view about personal identity *strictly so called*; the other, a view about personal identity *as integrity*. Let me begin by explaining this two-part view of persons and their identities ('The Two-part View').

The proposal about personal identity *strictly so called* says that the identity conditions over time which apply to us are conditions for the identity of the individual human animal. Persons (in this sense) are substances of a recognisable and familiar biological type – the species *Homo sapiens*. The ethical importance of persons in this sense correlates with the deontological requirements of the Threefold Schema, inasmuch as it is strict personal identity (meaning animal identity) that determines the bounds of the ethically basic notions of personal agency, responsibility, and moral significance, recognition of which is essential to a proper responsiveness to the basic goods that individual humans instantiate (2.2).

Meanwhile, the proposal about personal identity *as integrity* says that being a person means being a narrative. To be a person is to live a life, and lives can have more or less integrity or order to them: part of living well is to live a life that makes narrative sense, that has the shape and the integrity of a well-organised, happy narrative. Consider choices between options which are equally available to the agent within the constraints of the Schema. Practical rationality meets (or should meet) these by posing questions about how the options in question will affect *the shape of the agent's life*. When it is known that a given option isn't simply forbidden as being a violation of some good, the right question for practical rationality to ask about that option is not as determinate or fixed as 'Will doing this maximise [something]?' Nor is it as indeterminate and unfixed as 'Do I feel like doing this?' The right question to ask is, roughly, 'What kind of a person will I be if I do this?' or 'How does doing this fit into the shape of my life so far?' The idea is that the agent should view the choice before him as a *self-constituting* choice: a choice about what sort of person to become or go on being.[1]

This is the sense in which the Two-part View proposes that we see one aspect of *personal identity* as *personal integrity*, and personal integrity as *integrity of narrative*. This part of the Two-part View picks up a sense of 'identity' more used in sociology than in analytic philosophy; but a sense which is none the worse for that, provided we remember that it isn't the same as strict or logical identity.

On the Two-part View personal identity strictly considered has an ethical importance that correlates with the basis of ethics in the Threefold Schema. Likewise, identity as integrity has an ethical importance which correlates with the superstructure of ethics – the part of the subject about what goes on within the constraints of the Threefold Schema. There are considerations that can make it rational for an agent to choose one way rather than another, even when the Schema itself places no rational constraints upon choice. These considerations concern the rational agent's continuing project of seeking *narrative integrity over time* – their project of finding or creating their own personal identity in the second sense identified above.[2]

If the Two-part View can be established, it will have important consequences. First it will corroborate the Threefold Schema of chapter 3, and the distinction between the Schema and what I address in chapters 5 and 6 – the narrative part of ethical rationality. If that distinction in ethics correlates closely with a distinction about persons, that sheds interesting theoretical light in both directions and on both distinctions.[3] Another corollary of establishing the Two-part View is this: if it's right to see persons as substances of a certain sort, as individual human animals, then that is an important thesis in the philosophy of personal identity. (It's often called *animalism*.)

So can my Two-part View – Animalism plus Integrity – be established?

To begin with, the Two-part View needs to have an answer to the reductionism of Derek Parfit. Reductionism holds that questions about personal identity are 'empty questions', because personal identity relations are always reducible to other relations: only these other relations would need to be mentioned in a complete but maximally economical taxonomy of reality. If reductionism is right, it contradicts my metaphysical thesis, Animalism, and indeed any view of strict personal identity which takes personal identity to have a basic reality of its own.

Parfit also presents ingenious arguments for the claim that, because strict personal identity has no basic reality of its own,[4] therefore (a) it isn't what really matters ethically, and (b) if identity as integrity matters ethically, it isn't the only thing that matters or what matters most. If his arguments are right, they contradict my ethical claims not just about Animalism, but about Integrity too.

In 4.2 I try to show that substantive conceptions of strict identity can survive Parfit's arguments, by refuting his arguments. In 4.3 I try to do the same for the notion of identity as integrity. In 4.4 I defend Animalism, my view of persons as substances, more directly. In chapters 5 and 6 I turn to the notion of Integrity.

4.2   AGAINST REDUCTIONISM

Parfit himself has recently put his metaphysical argument for reductionism about personal identity like this:[5]

> (1) When experiences at different times are all had by the same person, either this fact consists in other facts, or it does not. (2) If this fact consists in other facts, some Reductionist view is true. (3) If this fact does not consist in any other facts, persons must be entities of the kind believed in by Metaphysical Non-Reductionists. Therefore (4) either persons are such entities, or some Reductionist view is true. But (5) persons are not such entities. Therefore (6) some Reductionist view is true.

Consider this argument's premiss (2). I claim (2) is a *non sequitur*. I agree with Parfit that facts about personal identity and persistence 'consist in other facts'. Like him, I don't wish to entertain the metaphysically extravagant hypothesis of a 'simple self' *à la* Descartes (or Swinburne). What I dispute is Parfit's inference from 'All facts about personal identity consist in other facts' to 'Some [Parfitian] Reductionist view is true'.

Point (2) is a *non sequitur* because facts about the identity and persistence of *virtually anything* can, if you like, be seen as 'consisting in other facts'. Just like the non-reductionisms Parfit attacks, Parfitian reductionism needs the claim that there is at least one sort of thing facts about which don't consist in facts about anything else. Non-reductionists want facts about the identity and persistence of *persons* not to consist in any other facts. Parfit wants facts about the identity and persistence of *person-components* (for example, the relata of what he calls 'R-relations') not to consist in any other facts. But what's sauce for the non-reductionist is sauce for the Parfitian. If non-reductionists face a dilemmatic choice between a retreat into mysteries about irreducibility and the admission that persons' persistence consists in other facts, then Parfitians face a dilemmatic choice between a retreat into mysteries about irreducibility and the admission that person-components' persistence consists in other facts.

This follows only on the assumption that 'the identity and persistence of *virtually anything* can, if you like, be seen as consisting in other facts'. (Let's call this assumption 'The Assumption'.) If we restrict ourselves to composite spatiotemporal continuants (CSCs), The Assumption seems to me an evident truth[6] – and, indeed, one in formulating which we can drop the word 'virtually'.

Why can facts about the identity and persistence of any CSC be seen, if you like, as consisting in other facts? Because there are no obviously legitimate restrictions on which facts are to be counted as *the* unique set of irreducible or brute facts – no more than there are obviously legitimate restrictions on which existents are to be counted as *the* unique set of irreducible or brute existents. Parfitian reductionism tells us that 'though persons exist, we could give a *complete* description of reality *without* claiming that persons exist' (*RP* p. 212): we need mention only person-components and their arrangements. But why stop at omitting persons? Aren't there plenty of other sorts of entity we might equally omit from some inventory of reality that we chose to offer? Undeniably the existence of, for example, a tree during any period 'just consists in' the suitably arranged existence of its trunk, roots and branches, the transpiration of water and other processes of growth . . . So why not argue that arboreal identity 'just involves' the suitably arranged continuity of such items; that all such items can be described without subordinating them to some further item *the tree*; and so that the sort *trees* can, if we like, be eliminated from our world inventory?

Indeed, why not offer similar moves for any sort of CSC whatever? Because (apparently) everything we might want mentioned in any world inventory is composite, we can, if we like, construct inventories that omit all sorts of sorts of CSCs. Persons are one such omissible sort. But until we see arguments showing that any inventories are preferable to others, or that there's any sort of CSC which must appear in every inventory, we can't count the failure of the sort *persons* to appear in every correctly compiled world inventory against that sort. Nor can we avoid the conclusion that just the same kind of omissibility applies to the sort *person-components*. If so, the fact that persons consist of components of other sorts can't be used to show that it's these other sorts of things and their relations which are irreducible, and so which 'really matter'. For *pari passu* it isn't these components but *their* components that are irreducible and really matter; and so on indefinitely. The reductionist suggestion seems to be that we should test whether sorts of items are irreducible and 'really matter' by applying the test of whether they must occur in a complete description of reality. But this 'Complete Description Test' leaves persons and their components on precisely the same footing.[7]

How might Parfitians deal with this criticism? Three tactics suggest themselves. First, they might somehow mitigate their apparent commitment to The Assumption sufficiently to allow them to argue for a view of the nature of world inventories that entails that facts about (or existents such as) person-components like R-relata <u>must</u> appear in any correct and complete world inventory, but that facts about (or existents such as) persons don't or can't appear. Hence person-components pass the Complete Description Test, but persons don't. Parfit would probably be inclined to sympathise with such an argument,[8] so it would be interesting to see one; but so far, we haven't.

Second, Parfitians might deny that person-components are composite. Parfit himself, I think, would reject this move. He holds that there may be some non-composite entities, but that these are probably found at subatomic levels. Their discovery is therefore a matter of interest mainly to the physicist, not the philosopher of personal identity.

Third, Parfitians might deny that person-components are spatiotemporal continuants. I gather that Parfit is inclined to make this move, at least in the case of 'R-relata' like intentions and memories. Such a move faces at least two difficulties. (1) Even if R-relata aren't spatiotemporal, it doesn't follow that they aren't composite continuants. (A continuant has to be temporal; but why does it have to be spatial?) But if they are composite continuants, then it can still be true that facts about them consist in nothing over and above facts about their components (whether or not *these* are spatiotemporal). To show that R-relata pass the Complete Description Test, it isn't sufficient to claim that R-relata, or their components, aren't spatiotemporal. So far as I can see, their being non-spatiotemporal would matter only if it *entailed* their being non-composite. (2) It seems, anyway, that R-relata *are* spatiotemporal continuants. Why can't we say that intentions and beliefs, etc., are located in, and can endure through, space and time? (Consider, for instance, propositional attitudes with indexicals in them: how could these fail to be spatiotemporally located?) The only obvious motivation for wanting to deny that intentions and beliefs are spatiotemporal is a sort of dualism. But even dualism doesn't *need* this denial (indeed is probably better off without it). Even dualists can say that my beliefs and intentions etc., like my soul or Ego, normally go where my body goes. Parfitian reductionists too seem quite happy in practice to trace spatiotemporal courses for psychological items. So even dualists and reductionists should not be much alarmed by the idea that R-relata are spatiotemporal continuants – in just the way (whatever they think it is) that minds are.

So perhaps the second claim, that person-components aren't themselves composite, is the one the Parfitian ought to insist upon after all. Perhaps this might be done by appealing to the notion of *emergence*. Perhaps 'emergent' entities, if they aren't hopelessly mysterious, have no components at the lowest level of analysis at which they emerge. So mightn't Parfitians suggest, for example, that 'R-relations' – continuities or connectednesses holding between psychological items such as propositional attitudes – appear as lowest-level emergents and so *can't* be reduced to any sorts of relations between still-lower-level things in which they consist?

Not plausibly. First, this (unattractively dualist?) line leaves it open to a hard-nosed non-reductionist like Swinburne to retort that persons are emergent too in just the same way, one level of analysis up. Second, and more importantly, this line of thought gets its attraction from the fact that propositional attitudes look like simple items, consisting only of logical parts (attitudes and propositions). But strictly speaking, propositional attitudes in this sense are abstract entities. What we need to understand to understand R-relata are mental entities – *holdings of* propositional attitudes. It would be a *non sequitur* to argue that these are simple because the abstract entities are. The way to understand these mental entities is to ask what has to happen for someone to hold any propositional attitude. The answer to this will either treat such holdings as 'brute facts' – which leads us back into mystery – or else specify some facts of a different sort from the holding of the attitude

itself. This specification will be either an incomplete analysis of what
it is to hold a propositional attitude – in which case more work needs
to be done; or else a complete one – in which case we could if we
chose give a complete description of the holding of the propositional
attitude without talking about holdings of propositional attitudes as a
'further fact' beyond our specification. This would suffice to show that
R-relata can be understood as composites, and therefore open the way
to the claim that they fail the Complete Description Test in just the
way that persons do.[9]

The upshot is that persons and person-components are on the same
footing relative to the Complete Description Test. The considerations
that might persuade us that persons fail that test can equally well be
applied to persuade us that all CSCs, and in particular person-components, will fail it if persons do. So step (2) in Parfit's argument (p. 108)
really is a *non sequitur*. Because we can say that any CSC consists in
nothing over and above its components, persons aren't specially vulnerable to this point, nor are person-components specially immune to
it. Thus the Complete Description Test gives us no argument for
reductionism. There is no reason, of the sort which has been on offer
so far, to think that person-components like R-relata are 'what really
matters'.

But mightn't other sorts of reasons for thinking that be offered?
Even if Parfitians[10] accepted that (2) had been refuted, mightn't they
argue like this?

> *Because* R-relations are what matters ethically, *therefore* we should
> stop taking talk about persons to be ethically basic or irreducible.
> All that's been shown to date is that persons and R-relata are 'on
> the same footing'. Even if we accept that, we're still free to argue
> (1) that a *better ethics* emerges if we concentrate on R-relata and
> ignore persons than if we do the converse, and so (2) that we
> *should* concentrate on R-relata and ignore persons.

In 4.3 I consider three possible arguments for (1) and (2), from (a)
the advantages of division, (b) *liberation from the self*, and (c) *integrity*.

4.3 WHAT MATTERS ABOUT PERSONAL IDENTITY

(a) *The advantages of division*

Instead of regarding division [into two separate continuants of my
experience] as being somewhat worse than ordinary survival, I

might regard it as being better. The simplest reason would be . . . the doubling of the years to be lived. I might have more particular reasons. Thus there might be two life-long careers both of which I strongly want to pursue. I might strongly want both to be a novelist and a philosopher. If I divide, each of the resulting people could pursue one of these careers . . . (*RP* p. 264)

Personal division, says (a), is a possible way of having my time again, or of resolving dilemmas by having my time twice at the same time. This possibility makes for a better ethics by bringing a hopeful prospect into view. So the possibility of personal division counts in favour of (1) and (2).

Problem-solving by division, however, seems impossible for at least three reasons. First, any close psychological continuant of me presumably shares my psychological characteristics. But then if I am – pardon the phrase – torn between two alternative careers, shouldn't my closest successors inherit the whole of this indecision from me – not one half each? A person divided between two ambitions is in a *single* mental state, that of indecision, not in a conjunction of two different mental states neither of which is indecision. Hence there isn't even in principle a line along which for example a surgeon might cut to get the neat division and deconditionalisation of previously conflicting wishes which division requires.

Second, why should half-me A think that he's given any reason to choose life-plan A over life-plan B by the mere fact that half-me B has chosen life-plan B; or even by the fact that life-plan A was what I intended for half-me A? What has anyone *else's* choice got to do with A's decision over life-plans?

The third reason why it's impossible to solve decision problems by division applies only if we accept both *Objectivism* and *Pluralism* about the good. Granting those assumptions, as Parfit evidently does,[11] it is the most decisive reason of these three. *Objectivism* about the good is the belief, defended in 2.4, that to say that 'There is a good or goods' is to state a fact of some sort. *Pluralism* about the good is the belief, defended in 1.2, that practical choice is between many different, multiply instantiable goods. If we accept these beliefs, we may perhaps grant that conflicts between subjective preferences can be resolved by division. But we must deny that division can also resolve conflicts between objective ethical values.

Objective values apply to each and every moral agent in the same way. Every moral agent is equally confronted by just as many different goods, and just as many different instantiations of each good. Hence division makes no difference to the structure of ethical choices. Because all post-division selves have all the same goods to choose between as pre-division selves had, division doesn't prevent opportunities for dilemma. It multiplies them, by multiplying the number of people who face them.

Division could resolve a dilemma between (Parfit's example) a lifetime as a novelist and a lifetime as a philosopher only if no objective goods were in conflict in such a choice. Objectivism says that this isn't so (or needn't be). My incompatible desires to be a novelist and to be a philosopher can both be grounded, not just in my psychology's quirks, but in my responsiveness to the different goods confronting me. My dilemma then isn't only structured by my desires; it is also, and more deeply, structured by the goods that ground those desires. Even if I do divide, each of the resulting people is still equally subject to the rational 'pulls' of those two different goods – and so no more able than me to solve the dilemma by any rational means.[12]

Still, the dilemma might be solved by irrational means. I could for example ensure somehow that one of the resultant selves has the appropriate beliefs, aptitudes and desires, whichever those are, only for a career as a novelist, while the other resultant self has the appropriate beliefs (etc.) only for a career as a philosopher. But *which* career as a philosopher? A career in (say) philosophy of mind, or in philosophy of mathematics? Both careers have value of quite different sorts; so there could be a dilemma between them too, as before. We might perform another division to solve this dilemma, but then the same question applies again: if a career as a philosopher of mind is my choice, which one?

There seems no end to this regress of divisions. The reason why is in the structure of Pluralism, which has the ethical choices available to any agent forming a mathematically dense array. Given Pluralism, there are indefinitely many different goods around for an agent to choose between; and uncountably many different ways of instantiating those goods within a life. So at no level of individuation of lives does it become clear that the possibility of dilemmas between different lives has faded out of the picture.

Suppose this can be got round. Suppose it is at least a logical possibility that iterated Parfitian divisions might (at possibly infinite length) lead to a situation where, for any member L of this set of all possible ethical lives, one of the resultant selves has the necessary moral beliefs, aptitudes and desires for nothing but L. Even then, notice first what we haven't gained, and second, what we have lost.

We haven't gained a reason for thinking that this scenario anywhere shows an agent with a full and rational responsiveness to every good. It's true that the original self has ensured – conceivably on purpose – that every instantiation of every good will be responded to by some successor self of hers. But it's also true that the original self has ensured that every one of her successor-selves will lack choices and forms of responsiveness to good which she herself has, by making sure that they lack the necessary beliefs etc. to pursue options which they aren't 'designed' to pursue. This means that all such successor-selves are desensitised to certain sorts of good (increasingly so desensitised, the closer one gets down the R-relations towards the terminal selves) and thus that all such successor-selves lack full responsiveness to the kinds of good there are. It also means, apparently, that the original self has deliberately so desensitised all her successors. But isn't there something morally dubious about this process of progressive ethical self- (or selves-) anaesthesia?

Connectedly, what we have lost comes down to two items. The first is the idea that anything might *depend* on ethical choice. Because all ethical options are realised somewhere in the family tree of selves – and because therefore no instantiation of value can ever be lost – ethical choices for successor-selves in the scenario are never important in a way that such choices are always important for us. More radically (the second missing item), it's dubious whether there are *any* real ethical choices in the scenario once it has begun. It's part of the hypothesis[13] that, beyond the original self's choice to begin the process, every self in the process has no serious alternative to the path which it actually pursues. At the limit, each terminal successor-self is responsive to only one instantiation of good, and deaf to the goodness of every other possible life. But then such selves don't choose the lives they live; they roll into them like marbles into slots. For such selves there is no gap between moral capacity and moral actuality. Put another way, such selves buy freedom from dilemmas at the price of freedom.[14]

(b) *Liberation from the self*

[Because] I changed my view [from non-reductionism to reductionism] . . . there is still a difference between me and other people. But the difference is less. Other people are closer. I am less concerned about the rest of my own life, and more concerned

> about the lives of others. When I believed the non-reductionist
> view, I also cared more [that after] my death, there will be no one
> living who will be me . . . [But] instead of saying 'I shall be dead',
> I should say, 'There will be no future experiences that will be
> related, in certain ways, to these present experiences'. Because it
> reminds me what this fact involves, this redescription makes this
> fact less depressing. Suppose next that I must undergo some
> ordeal. Instead of saying, 'The person suffering will be me', I
> should say, 'There will be suffering that will be related, in certain
> ways, to these present experiences' . . . the redescribed fact seems
> to me less bad. (*RP* 281–2)

This argument cites two ethical advantages of reductionism which
Parfit thinks aren't shared by non-reductionism, to do with *egoism* and
fear of the future.

No doubt the non-reductionist can't argue against *egoism* as the
reductionist recommends. But there are plenty of other ways of arguing
against it: for example, as I argued on the basis of Pluralism in 2.3.
Because you don't need to be a reductionist to argue like this,
reductionism is only corroborated by our felt need to refute egoism if
no such argument is plausible.

As for *fear of the future*: given the undoubted fact that people who
haven't signed up for any philosophical view about personal identity
do fear death and pain, we might find in Parfit's remarks the dilemma
that his proposed redescriptions are either inaccurate or comfortless.
Suppose I find less to frighten me in the idea that 'There will be no
future experiences that will be related in certain ways to these present
experiences' than in the idea that 'I am going to die'. We might say
that this can be only because I *don't* think that these ideas mean the
same. If Parfit persuades me that they *do* mean the same, perhaps I'll
decide that they are equally frightening too. Or we might say that it
doesn't make much difference to such fears whether non-reductionism
or reductionism is true. If it is reasonable for a non-reductionist to fear
the end of the person which he believes he is, why isn't it reasonable
for a reductionist to fear the end of the set of R-relations which he
believes he is?

Parfitians may rejoin that all this misses the point. What is the *ground*
of any person's fear of death or pain? Surely his perception that
something bad is going to happen *to him*. Reductionism *can* make a
difference to this perception, by undermining the meaningfulness of
the words 'to him'.[15] Once I see that there's not much more reason to

fear future pain 'to me' than there is to fear any other future pain I will, in Parfit's phrase, be 'liberated from my self'.

Even if we accept this, we may still wonder whether it shows that reductionism is a more cheery position than non-reductionism, and so has the edge over it ethically. If unravelling the self lessens our fears, presumably it also lessens our hopes. If reductionism decreases my unhappiness by detaching me from expected pain, presumably it also decreases my happiness by detaching me from expected pleasure.

In any case the argument doesn't show that reductionists have less reason to fear (or hope for) the future than non-reductionists. What it shows is that a reductionist has less reason than a non-reductionist to fear the future *because it will be bad for him*. But this isn't a reductionist attitude to the future anyway. The reductionist's attitude to the future isn't that it will be good or bad *for him*. It is that it will be good or bad *for someone*. This certainly means that the reductionist lacks a reason which the non-reductionist has for fearing the future, arising from the non-reductionist's concern for himself. Conversely, it also means that the reductionist has a reason which the non-reductionist doesn't have to fear *anyone*'s pain or death (including his own), arising from the reductionist's concern for any future self. (Unless the reductionist is merely callous about suffering; which he's presumably meant not to be.) Hence reductionism can't reduce the total amount of fear of the future. At most reductionism redistributes that amount. (Similar points apply to hope.) If this means an increase in empathy, no doubt that's a good thing. Whether such increases in empathy are possible *only* if we adopt reductionism is, as with the refutation of egoism, surely a different question.

A different point about both of the alleged ethical advantages of reductionism discussed so far is their inconsistency with the third advantage, integrity. Integrity really is an advantage of reductionism. But it can't be argued for in the same breath as the alleged advantages of division and liberation from the self.

(c) *Integrity*

On the non-reductionist view, the deep unity of each life is automatically ensured, however randomly, short sightedly, and passively this life is lived. On the reductionist view, the unity of our lives is a matter of degree, and is something that we can affect. We may want our lives to have greater unity, in the way that an artist may want to create a more unified work. And we can *give*

our lives greater unity . . . [in this respect] the reductionist view
gives more importance [than non-reductionism] to how we choose
to live, and to what distinguishes different people. (*RP* p. 446)

I'm happy to agree that what Parfit calls 'the unity of our lives', and
I call integrity, is an ethically crucial notion. Recall the conflicts between
goods which I, following Parfit, examined above. The decision
between the different lives of for example, a philosopher and a novelist
is, says Objectivism, not just a decision between subjective preferences,
but also between objective goods. Moreover (says Pluralism), such
goods can be reconciled or commensurated only to a degree. Decisions
like the novelist-or-philosopher choice[16] aren't made algorithmically, by
deciding which way we should go to maximise the good. It is a corollary
of Pluralism that in such decisions no maximising algorithm is available:
1.2, 3.1 to 3.2.

So the Problem of Reconciliation arises again: how are such decisions
to be made if not by attempting to maximise? What *other* kind of
rationality could they have? Aren't they, really, just irrational or
random? The concept of integrity can be used to answer this. We can
reply that the rational agent typically seeks to give her life a clear
narrative unity and shape by her choices among goods. So her choice
between novel-writing and philosophy can be made, not by asking
'Which of these two lives is better?', but by asking 'Which of these
two kinds of person do I want to be?'.

The agent seeks, in either alternative, to create a fitting way of
carrying on the narrative of her own life, and to give it the organisation
and shape of a certain sort of story. Choosing like this isn't choosing
by reference to any maximising criterion. But it isn't choosing randomly
or irrationally either. Such ethical choices aren't so much like compari-
sons of two measurements as like choices about how to carry on a story.
But carrying on a story is no less a rational process than measuring is.

Integrity in this sense isn't a *dispensable* objective for a rational
person. Parfit writes that 'We *may* want our lives to have greater unity,
in the way that an artist *may* want to create a more unified work'. But
a work of art that lacks *any* real unity is just a mess. A good artist
necessarily seeks to give his work unity. Unity may not be the only
canon of artistic excellence; but it is one of the canons. Likewise the
integrity, the achieved narrative unity, of a person's life isn't the only
thing needed to make it a good life; but it is one of the things. We may
sometimes want our lives to have *greater* unity – or we may not,
depending on circumstances.[17] But if we're rational at all, we must

want our lives to have *a high degree of* unity. As Parfit rightly says, the alternative is randomness, short-sightedness, and passivity.

If integrity is a necessary condition for a good human life, there is an inevitable conflict between this ethical advantage of reductionism and the other two alleged advantages concerning self-division and liberation from the self. If there can't be a good life without a conscious effort on the agent's part to make as much connection as she possibly can between the different (temporal and other) parts of that life, it can't be consistent with this effort for the agent to encourage herself to reflect that future pains matter less because she isn't deeply connected to them, as she would be if non-reductionism were true. Again, if a life can't be a good life without a high degree of narrative unity, it can't be a good one if it divides in two. Choices between different ways my life could go are constitutive of my character – of my *identity* (in the non-strict sense of that word). To try to choose *both* options by splitting and becoming a philosopher and a novelist is to find a way of ducking what is certainly a hard choice. But it is also to miss out on an interesting and important opportunity for *self-definition*. It is to fail – so far as this choice goes – to become anything to which narrative rationality could even begin to apply.

I've considered the possibility that Parfitians might argue that '*Because* R-relations are what matters ethically, *therefore* we should stop taking persons to be of basic ethical significance'. But the ideas about integrity which Parfit himself advances in corroboration of reductionism can be spelled out in the way I've just suggested. So developed, these ideas don't show that 'a better ethics emerges if we concentrate on R-relata and ignore persons'. Instead they strongly suggest that the notion of a human life lived with a high degree of narrative coherence is ethically indispensable. But this notion is just one way of understanding the notion of a *person*.

Still, it seems a decidedly reductionist way of understanding that notion. Personhood so understood is something that comes in degrees, and consists in nothing over and above the connections between the different sorts of components of personhood. For this notion of personhood, identity means no more and no less than narrative coherence: I continue being 'the same person' in this sense just so long as my narrative continues in a clear and coherent way.

But what this point shows – to reiterate what was established in 4.1 – is not reductionism, but the claim that this notion of 'the same person' is emphatically not the same as the notion of 'the same person' relevant to the problem of strict personal identity. That isn't to say that this narrative notion of sameness of person (or better perhaps of personality) isn't useful and important ethically speaking: we have already seen one of its uses and some of its importance. Nor is it to say that there is available any other notion of sameness of person more relevant to the main debate about personal identity which isn't vulnerable to objections like the empty question cases that Parfit puts up against non-reductionism about personal identity.

For instance, we might wish to say that the main debate about personal identity isn't a debate about narrative integrity in the sense I've just explored, but about the conditions under which we have or haven't got *the same human animal* (4.4). But if we do say this, we must concede something parallel to what I've just said about the narrative conception, namely this: On the animalist conception, personal identity means no more and no less than biological coherence. I carry on being 'the same human animal' just so long as the living organism which I am continues existing in a clear and coherent way. That naturally means that there will be what Parfit might call 'empty-question' cases: cases where such continuity is so puzzlingly compromised that there's nothing to say about whether my identity is sustained or not. These cases will be (so to speak) the right ones for personal identity to break down in, however, unlike the cases in which the narrative relations would break down. Division of the components of a *personality* doesn't furnish any empty-question cases for personal identity. Division of the components of a *human animal* does – and should. To admit the possibility of such empty-question cases is – as argued in 4.2 – only to agree to a corollary of the kind of reductionism that anyone is obliged to accept who agrees that any CSC consists in nothing over and above its components. But this isn't the sort of reductionism that Parfit was hoping to prove.

4.4 PERSONS AS SUBSTANCES

The rejection of reductionism opens the way for the Two-part View's thesis that personal identity – in both senses – does matter deeply; and for the thesis that personal identity, strictly so called, is a matter of identity of substance. In 4.4 I want to say something in favour of the view of persons that this last claim entails (and is entailed by): that persons are human substances. I also want to say something about the ethical status of persons as human substances. These matters aren't easily dealt with briefly, as they land us right in the middle of a complex and important debate in applied ethics: they will occupy the rest of this chapter. In chapter 5 I return to the other part of the Two–part View, the thesis that persons (in a different sense) are narratives, and to the ethical importance of being such a narrative.

My claim about persons as substances, then, is that when we talk about personal identity in the traditional way, taking 'personal identity' in the strict and logical sense and not as having to do with such novelties as the notion of integrity that I've been exploring (3.5, 4.1, 4.3), we mean to be talking about the identity over time of nothing other than living human animals. The reason why is simple: it's because we *are* nothing other than living human animals. Because we are individual biological substances, if it is *our* identity over time that we mean to be talking of, to discuss the identity-conditions over time of anything else but individual biological substances of the species *Homo sapiens* would be an irrelevance.

(a) *The notion of a substance*

But what is a substance? Crudely but intuitively, an individual substance is just a *thing* – a thing, that is, as opposed to a *stuff*. A stuff is a non-individual substance, which goes with an uncountable noun not a count-noun. Thus 'dog' names an individual substance, but 'gold' names a non-individual substance. Again, a substance is a thing as opposed also to a property, which is no sort of substance, individual or otherwise: 'dog' and 'gold' name substances, 'heavy' and 'yellow' and 'tame' and 'stupid' and 'fond of mutton bones' name properties[18] *of* substances.

More exactly, an individual substance is a particular thing of a particular kind. Such individual substances have at least nine important features:

1 Individual substances, like properties and non-individual substances, are things that can or do go on existing in space over time. They do this at a more fundamental level than either properties or non-individual substances, because no property goes on existing except by going on existing in or belonging to a substance, and because no non-individual substance goes on existing except by being the same portion of for example gold. The unity of for example a single dog is a more distinct and genuine unity than that of a single portion of gold. There are obvious and easily generated borderline cases of the continued existence of a portion of gold: if I melt it down or alloy it, how much addition of copper or of more gold will make it cease to be the same portion? By contrast if there are borderline conditions of the continued existence

of a dog, these are – without much philosophical ingenuity – neither obvious nor easily generated. Thus an individual substance has clear identity-conditions, so that we know one dog from another, and the same dog again, with a definiteness which isn't available in the other two cases.[19]

2 Hence an individual substance is readily countable with integers, so that 'one dog, two dogs' is perspicuous, but 'one gold, two golds' isn't, and neither is 'one yellow, two yellows'. If you think this last *is* perspicuous, that's probably because you automatically take it to mean yellow *thing*, that is yellow individual substance, or else yellow *stuff*, that is yellow non–individual substance. Or thirdly and most plausibly, you might take it to mean yellow *shade*, that is particular quality of yellowness. But notoriously, the conditions under which two samples of yellow count as the same shade of yellow are no clearer than those under which some portion of gold counts as one and the same portion. The reason is the same: it's because the numbers that measure sizes of stuff-portions and ranges of colour-shades are the real numbers not the integers.

3 Any individual substance provides a suitable answer to the basic metaphysical question 'What is it?' 'It's a dog' is an example of a good answer to this, as is 'It's gold'. 'It's *a* gold' isn't a good answer, and neither is 'It's *dog*'. Nor, for different reasons, is 'It's brown' a good answer. This merely prompts the retort 'Yes, but a brown *what*?' and this, of course, is a request for the name of an individual substance which *bears* this brownness, for example, 'A brown dog'.

4 Individual substances exist so long as they retain their essential properties, that is, precisely those properties in the absence of which they necessarily don't go on existing. But not all their properties are essential to them, as they are for example to *precise* shades of yellow or other bundles of properties. Some things have some properties that are merely incidental. This distinction has the important pay-off that it makes an individual substance a possible subject of change as well as of destruction. A dog can be fed to obesity; it can also be fed to crocodiles. In the former case we still have one and the same dog, but with an incidental change in its shape and size. In the latter the dog itself ceases to be. Its essential properties, in particular its being alive, are destroyed by the crocodiles.

5 In general, individual substances of a given kind have a characteristic way of coming into existence, and a characteristic way of being destroyed.[20] By (4), the conditions under which a substance is created or destroyed are necessarily connected with the sorts of circumstances which make it true that that substance's essential properties are brought into being or taken away. For individual substances which are alive, like dogs, this has the corollary that the individual dog's *being alive* is one of its essential properties. (Indeed, that is its essential property *par excellence*. As Aristotle remarks in *de Anima*, 'For living things, to be is to be alive'.)

6 Among the most interesting characteristics of individual substances is the role they characteristically play in causal explanation, *qua* members of a given substance-kind, a given natural kind with certain essential properties, powers, capacities, tendencies and dispositions (2.4). The reason why an animal has puppies is because it's a dog, and dogs can have puppies; and the reason why a dog can have puppies is because that's what dogs are like. It is an essential feature of the species *dog* that any dog, if female, has – at least potentially – a capacity to have puppies, if she mates and if nothing (like a trip to the vet's) intervenes to prevent her. Anything that didn't have this capacity, not even potentially,[21] wouldn't be a (female) dog at all. This is one sort of scientific explanation – though not of course the only sort, nor a complete one even of its sort – of why dogs have puppies, at bottom resting (like so many good scientific explanations) on the Principle of Least Astonishment.[22] Individual substances come in natural kinds, and natural kinds are a key category for at least some sorts of scientific explanation (for example, in zoology and biology).[23]

7 When the essential properties are taken away, then strictly no part of the individual substance remains.[24] What remains is the matter from which the substance was composed, which means either new individual substances, new things, or else non-individual substances, stuffs, which may be new but may also have been present in the individual substance. Thus, when a dog dies, this sad event produces a canine corpse, which is *not* an individual substance, but a collection of doggy stuffs – dog fur and dog bone and dog brain and so on. By (5) it was an essential property of the individual substance which was the dog that it should be an *alive* dog; so for it to cease to be alive is for its identity conditions to fail. Thus, there is an important sense in which a canine corpse is not a dog at all. 'Dead dog', grammatically, is not so much like 'brown

dog' as like 'model dog' (or 'ex-parrot'). 'Dead', in fact, is an alienating[25] adjective, like 'model' or 'ex-' or 'forged'. From 'X is a brown dog' it follows that 'X is brown and X is a dog', but from 'X is a dead dog' it no more follows that 'X is dead and X is a dog' than it follows from 'X is a forged banknote' that 'X is a banknote and X is forged'. All of which tends to show that it is more obvious with an individual substance than it is with a property or a non-individual substance when we have an end of it.

8 The thoughts about individual substances' countability-with-integers developed in (2) have a further interesting corollary. That individual substances are countable with integers means that each such substance is itself a *natural whole individual*. Thus, the notion of an individual substance is sharply distinct from that of a substance-part, and from that of a collection of individual substances. Because any individual substance is a whole in itself, no part P of any such substance S is itself an individual substance. For if P were an individual substance, then P on its own would be a whole in itself. Hence S wouldn't be a whole in itself, but a congeries or collection of things having the individual substance P as a part. Conversely, if S *is* an individual substance and P is a part of S, P can't itself be an individual substance: for if it were, how could S be an *individual* substance, *one* whole-in-itself, rather than two or more?

Thus, no individual substance is composed of or constituted by any other individual substance(s) – even though new individual substances can replace old ones when those cease to be, as in the case of the splitting amoeba. Rather, as in the dog case, the components of any individual substance are non-individual substances and properties (some incidental and some essential).

9 Hence, further, two different individual substances can't be in the same place at the same time.[26] And so there is always only one definitively right complete[27] answer to the question 'What is it?' asked of any thing, for there is always only one individual substance in front of the questioner. In this respect individual substances are unlike non-individual substances and properties. Two non-individual substances can be in the same place at the same time, or sort of, in at least two ways: (a) if they are mixed well enough: for example, tea, which is mixed water and milk and leaf extracts; or (b) if one non-individual substance is constituted by some other non-individual substance(s), as the stuff water consists in a chemical compound made, in the ratio 2:1,

out of particles of two other stuffs, hydrogen and oxygen. Likewise with properties: for example, there is nothing to stop the simultaneous copresence of heat, wetness, fragrance, sweetness etc. (as in my tea-cup).

From all this it also follows that individual substances are spatiotemporal individuals, and hence that they are what are usually called[28] physical objects.

(b) *The priority of substances in ontology; and in ethics*

Next, to this account of what an individual substance is let me add a general claim about what ought to be in our ontology:

(O) What is basic to a correct ontology is what is most fundamentally real; and what is most fundamentally real is what is most clearly:

- (a) a good answer to 'What is it?',
- (b) a natural individual,
- (c) countable with integers,
- (d) reidentifiable over time, and
- (e) existent in its own right, that is, such that its existence doesn't presuppose the existence of anything else that more clearly satisfies (a–d).

From this ontological claim (O) plus my account of individual substances in points (1–9), it follows that individual substances are what is ontologically prior, most fundamentally real. It obviously follows from points (1–7) of that account that individual substances satisfy (a–d) better than non-individual substances or properties. And it follows quite clearly from points (7–9) that individual substances also satisfy (e) better than non-individual substances or properties. The components of any individual substance, I said, aren't other individual substances: they are non-individual substances and properties. But, by (1–7), these satisfy (a–d) less well than individual substances do. So individual substances satisfy (e), and properties and non-individual substances don't. Hence it is at the level of individual substances – not at any lower level of stuffs or properties composing substances, nor at any higher level of properties supervening on substances – that we reach the sort of things that are most fundamentally real.[29] This must be so unless there is some other sort of existent around besides the three sorts considered so far: individual substances, non-individual substances, and properties. But what might this other sort of existent be?[30]

Next, consider the thesis of Symmetry. This states that what is most metaphysically or ontologically important or deep is most ethically important or deep as well. So, for instance, the most basic truths about what we may or may not do to something depend on which truths are most basic about what that something *is*. *What is metaphysically prior is also ethically prior.*

The thesis of Symmetry seems closely connected with the widely accepted thesis of the Supervenience of the ethical on the non-ethical: the thesis that every change or state of affairs in the way things are ethically depends logically upon some change or state of affairs in the way things are non-ethically.[31] Supervenience says that if something is ethically good, this must be in virtue of some non-ethical properties which it has; and if it ceases to be ethically good, this must be because it ceases to have some non-ethical property. If we accept Supervenience, this view about the ethical importance of actual or counterfactual *changes* to a thing, we should also accept Symmetry, a view about the ethical importance of the actual or counterfactual *relations between the different statuses* which a thing or state of affairs has. The two go together because Symmetry explains how and why at least some changes at the factual level matter at the moral level, as Supervenience predicts.

Just as various sorts of answer are possible to the basic metaphysical question regarding any thing – 'What is it?' – which reveal the nature of that thing to a greater or lesser degree, so also various answers are possible to the basic ethical question 'How should it act or be acted on?' which, insofar as they are true, bring to light different ethical aspects of the thing. The point that Symmetry makes is that the two sorts of answer run in parallel. For example, it's true of me that I am a cousin, a father, a philosophy lecturer, an Englishman, a thirty-something, a husband, and a member of the Royal Society for the Protection of Birds. So it would be a kind of (non-definitively) true answer to 'What is it?' as that question applies to me, to say 'It's a cousin/father/philosophy lecturer/Englishman/thirty-something/ husband/member of the RSPB . . .' (etc.). None of these answers to 'What is it?' gets at the most fundamental truth about me, however, even if they do all get at truths about me.[32] For the most fundamental truth about me is that I am a *human*. (More about that in a moment.) Symmetry says that what is the *best*, the most definitively right, answer to 'How should it act or be acted on?' depends on what is the best, the most definitively right, answer to 'What is it?'[33] So about me, Symmetry says that the most important way of seeing me is as a human being. That is the determinant of my moral status which overrides all other determinants. It's true, of course, that my being a cousin, a father, a philosophy lecturer, an Englishman, a thirty-something, a husband, and a member of the RSPB are all facts about me that could be used to say what I am, and which can also determine secondary ethical statuses for me of various sorts. But because (to anticipate 4.4(c) to 4.4(d) a little) my being human is the metaphysically most basic fact about me, so it is my being human that matters most in assessing my moral status. The duties and rights that attach to me in virtue of my human status override every other sort of duty or right that I might be seen as having in virtue of some other status that I also have.

So we should accept both Supervenience and Symmetry. Nearly everyone accepts Supervenience; indeed, it is hard to see how to argue against it, at least in the modest form that I'm here committed to. If Symmetry is a corollary of Supervenience, the grounds for accepting Symmetry are just as strong as the grounds for accepting Supervenience. But there are quite good independent reasons for accepting Symmetry anyway, even if Symmetry isn't strictly a corollary of Supervenience.

We have already argued for the ontological priority of individual substances. So Symmetry now adds the extra premiss needed to make the next inference: from the ontological priority of individual substances to their ethical priority.

(c) *Individual human animals as ethically basic*

The next point seems to me quite uncontroversial – though it is shortly going to do a great deal of work. This point is that one example of a (fundamental) kind of individual substance is *human* individuals.[34]

Consider again the criteria of individual substance which we already have. Like dogs, and unlike gold or yellowness, human individuals are countable continuants and individual, integral wholes in their own right. When we're presented with an appropriate object, saying 'It's a human being' answers 'What is it?' extremely well – indeed more definitively than any alternative I can think of. Humans are clearly capable of undergoing some but not all changes without ceasing to exist: so a distinction between their incidental and essential properties applies to them. It seems to be essential to a human's continuing existence to be alive; and *that something is a human being* certainly suggests an appeal to a natural kind and an explanatory framework known to science (in particular, to biological and medical science). Again, human individuals are (normally) readily reidentifiable, and (normally) what we most readily seek to reidentify. Their existence doesn't presuppose the existence of anything else which satisfies the other criteria of individual substancehood better than 'human individual' does. Nor is a human composed of anything else of this sort. Hence the presence in one spatiotemporal location of one human individual excludes the presence there of any other individual substance, including any other human individual.[35]

In all these ways human individuals seem to fit nicely into the category of individual substance. I will therefore make three further inferences without further comment. First, human individuals *are* individual substances. So, second, human individuals are as a category ontologically basic. So, third, human individuals are as a category ethically basic.

Next, what does it mean for a category or its members to be ethically basic? To identify some category as ethically basic is to identify it as a category that plays a basic role in our assignments of value, rights, duties, and other forms of moral considerability. For the category of human individual substances to be ethically basic is for that category to be the one that defines all and only those to whom we have the most fundamental moral commitments which we recognise anywhere in the relevant moral territory. These, of course, are the kinds of commitment grounded by the Threefold Schema, and its recognition – on which we are now converging from a different starting point – that individual humans are instances of one kind of basic good (2.2).

There are two reasons why I add the words 'in the given area' and 'in the relevant moral territory'. First reason: my argument so far entails that being a dog is an ethically basic property if it entails that being a human is an ethically basic property. I accept this entailment; but I point out that, just as the basic goods can differ in their demands on agents (3.4), so being ethically basic *in one area* can bring with it a quite different moral status from being ethically basic in another. For the moment, that's all I shall say about the ethical basicity of dogs. It is indeed the case that that which most matters ethically about dogs is their caninity. It doesn't follow from that that their caninity matters ethically in just the same way as our humanity matters.[36]

The second reason why I add the above riders is that there are other ways besides that proposed here of cutting up 'the relevant moral territory', that is the moral territory within which *we* (as opposed to dogs) have to find some sort of moral considerability if we are to find any. In particular, my proposal that that which is ethically basic is membership of the category of human individual substances has to compete with proposals which say that what is ethically basic is membership of some other category, usually called – confusingly enough, given the shape of the argument so far – the category of *persons*. I'll now consider and criticise views of this sort (forms of personism as I shall call it, following Jenny Teichman).[37]

(d) *Personism*

Within the moral territory relevant to *us*, it's obvious that there is *some* category of beings which is ethically basic in what I take to be the strongest sense of that phrase in any territory. Almost all of us agree that (unlike, perhaps, dogs or hamsters) the beings in *this* category, whatever it is, have a virtually absolute right[38] of some sort not to be killed barring very special circumstances. It is usual to regard those who don't agree even with this much as dangerous lunatics.

Let us take this broad agreement as evidence, which I won't dispute further, that there is some category in this moral territory which really does have this special sort of ethical basicity, grounding a fundamental right not to be killed. Very well; but exactly *what* is the category in question? Where precisely are its boundaries? As noted, many popular answers to this inquiry invoke a category of 'persons' which is supposed to be a different one from the category of human individuals. But none of the categories that the personists propose has any claim whatever to ethical basicity, for the simple reason that none of them has any claim to ontological basicity.

What – to ask it again – is a 'person'? My view, outlined above, is that in one sense 'person' means the same as 'human individual'; in another, it means a self who is constructing himself or herself as a narrative. The present point is that if 'person' is used to mean 'human individual', then I have no reason to dispute its ontological and ethical basicity. The same isn't true if 'person' is used to mean either a self-constructing narrative – or any of the following things:

1 'A person will be any being capable of valuing its own existence.' (John Harris, *The Value of Life*, p. 18.)
2 'What properties must something have in order to be a person, i.e. to have a serious right to life? . . . An organism possesses a serious right to life only if it possesses the concept of a self as

a continuing subject of experiences and other mental states, and believes that it is itself such an entity.' (Tooley (1972).

3 'I propose to use "person", in the sense of a rational and self-conscious being, to capture those elements of the popular sense of "human being" that are not covered by "member of the species *homo sapiens*".' (Peter Singer, *Practical Ethics*, 2nd edn, p. 87)

4 'The sanctity of life [doctrine] ought to be interpreted as protecting lives in the biographical sense, not in the biological sense . . .' (James Rachels, *The End of Life* p. 26)[39]

5 ' . . . we must consider what person stands for; which, I think, is a thinking intelligent being that has reason and reflection and can consider itself as itself, the same thinking thing in different times and places . . . Thus it is always as to our present sensations and perceptions, and by this everyone is to himself what he calls *self* . . . For since consciousness always accompanies thinking, and it is that that makes everyone to be what he calls *self*, and thereby distinguishes himself from all other thinking things: in this alone consists personal identity.' (John Locke, *Essay* II.27.9)

6 'What then am I? A thing that thinks. What is that? A thing that doubts, understands, affirms, denies, is willing, is unwilling, and also imagines, and has sensory perceptions.' (Descartes, *Meditations* II)

My first comment on these six proposals about the meaning of 'person' is that not one of them gives us any good reason to think that 'persons', in any of these senses, are individual substances as I've defined that term. Indeed Singer, by explicitly denying in his very definition that 'person' means 'human individual', goes out of his way to avoid giving us such good reason. As for Tooley, it's by now a traditional comment on his view that anyone who accepted Hume's or Parfit's views of personal identity would seem to fail Tooley's test to qualify as a person 'with a serious right to life'.

Leaving these relatively minor points aside, let's reapply to these proposals 1 to 6 about the meaning of 'person' the tests used above to show that human individuals are individual substances. It will quickly emerge, by way of a question-and-answer session, that in none of the senses used in 1 to 6 are 'persons' individual substances.

Question 1: If 'persons' doesn't just *mean* 'human individuals', are 'persons' countable continuants, or readily reidentifiable?
Answer: Very unclear. How do we go about counting 'persons' *without* counting human individuals? What are the boundaries of a 'person', if they aren't the boundaries of a human individual? Why couldn't one 'person' be part of another? What would be the difference between 'personal' continuity and 'personal' replication?

Question 2: Is 'It's a person' ever a good – let alone the best – answer to 'What is it?'?
Answer: Extremely unclear – unless, as before, 'It's a person' means (as it often does) 'It's a human individual'.

Question 3: Can 'persons' undergo some but not all changes without ceasing to exist, so that there is a distinction between their incidental and essential properties?
Answer: Hard to tell; perhaps.

Question 4: Is it essential to a 'person''s continuing existence to be alive?
Answer: Presumably: but what *is* the notion of an essential property as applied to 'persons'?

Question 5: Does *that something is a person* suggest an appeal to any natural kind, or an explanatory framework known to science (in particular, biological and medical science)?
Answer: No.

Question 6: Does the presence in one spatiotemporal location of one 'person' exclude the presence there of another individual substance or person (or 'person')?
Answer: There's no obvious reason why it must. Cp. the answer to Question 1 above.

Question 7: Does the existence of 'persons' presuppose the existence of anything else which satisfies the other criteria of individual substancehood better than 'person' does? Is a person composed of anything else of this sort?
Answer: Yes to both questions. Unless dualism is true, the existence of 'persons' presupposes the existence of human (or similar) individuals, which satisfy the criteria of substancehood much better than 'persons' do.

To expand on this last point. 'Persons' as defined in (1–6) look, in every one of these cases, not so much like a category, as like that subset of the category of human individuals which happens to possess certain further properties. If a person isn't an individual human animal, but (5) 'a thinking intelligent being' or (6) 'a thing that thinks' or (4 – implicitly) 'a thing that has a biography', or (3) 'a rational self-conscious being' or (1) 'a being capable of valuing its own existence' or (2) 'an organism with a concept of a self', then the first and most obvious question about persons so defined is simply: 'Yes, but what *sort* of being, or thing, or organism?' And the answer to this will be (usually):[40] 'A *human* being/thing/organism'. But then in picking out such properties as capacity to value one's own life, or self-consciousness, or having a concept of self, we weren't picking out the defining or essential properties of any *new* category of individual substances, called 'persons'. Rather we were picking out the non-defining or non-essential properties of *the same old* category of individual substances: namely human individuals. If that's right, and if the thesis of Symmetry is also correct, then how can it be reasonable to rate the possession by human individuals of these incidental properties as of more ethical importance than the possession of the essential properties, such as being alive, which *define* the category of human individuals?

This brings me to my third point about revisionism regarding the sense of 'person', which is that if it fails to dislodge or replace the notion of 'human individual' then it fails to achieve anything at all. As the practice of Singer, Tooley, Glover, Rachels, Harris *et alii* demonstrates, the whole *point* of their deploying 'person' instead of 'human individual' is that, at the cost of some appearance of special pleading (and of sharing Humpty Dumpty's attitude to words and their meanings), it allows the revisionists to get to their novel conclusions in bioethics, for example, about abortion, euthanasia and infanticide. But if (a) human individuals are individual substances and 'persons' (in any other sense) aren't, if (b) Symmetry is correct, and if (c) it follows from the Three-fold Schema that among the most basic and inalienable rights that human individuals have is a right not to be killed, then none of this revisionist programme in bioethics can even begin. Given a mild dose of revisionism, there is (apparently, anyway) some sense in saying that a neonate or a foetus or a woman in a PVS is not a *person*. Leaving confusions aside, there is none at all in saying that in any of these cases what we have isn't a *human individual*. Unfortunately for the revisionist, it's as plain as daylight – despite many attempts to obscure it – that human individuals normally[41] begin at conception, carry on to have or not have whatever experiences they may and to acquire or not acquire whatever capacities they may, and then die.[42] So if it's really human individuals that basically matter in ethics, as the thesis of Symmetry suggests, then the special pleading which introduced the revisionist's notion of 'persons' hasn't even bought him any novel conclusions.

Of course, as I've already hinted, there is still *one* way left out of this mess for revisionists about persons. They can still say that there is indeed a sort of individual substance that comprises all and only 'persons' in their special sense, and claim that this sort is non-co-extensive with humanity or indeed with anything physical. That is, the revisionist can become a dualist. (It is because of this possibility that my list of revisionist proposals about the meaning of 'person' ends with Descartes.) I think dualism is wholly untenable. Apart from everything else, it's so *gratuitous*. What's the point of supposing there to be a mental substance for mental properties to be properties of, when we can just as well suppose that the mental properties are properties of the physical substance – the human individual – and thereby avoid the postulation of a whole realm of unnecessary mental entities?

I recognise, however, that someone who wanted to avoid certain conclusions in bioethics might well feel an urge to posit just such an extra realm if they took seriously the kind of threat to making 'persons' ethically basic that I have tried to press here. Whether such adhockery is legitimate or not, it certainly seems that something like the ghost of Descartes' dualism must be haunting the thoughts of those who think that there can be any substantial sense of 'person' which can easily be separated from the biological and physical sense of 'human individual'.

What I've tried to show in 4.4 is that, given Symmetry and an account of individual substances which makes individual humans individual substances, three conclusions quickly follow.

First: the conditions of personal identity must be the conditions of identity for individual human animals. Second: if persons are human animals, then their basic ethical status must be given by that fact. The deontological requirements that the Threefold Schema reports about the status of persons, and in particular about the requirement not to murder them, must apply to nothing other than individual human animals. Other senses of 'person' – such as the sense I am developing, in which persons are self-constituting narratives – may also be ethically significant; but not in *this* way. No other sense of 'person' has the fundamental ethical significance that 'person' in the sense of 'individual human being' has.

Third, and as a corollary of this, it also emerges from our argument that there's no proper use in bioethics (or anywhere else for that matter) for a category of persons, separate from the category of human[43] individuals, which is supposed to collect any basic ethical status.

So anyone who, because of their revisionism in bioethics or for whatever other reason, wants to reject these last two conclusions must reject (1) the present account of individual substances or (2) the claim that humans are individual substances, or (3) the thesis of Symmetry. If they reject (1) they owe us an account of how metaphysics goes if it isn't based on the notion of individual substance. If they reject (2) they owe us an explanation of what else human individuals might be if they aren't individual substances. And if they reject (3) they owe us an account of how Symmetry can fail to be true if Supervenience is; or else of how it is that, despite appearances, neither of these fundamental claims about ethics is right. I don't say that none of these tasks can be achieved: but I do say that they are in the way of anyone who disagrees with the case that has been made out, however sketchily, in 4.4.

This completes my defence of the first claim made by the Two-part View outlined at the beginning of this chapter: that in one sense 'persons' are just individual human substances, and have a basic ethical status which is cashed out by the Threefold Schema's requirements about respecting persons as a kind of instance of basic good which is correlative with the substance account of their nature. The second claim made by the Two-part View is that in another sense 'persons' are narratives, and have an ethical importance correlative with being such narratives, which is made sense of by the operations of narrative rationality within the constraints of the Threefold Schema. In chapter 5 I shall discuss this second claim in more depth.

ENDNOTE: WILLIAMS ON ABORTION

Bernard Williams is (as they say) a 'liberal about abortion'. Unlike many such 'liberals', he isn't a personist: wisely, he bases nothing at all on claims about the ethical importance of possessing some arbitrarily determined set of 'personal qualities'. Rather, what he disputes is the claim, which I subscribe to in 4.4(d), that we have the same individual human being, in any normal life, from the moment of conception onwards:[44]

> An embryo[45] which, if all goes well, will develop into a human being is certainly a human embryo, but that does not imply that it is itself a human being ... It is thus not true to our

experience . . . that the embryo has to be seen as a human being, and there is much in our experience to make natural the description which many would give, that the embryo is something that develops into a human being. So what basis is there for insisting that, despite these appearances, it must be a human being? . . . The idea is that since 'human being' is an absolute term – that is to say, nothing is more or less of a human being – it must be unacceptable to have a situation in which there is no definite starting point to something's being a human being, or only an arbitary imposed starting point. [However,] very many terms, such as the names of many artefacts, are 'absolute' in this sense, but no one would insist on imposing a definite moment for the start of their being the sort of thing that they come to be. (Bernard Williams, *Making Sense of Humanity*, pp. 221–2)

Williams invites us to see gestation as a process of creation. At the end of it, we have a human being. At the beginning of it, and for a vague and unspecified length of time during the process, we haven't. So thinking that we do have a human while gestation is still in progress is a mistake, like the mistake of thinking that the lump of clay on the potter's wheel is a vase from the moment it hits the wheel.

Williams's analogy with artefacts goes lame in two ways, however. First, there's no obvious need to define a moment by which any lump of potter's clay becomes or has become a pot. But there is a need to define a moment by which the foetus has become a human being if one wishes, like Williams himself (I take it), to say that very late abortion is impermissible. This makes it harder than Williams admits for him to avoid problems about 'slippery slopes'.

Second, and more importantly: presumably it is beyond dispute (certainly Williams seems not to dispute it) that from the conception of a human being or future human being X to his or her death, we have the same living organism. But this means that whereas there is no vase at all until late on in the clay-shaping process, in the process of the gestation of the human being X there is a living organism from the very moment of X's conception – namely C, the conceptus that will become X.

Now that living human organism C is strictly identical with X, the human being who is, in Williams's terminology, created by the gestational process: X and C are the same living human organism. (C is not just a *vehicle* for X, as some sorts of dualist might think. Nor does

C merely *constitute* X, as the clay that becomes a vase constitutes that vase. Here there is a third disanalogy with the case of artefacts.)[46]

Hence Williams has a choice between three alternatives. He must say:

1 that embryology provides us with a counterexample to Leibniz's Law's exclusion of relative identities, by giving us a case where C is the same living organism as X, but <u>not</u> the same human being as X (because, at least just after conception, C isn't what Williams calls a human being at all).

Or else

2 that the process which is the creation of the human being X (that is, gestation) is also the process which is the creation of the living organism C.

Or else

3 that 'human being' is what Wiggins calls a 'phased sortal'. (Phased sortals are a category of sortals introduced by Wiggins to prevent apparent breaches of Leibniz's Law of the sort described under (1). In Wiggins's own words: [we] 'need to distinguish between sortal concepts that present-tensedly apply to an individual x at every moment throughout x's existence, <u>e.g. human being</u>, and those that do not, e.g. boy, or cabinet minister'.)[47]

Presumably Williams won't opt (1) for a breach of Leibniz's Law. Enough has been said in the literature (especially by Wiggins in *Sameness and Substance*) to make this option an obvious non-starter.

But (2) clearly won't do either. A one-month-old embryo – indeed a one-day-old embryo – isn't in the process of becoming a living organism. It *is* a living organism; and not the same living organism as the sperm and/or egg it came from, either. (This is an important point, given the common but mistaken claim that we might as well ascribe rights to a sperm or ovum as to a newly conceived zygote. That claim is mistaken because it rests on a misunderstanding of the identity conditions for human substances.)[48]

This leaves us with (3). Notice first that, in one perfectly respectable sense of 'human being', (3) is just false. If 'human being' means what we might most naturally expect it to mean, namely 'individual of the human species', then 'human being' is no more a phased sortal than is 'dog' or 'individual of the species "cabbage-white butterfly" '.[49] Moreover, there's no more reason why, in this sense, unborn babies of whatever gestational age shouldn't qualify as human beings than there is reason why, in this sense, cabbage-white caterpillars or pupae shouldn't qualify as cabbage-white butterflies, or puppies (born or unborn) as dogs.

If, despite the comments of the last paragraph, we do decide to take (3)'s proposal seriously, then we are putting the predicate 'human being' on the same analytical level as other predicates like 'boy', 'youth', 'old man', 'toddler', and so forth (though certainly 'human being' in this sense is a predicate with a more generously inclusive scope than these other examples). We are also putting 'human being' on the same level as 'person' in the personists' sense, which ironically suggests that Williams's argument has come full circle. Moreover, if we treat 'human being' this way, what reason is there to think that 'human being' in this sense will be any more capable of providing a basis for the assignment of basic human rights than 'toddler' or 'youth' (or 'person' as meant by personism) is?

A quite general reason for doubting that any phased sortal could be used as a basis for the assignment of basic human rights comes from the Thesis of Symmetry (4.4). Basic human rights are assigned in virtue of one's basic human nature. But phased sortals aren't the right kind of thing to pick out that basic human nature. Necessarily so, because what they're designed to pick out is phases in the life of an individual possessing the basic human nature, not that human nature itself.

So to think that 'human being', if used (as Williams proposes) as a phased sortal, could give any such basis would be uncomfortably like thinking that the difference between, say, toddlers and other humans marked a basically significant moral difference. Such distinctions are typically condemned – with justice – as being arbitrary; the word that springs to mind is 'ageism'. Given the thesis of Symmetry, we lack an explanation of why and how 'human beings' (in Williams's sense) are sufficiently morally different from other instances of *Homo sapiens* to justify their receiving basic human rights when other members of the species, such as very young foetuses, don't.

NOTES

1. 'To want to be rational is to want to be a person': Raz (1997) p. 224. To an extent Raz is drawing, as I am, on philosophical resources made available by Harry Frankfurt's classic articles in this area, especially 'Freedom of the will and the concept of a person', in Frankfurt's *The Importance of What we Care About* (Cambridge, CUP 1988).
2. Readers of Chappell (1997) will see that my views about persons have changed. I no longer want to abandon the very term *person* to the personists. Like abandoning the term *rational* to the rationalists, that seems bad tactics; also unnecessary, because we can argue instead

about how to use the word *person*. This terminological point aside, the argument of Chappell (1997) supports the argument of 4.4.

3. Also, if it's right to see persons as narratives, continuing and self-constituting stories, then there are interesting connections between the present broadly analytic inquiry and a body of work in continental philosophy that begins with Sartre.

4. I say 'of its own' because Parfit consistently disowns the claims that persons or personal identity aren't real. But he does seem to hold that personal identity has no reality *of its own*. The reason for this distinction should become clear in 4.2.

5. Parfit's latest statement of reductionism is in his forthcoming *Practical Realism*. This book isn't published as I write – but Parfit himself has kindly sent me over 100 pages of his drafts for it. I refer to these as PD. What I quote here is the summary of his argument that Parfit gives at PD p. 62, in the course of a response to John McDowell. So far as I can see this argument could equally well have been made out in *Reasons and Persons*. Cp. *RP* p. 275: 'On the Reductionist View that I defend, persons exist. And a person is distinct from his brain and his body, and his experiences. But persons are not separately existing entities. The existence of a person, during any period, just consists in the existence of his brain and his body, and the thinking of his thoughts, and the doing of his deeds, and the occurrence of many other mental and physical events . . . Personal identity . . . just involves physical and psychological continuity . . . both of [which] can be described without claiming that experiences are had by a person.'

6. Even if readers' particular views about mereology don't make The Assumption seem evidently true to them, I gather that The Assumption isn't in dispute between Parfit and myself.

7. There is an analogy here with the debate about universals. Many nominalists (e.g. Quine) have insisted that we don't have to posit universals, for example, of redness *because* we can paraphrase them away into ontologically uncommitting talk of different things being red. But as Mellor and Oliver point out in their introduction to (Mellor and Oliver 1997), this popular paraphrasing move is rather inconclusive even if it works (which has been much questioned: for example, by Loux, *Substance and Attribute* ch. 4, and by Jackson in (Mellor and Oliver 1997). For if a paraphrase from universal-invoking discourse into particulars-only discourse is possible, then a paraphrase from particular-invoking discourse into universals-only discourse seems equally possible: ' . . . parodying Quine, we might add that it is only "a popular and misleading manner of speaking" to say that there is some one thing which *F*-ness, *G*-ness and *H*-ness all have in common when *a* is *F* and *G* and *H*' (Mellor and Oliver p. 15; for Quine v. pp. 74–88).

8. My judgement about this, and about various other questions raised in the next few paragraphs, is based on comments Parfit has kindly offered me in private correspondence. I hope I haven't misrepresented his views.

9. A third problem: 'simple' and 'complex' are, as Wittgenstein pointed out (*Investigations* I, §47), purpose-relative terms. What's simple relative to one purpose (e.g. the smallest sort of part mentioned in a 'Build your own Jumbo Jet' kit) obviously isn't simple relative to some other purpose; even the smallest wing-nut can be sawn in half. This makes the reductionist's quest for simple person-components even more hopeless. The kind of simplicity he's after can't be non-purpose-relative – there is no such simplicity; but it can't be purpose-relative either – even a person is simple relative to some purposes. Is the question whether persons or person-components are simple relative to the purposes *of metaphysics*? 4.4 argues that it is persons (= individual humans), not their components, which are simple in that sense. The fact that persons have components into which they can be broken up in no way tells against this conclusion, any more than sawing some wing-nut in half proves that it isn't a single Jumbo-jet part.

10. I don't imply that *Parfit* ever argues like this; only that he could do even if he rejected step (2).

11. *RP* Appendix I's 'Objective List theory', which Parfit tentatively accepts in combination with what he calls 'hedonism' (*RP* p. 502), is apparently both Pluralist and Objectivist.

12. But what *would* count as a rational means of solving such a dilemma? My own account of that, going under the name of *Narrative Rationality*, begins to appear in the later part of this section and in chapters 5 and 6.

13. Because it is by the options actually taken that the paths, and the selves pursuing them, are individuated.

14. Cp. Slote, *Goods and Virtues*, p. 46: 'Consider . . . a child at primary school who plans to go to a certain medical school and become a surgeon. [Such children's] vast predetermination

is likely to seem suspect . . . If the child's father went to that medical school and is a surgeon, we shall wonder whether the child doesn't feel some sort of more or less explicit pressure to be like his father which one hopes will eventually dissolve. And will we not think that his plan may well collapse when he does go to college, or before, and, more to the point, that if it does not, that will mean that he is probably not allowing life to influence or change him, that he is too rigid? His planfulness will in that case prove positively detrimental to his development: it will prevent him from seeing, for example, whether he might not prefer pure science, or the law, to medicine, or prefer another branch of medicine, in the light of subsequently uncovered and developed interests and talents.'

15. I ignore the possibility that reductionism might be meant to abolish the fear of death altogether. Even if this is right (there's little evidence that it is) the problem I indicate still arises regarding future pain.

16. Recall that I'm *not* claiming that all choices between goods are of this type: only those made within the constraints of the Threefold Schema.

17. Perhaps I hold that my life so far has *too much* unity – the unity of someone who breaks the law all the time. So perhaps I want a clean break from my criminal past – or even what detective novels call 'a change of identity'. Fine, but this doesn't show that narrative integrity isn't a necessary condition of a good human life; just that it isn't a sufficient condition.

18. The last property is relational: '—— is fond of ——' is a two-place predicate, and hence in Aristotle's terms in the category of relation not quality. I follow Frege in rejecting Aristotle's distinction between these two categories. What *really* matters is the distinction between the category of substance (object in Frege's terms) and all the other categories (the concepts or functions, in Frege's terms: or as I call them here, the properties).

19. And where it begins to be unclear whether we have one or two individual substances is where the category of individual substances begins to shade into that of non-individual substances. This is why it makes more sense to ask 'How much grass?' than 'How many grass plants?'. Here my bias towards the charismatic megafauna is naked and unashamed. If my account of individual substance makes it turn out that individual tigers, human beings, dolphins and elephants etc. are paradigm examples of individual substances but individual pear trees or amoebas or bee-swarms or lawns of grass aren't, then so much the better for my account.

20. So the substances I have in mind aren't indestructible, like Leibniz's or Spinoza's 'substances', or the basic existents in the metaphysics of Wittgenstein's *Tractatus*. On the contrary they are mortal, all too mortal.

21. The essential conditions for any creature X to be a member of a natural kind K stipulate the presence in X neither of certain activities characteristic of K, nor even of capacities for activities, but merely of potential capacities for those activities. Thus, a dog that does not *actually* produce puppies (with another dog's help) is still a dog. A dog that doesn't have a *capacity* to produce puppies can still be a dog too: perhaps it is itself a puppy, or a neutered or senile adult dog. But a 'dog' that doesn't even have a *potential* to produce puppies – one which doesn't have anything in its make-up which might develop, or have developed, into a puppy-making capacity – such a creature isn't a dog at all. For one reason why this fine distinction matters see Harris, *The Value of Life* p. 26. Harris wants to define a class he calls 'persons' by reference to capacities, not potentials. Our 'dogs' example illustrates a striking point about this proposal: that there are no natural kinds which are picked out in Harris's way. Therefore Harris's kind 'persons' is not a natural kind, but (perhaps) an achievement kind, like (to take Harris's own parallel) 'French speaker'. This point becomes important once we accept the thesis of Symmetry [4.4(c)].

22. It is, to put it mildly, no surprise to hear that something has puppies because it's a dog. But first, to say this doesn't have to be merely to make a linguistic remark about the meaning of 'puppy' and 'dog'. Second, I hope that the studied jejuneness of my example, taken as stating a more than linguistic truth, won't conceal its serious point. This is that a great deal of scientific explanation has precisely the form of this example – that of the subsumption of the particulars under their natural kinds. A more revealing explanation of why this thing has puppies wouldn't, I think, have to make any other sorts of connections. It would just have to make more connections of the same sort, by reference either to the parts of this dog, or to the evolutionary history of all dogs (or all mammals), or both.

23. Wilson (1992), pp. 37–8: 'Since antiquity biologists have felt a compelling need to posit an atomic unit by reference to which diversity can be broken apart, then described, measured, and reassembled . . . the species concept is crucial to the study of biodiversity. It is the grail

of systematic biology. Not to have a natural unit such as the species would be to abandon a large part of biology to free fall, all the way from the ecosystem down to the organism.' (Thanks to Kate Rawles for the reference.)

24. But cp. the points made about the relativity of 'simple' and 'complex' in Note 9.

25. Cp. Geach, 'Good and Evil', in Foot, (ed.) *Theories of Ethics*.

26. There is currently debate among metaphysicians about whether two or more artefacts, like the ship of Theseus and some other ship, can be in the same place at the same time: see Hughes (1997). Because artefacts are (roughly) individuals, yet not individual substances, no part of the present argument hangs on the outcome of this interesting debate.

27. 'Complete' is in this sentence because 'It's a mammal' is perfectly *correct* as an answer to 'What is it?' asked of a dog; but not *complete* if, as I shall here assume without arguing the point, 'dog' is the name of a natural kind and 'mammal' only of a family of natural kinds.

28. It can be argued that 'spatiotemporal individuals' – or 'individual substances' – is a better name for the items in question than 'physical objects'. Because we tend, thanks to Descartes, to see 'mental' and 'physical' as mutually exclusive determinates of one determinable, calling the items 'physical objects' tends to create a pseudo-problem about how any physical object can have mental properties like thought and sensation. If we talked about spatiotemporal individuals instead, the obvious question would be not 'How can they?' (though the how would, of course, still be an interesting issue), but 'Why on earth shouldn't they?' I can't pursue this here, though the point will crop up again at the end of 4.4; cp. Mellor and Crane (1990).

29. This thesis about what's most fundamentally real doesn't have to be in conflict with modern physics. Some philosophers under, e.g., Quine's influence apparently think that what modern physics is most concerned with is what is most real. I'm committed to denying this, because I do *not* hold that what is most real is tiny energy-packets or quarks or neutrons or whatever, but the medium-sized dry goods like dogs and trees and hamsters and human beings that have such basic physical particles as their (perhaps ultimate) constituent matter. (Cp. (6–8) in main text.) A physicist, however, can agree to this without besmirching his professional reputation – just as an economist could happily agree that the entities recognised by economics are metaphysically less basically real than the entities recognised by certain other disciplines, biology and physics for example, without thereby ceasing to be a good economist. Physics isn't, I suggest, concerned (like metaphysics) with what really exists, but with what what really exists is made of. That is a different question, which is why physics and metaphysics aren't in conflict here: even though physics nowadays often looks far more meta – than metaphysics.

30. It might be God. But that possibility is hardly going to affect the present argument.

31. Compare 2.4, which asks what the *inferential* relations between 'fact' and 'value' are. 4.4 asks a different question: how changes in the factual and its relations affect changes in the ethical and its relations.

32. Some truths about me, e.g. that I am the first person ever to have thought of the twenty-second largest codfish in the Sargasso Sea on 1 January AD 100 are of course of no ethical importance whatever. But this is no counter-example to Symmetry, because such truths about me aren't metaphysically important either. Such truths have almost no conceivable bearing on our account of how I should act or be acted on, *precisely because* they have almost no conceivable bearing on our account of what it is to be the creature that I am. (There are irrelevancies to do with Supervenience too: not every factual change matters for ethics.)

33. Returning to the issue of scientism, this point too may help us to see that metaphysics isn't just the physics of the Stone Age, but deserves to be treated as an autonomous discipline. Physics-led scientism claims (to put it crudely) that what everything *really* is, including ourselves, is just a bunch of atoms. Biology-led scientism claims (to put it crudely) that what everything that lives *really* is, including ourselves, is just a bunch of selfish genes. Humanely speaking, these are notoriously bewildering and estranging claims: why? Perhaps part of the reason is this. In line with Symmetry, our decisions about how to interact with things depend on what we think those things really are. But we have *no idea* how to interact with bunches of atoms or of selfish genes. Hence our bewilderment when we are told – falsely – that these phrases describe what humans really are.

34. For more or less recent support for this claim see: Williams's title essay in *Making Sense of Humanity*; Wiggins, *Sameness and Substance*, for the general notion of a fundamental kind and for *being human* as one such kind; and now Christopher Peacocke's passing invocation of

Wiggins in Peacocke (1997) p. 540 (underlining added): 'One plausible constitutive principle [of possibility] concerns the fundamental kind of an object, where for instance <u>your fundamental kind is the kind *human being*</u> and the fundamental kind of New York is the kind *city* . . .'

35. Pregnancy is not a counter-example to this. The mother and the foetus do not occupy the same location – any more than a garden and the wall around it occupy the same location.

36. Speciesism, as I would defend it, says that insofar as the human species is privileged compared with other species, the reason for this special status is that humans have a uniquely creative and directive role in nature. That doesn't entail a right simply to violate the goods represented by other species; but it does mean that what counts as a violation of the goods of other species is rather different from what counts as a violation of the goods represented by the human species. Cp. my (1996c).

37. Teichman uses this term in her *Social Ethics*. For an argument similar to the present one (of which I was, I'm ashamed to say, unaware when I first wrote 4.4), see her (1985), esp. 184: 'Person is not the name of *a* natural species; nor is it the name of a broad natural kind . . . Being a human being, i.e. a human animal, is a sufficient condition of being a person. What it is to be a human animal may perhaps be a further question; I use the term here mainly to rule out, on the one hand, mere human matter, such as human finger-nail parings . . . and on the other hand, any thesis to the effect that being a human animal is not enough, that one must also for example have an immortal soul, or an IQ of 120.' On this last point Teichman also writes (p. 180–1): ' . . . one can have a rational nature even if one happens to be quite irrational or even mentally defective . . . The idea that a creature can have a rational nature without being rational seems to cause problems in the minds of some people, but it does not appear to me to be any more intrinsically problematic than the idea that all cattle are mammals – even the bulls.' (I take it Teichman means that bulls don't suckle calves, as the etymology of 'mammal' suggests they might, but are still mammals.)

38. I'm not here proposing a formal theory of rights. All I mean by 'a right not to be killed' is this: anyone who has such a 'right' has it *owed to them morally* that others should abstain from acts of killing them.

39. To judge by its index, Rachels doesn't actually use the word 'person' anywhere in *The End of Life*. All the same, that book's whole programme is in effect a proposal about how to use the word 'person'.

40. Or perhaps will be 'An *intelligent alien* being/thing/organism'. In that case, we get back to the issue of what makes that alien species, as a species, to have its own sort of moral considerability. See Chappell (1997).

41. 'Normally' because monozygotic twins come from the same zygote, but neither of them sustains identity with it. The exception is interesting rather than problematic. It doesn't, e.g., give us the conclusion that the single zygote from which the twins later come isn't itself a human individual substance, with whatever rights that status brings. An 'indiscernibility argument' proves this. Compare a zygote Z1 which won't later divide into two with another zygote Z2 which will. Z1 is, by my criteria, *obviously* a human individual substance. But Z2 is, in all essential features, *exactly like* Z1 (unless Z2 has already started to divide into two). There is then no ground for asserting that Z1 is a human individual but denying that Z2 is a human individual; not at least until Z2 begins to divide, after which Z2 is still human, but plural rather than individual.

42. The best (indeed the only even prima-facie good) argument I know againt the view that human individuals begin at conception is Bernard Williams's. See the Endnote to this chapter for a discussion.

43. Or, again, 'intelligent alien'.

44. Support for the claim that we ought to shift the abortion debate from questions about persons in the personists' sense to questions about persons in the sense of human individuals comes from some surprising quarters. V., e.g., Williams's own remarks in the first epigraph to this chapter; also Churchland (1995), pp. 308–9): 'If the felt need to protect any foetus from abortion has its basis in a concern to protect and preserve an existing *self*, then that concern appears to be factually misplaced. If the neurobiological account of consciousness and the self emerging from current research is even roughly correct, then there can be no self, not even an unconscious one, until the foetus has developed a functional nervous system and has begun to configure its myriad synaptic weights so as to sustain an ongoing history of cognitive activity. Without a neural network in place there can be no self, neither an emotional self,

nor a perceiving self, nor a deliberating self, nor any other kind of self. A first or second trimester foetus is many things, to be sure, but an established self it is not.'

45. I don't here try to observe the medical distinction between 'embryo' and 'foetus'.

46. On the 'is' of constitution and its misuses, cp. Wiggins, *Sameness and Substance*, chapter 1 – but cp. *Identity and Spatiotemporal Continuity* pp. 48ff. We might, incidentally, feel the urge to add that even if C did merely constitute X, and wasn't the very same organism as X, it would still be true that $\overline{X}$ was necessarily derived from C. This would follow if we accepted the Kripkean thesis that, for any object Y, if Y's natural origin is actually O, then in every possible world Y's natural origin is O. (V. *Naming and Necessity*, pp. 112–14.) But why should X's necessary origin in C in any way justify the ascription of any sort of rights to C? If that's all there is to the relation between X and C – if X and C aren't, as I am claiming, identical – that relation can no more ground rights for C if X has rights than it can ground rights for the spermatozoon or ovum from which C was formed. (I mention this point because it seems to correspond closely to a familiar mares' nest of the pro-life literature, namely the claim that mere potentiality for human life grounds human rights. The standard and proper retort is that mere potentiality for human life grounds mere potentiality for human rights.)

47. Wiggins, *Sameness and Substance*, p. 24; my emphasis.

48. For what seems a related misunderstanding cp. Forbes, *The Metaphysics of Modality*, p. 133: 'For a general term to cover such antecedent entities, let us use the word "propagule"; the oak tree's propagule is its acorn, while a human's propagule is his zygote'. Forbes offers no argument for thinking of a human zygote as a separate entity from a human in the way that an acorn *is* a separate entity from the oak seedling that it develops into; nor could he. And he doesn't tell us what the principle of individuation is that might enable us, in any one case, to count 'human' and 'human propagule' as two entities; nor could he.

49. On at least one occasion, Williams himself seems to use 'human being' (or a near equivalent thereof, 'man') in this sense. V. *Problems of the Self* p. 232 (emphasis added): 'That all men are human is, if a tautology, a useful one, serving as a reminder that those who belong anatomically to the species *homo sapiens*, and can speak a language, use tools, live in societies, can interbreed despite racial differences, etc., are also alike in certain other respects more likely to be forgotten'.

So many hundred Hands in this Mill; so many hundred horse Steam Power. It is known, to the force of a single pound weight, what the engine will do; but, not all the calculators of the National Debt can tell me the capacity for good or evil, for love or hatred, for patriotism or discontent, for the decomposition of virtue into vice, or the reverse, at any single moment in the soul of one of these its quiet servants, with the composed faces and the regulated actions. There is no mystery in it; there is an unfathomable mystery in the meanest of them, for ever. Supposing we were to reserve our arithmetic for material objects, and to govern these awful unknown quantities by other means!

Charles Dickens, *Hard Times*, Bk 1 Ch. 11

'If a thing is a pleasure, a [human] wants it again. He might want the pleasure more often than the number of young that could be fed.'

It took Hyoi a long time to get the point.

'You mean,' he said slowly, 'that he might do it not only in one or two years of his life but again?'

'Yes.'

'But why? Why would he want his dinner all day or to sleep after he had slept? I do not understand.'

'But a dinner comes every day. This pleasure, you say, comes only once while [a creature like you] lives?'

'But it takes his whole life. When he is young he has to look for his mate; and then he has to court her; then he begets young; then he remembers all this, and boils it inside himself and begets wisdom.'

'But the pleasure he must be content only to remember?'

'That is like saying "my food I must be content only to eat".'

C. S. Lewis, *Out of the Silent Planet*, Chapter XII

[A] person, an individual self, may be defined as a human life lived according to a plan. If a man could live with no plan at all, purposelessly and quite passively, he would in so far be an organism, and also, if you choose, he would be a psychological specimen, but he would be no personality. Wherever there is personality, there are purposes worked out in life. If, as often happens, there are many purposes connected with the life of this human creature, many plans in this life, but no discoverable unity and coherence of these plans, then in so far there are many glimpses of selfhood, many fragmentary selves present in connection with the life of some human organism. But there is so far no one self, no one person discoverable. You are one self just in so far as the life that goes on in connection with your organism has some one purpose [or ideal] running through it . . .

Josiah Royce, *Philosophy of Loyalty*, Lecture IV, Sections IV–V

5

·

TWO CONCEPTIONS OF THE GOOD

I have set up a response to the Problem of Reconciliation which adds to the Threefold Schema the proposal that within the constraints of that schema, practical rationality can be narrative in its nature. In chapter 4 I suggested a parallel between this two-part answer and a Two-part View which we might take about persons; and defended that parallel, and the Two-part View, from metaphysical and ethical arguments for Parfitian reductionism about the self. I also suggested some further points in favour of the Two-part View's first thesis, that strict personal identity is a matter of identity of substance. In chapters 5 and 6 I spell out further what is involved in the second part of the Two-part View: the notion of identity as integrity, the narrative conception of the person.

My approach is indirect. Because there are always close links between conceptions of the self and of the good, it's convenient to begin by criticising a conception of the good that seems to go naturally with the Parfitian reductionism about the self criticised in 4.2 and 4.3, and also with the maximalism criticised in chapters 1 to 3. This is the List Conception of the Good (LCG), which I argue should be replaced by a Narrative Conception of the Good (NCG). My argument will make more explicit the connections that I see between conceptions of the self and of the good, so bringing us back to the narrative conception of the person. First, I'll indicate three features of LCG which reveal decisive criticisms of any version of it.

5.1 THREE CRITICISMS OF THE LIST CONCEPTION OF THE GOODS

'What makes someone's life go best?' That is the question posed by Parfit in Appendix I of *Reasons and Persons*, in an argument that picks up on terms framed right at the beginning of the book (cp. p. 4). Appendix I is an important and interesting part of Parfit's discussion.

But note immediately that which is apparently implied by Parfit's placing of this part of his discussion, aside from the main business of the book. This placing seems to imply that nothing much else in *RP* turns on which answer we adopt to the question 'What makes someone's life go best?'. The disputes between the three or four varieties of 'theories about self-interest' which Parfit considers in detail in Appendix I[1] aren't – he evidently thinks – bound to be important for the other areas of ethical inquiry that concern him. Such variety in 'theories about self-interest' may be interesting in its own right, and generate some engaging theoretical permutations. But it has no essential effect on most other important matters in ethics. For example, as Parfit explicitly claims at the outset of *Reasons and Persons* (p. 4), it need have no effect on our view of what rationality consists in:

> It would take at least a book to decide between the different theories about self-interest.[2] This book discusses some of the differences between these theories, but does not try to decide between them. Much of this book discusses the Self-interest Theory . . . this is not one of the theories about self-interest. It is a theory about rationality. We can discuss [it] without deciding between the different theories about self-interest. We can make claims that would be true on all these theories.

Here is the first distinctive feature of LCG: that, for many or even most theoretical (as opposed to practical) purposes, <u>it doesn't matter what you put into the list</u>. An account of moral rationality can simply bypass the vexed issues of which things are good (2.2) and objectivism (2.4) because, to put it bluntly, what the good is and how to get it are two separate questions. Given the intractability of the former question, we should concentrate our attention on the latter.[3] This thesis (call it the *Thesis of the Indifference of Ends* – TIE for short) is very familiar from plenty of other more or less consequentialist-minded ethicists besides Parfit. It is also a natural thesis for anyone to adopt who is committed to Hume's view that practical rationality is typically or essentially only instrumental rationality – as many consequentialists are (though not, as it happens, Parfit).[4]

The second distinctive feature of LCG, which I'll call the *Taxonomical Thesis* (TT), is the thesis that the human goods that there are – or if we accept monism about the good, that there appear to be – together constitute no more and no less than a list. We can have a (practically speaking) complete understanding of which goods are available for humans just by compiling some such taxonomy of things that might 'make someone's life go best' as I compiled in 2.2 – or such as Parfit compiles, though only I think to give some examples, at *RP* pp. 493, 499: ' . . . moral goodness, rational activity, the development of one's abilities, having children and being a good parent . . . eating, drinking, laughing, dancing, and talking to my friends . . . reading *King Lear* . . .'

As for the third distinctive feature of LCG, which I'll call the *Aggregation Thesis* (AT), this is closely connected with TT. AT is another view that must be very familiar to readers of recent consequentialist ethics. It's the view that goods can be summed, and hence that the goodness of a life relates to the number of goods (or bads) in it in, at bottom, a simply additive manner. Each good is itself quantifiable: one can have more or less of it. Different goods, if there are any, are interquantifiable: N amount of good A and M amount of good B can be more or less or the same amount of good overall as M amount of of good A and N amount of good B.

Consider, for example, Parfit's view that a good life would on the Desire Fulfilment Theory be one in which 'there is a very great sum of desire fulfilment'. Or again, take his view that a life which is, 'though not by much, worth living', is one about which 'there is nothing bad', and which 'each day contains a few small pleasures' (*RP* pp. 496, 498). Despite Parfit's own recognition (*RP* p. 493) that 'pleasure and pain are not two distinctive kinds of experience', the idea evidently is that of a head-count of something: if not a head-count of pleasures, then a head-count of fulfilments of desires of more or less self-centred scope; or else a head-count of items taken off Parfit's Objective List. A life worth living is one in which lots of items off the list of goods are found, and not many off the list of bads or evils. Of a bad life, a life not worth living, the opposite is true. Of a middling life, a life barely worth living, the items from the list of goods that are present in that life only just outweigh that life's evils as to their quality and quantity. What we're given, as the means of assessing the worthwhileness or otherwise of lives, is simply two lists. The suggestion is that good and bad lives are composed out of the items on these lists by simple aggregation from the lists.[5]

So we have the Thesis of the Indifference of Ends (TIE) – the view that the question of which things the goods are is very largely theoretically unrelated to other questions in ethics. We have the Taxonomical Thesis (TT) – the view that what's necessary and sufficient for an understanding of the human good is the compilation of a list or taxonomy of goods. And we have the Aggregation Thesis (AT) – the view that the goods contribute to a life's goodness in a straightforwardly additive manner. Three interesting, popular, and (perhaps) plausible theses: so what's wrong with them?

What's wrong with AT can be briefly stated given two distinctions:

Distinguish two ways in which, very generally, things can be counted or measured: (1) by simple quantity, or (2) by units of meaning or content. For example, contrast volumes of noise, numbers of pages, amounts of electrical power, and degrees of arc on the one hand, with numbers of scientific laws, or of universals, or of concepts, or of tunes on the other. All the things in the first group are, as such, countable only by simple quantity, and not by units of content. All the things in the second are, as such, countable only by units of content, and not also by simple quantity. It makes no sense to try to measure any noise – not even the noise of someone speaking – by measuring the amount of information conveyed to competent listeners by that noise. Conversely, it makes no sense to try to count or estimate the number of theses in this book by counting the number of its pages.

Connectedly, distinguish two sorts of putting-together or, as we might say, 'sum': arithmetical sums, and rational sums. Arithmetical sums are exemplified, unsurprisingly enough, by the kind of putting-together we find in '2 + 2 = 4'. Rational sums are exemplified by a quite different sort of putting-together. Consider, for instance,[6] the sort we find in syllogisms and other pieces of practical or theoretical reasoning. 'If all men are mortal and if Socrates is a man, then Socrates is mortal' would be one of the kinds of putting-together that I mean by a rational sum.[7]

Note that rational sums, unlike arithmetical sums, are in no sense 'means' or 'compromises' between their components. The arithmetical sum of +4 and −2 is +2, which is a kind of mean, or perhaps even compromise, between its components +4 and −2, because it's between those points on the numerical scale (though not half-way between, like the average of +4 and −2). By contrast, the rational sum of the components 'All men are mortal' and 'Socrates is a man' is (at least in one sense of my phrase 'rational sum') 'Socrates is mortal'. The relation of this sum to its components is utterly different from that seen in the arithmetical sum. It would be senseless to describe 'Socrates is mortal' as a mean (or compromise) between those claims.[8]

Where do goods fit in with these two distinctions? Well, goods are the kind of things to be counted or measured not as simple quantities, but as units of meaning or content. Taken together, they form, if anything, rational sums, not arithmetical ones. But all versions of AT depend on the denial of these two claims. *That's* what wrong with AT.[9]

This way of seeing things can be justified by giving some examples of its explanatory power. Here are seven.

First, it gives us a succinct explanation of some of the problems facing adherents of AT. Thus, for example, we can explain why the Global versions of Parfit's theories about self-interest are (or can be made) preferable to the Summative versions. The answer, apparently unavailable to Parfit, is 'Because Global theories of self-interest needn't embody the mistake of treating goods in simple-quantitative terms, as Summative theories must'.

Second, we can explain neatly why – as is clearly the case – twice as much of a given good isn't always twice as good.[10] The answer is that twice as much in *simple-quantitative* terms of some 'good' (shag-pile carpets or birdwatching excursions, or money, or even friends) is never guaranteed to be twice as much in *meaning-unit* terms. In those terms, it might even be less. (Cp. the economists' notion of 'diminishing marginal utility'.)

Third, we can explain why it seems wrong to say that, for example, the sum of a desire to be a philosopher and a desire to be a novelist must be a desire to be both a philosopher and a novelist, or to be something between, such as a writer of philosophical novels or a philosopher of the novel. That's no more true than it's true that the sum of a desire to be in Edinburgh and a desire to be in London must be a desire to be in Northallerton. It's no nearer the truth than Parfit's bizarre suggestion (Parfit 1973) that the sum of (a liking for Palladio and an intention to visit Venice) plus (a liking for Giotto and an intention to visit Padua) must be 'both tastes and both intentions', or that the sum of (hatred of red hair and Conservative voting) plus (love of red hair and Labour voting) must be indifference to red hair and floating-voter status.

(Notice, incidentally, that Parfit treats these two cases in opposite ways. He doesn't suggest that the sum of (a liking for Palladio and an intention to visit Venice) plus (a liking for Giotto and an intention to visit Padua) might be indifference to both artists and neither intention. Nor does he suggest that the sum of (hatred of red hair and Conservative voting) plus (love of red hair and Labour voting) might be both attitudes to red hair and both voting intentions. If such cases as these were amenable to arithmetical rather than rational summing, the first thing we'd need would be some decision between these two ways of arithmetical summing. One clear sign that they aren't amenable to rational summing is our lack of a good reason for either decision.[11])

What such sums are sums of is units not of quantity, but of conceptual content. That is why such sums, where doable at all, aren't arithmetical but rational sums. As already emphasised, the outcome of such a sum need in no way be a mean of or compromise between its components.[12] Quite often there is no sense in which the outcome of a rational sum *could* be such a mean or compromise. Even where there is such a sense, it's never guaranteed, by the mere fact that such a compromise is possible, that that compromise represents the best way to do the sum.

Thus, for example, the outcome of a rational sum between a desire to be a philosopher and a desire to be a novelist might (depending on other factors) be a desire to be both, half-time. It could also simply be a decision to be a philosopher all one's life. In quantitative terms, the result of the rational sum can appear to be influenced not at all by one of its original components.

Fourth: these thoughts about the difference between rational and arithmetical summing suggest some interesting points about conflict resolution – not only intrapersonal, as above, but also interpersonal. Some conflicts can, and others can't, be resolved by anything like arithmetical summing. If you want to get no less than £50,000 for your house and I want to give no more than £40,000, maybe our conflict can be resolved by my offering you £45,000. This is an arithmetical compromise. But if you want to marry me and I don't want to marry you, there is no compromise point between our positions, such as (say) getting engaged *pro tem*. Because you can't be married to me unless I'm married to you, our conflict can't be resolved unless either I come over to your viewpoint or you come over to mine. This conflict can be resolved only by rational summing – by my finding reasons to persuade you, or your finding reasons to persuade me. But then it will look to the arithmetical eye as if one of us has 'given in' to the other, because one of us has now adopted the whole of the other's position. This may be one of the things that bedevils political negotiations, such as the Northern Irish 'peace process'. Because some of the problems inevitably faced by such negotiations can be solved only by a move that looks like a caving-in of one side to the other, but is in fact a rational summing across their two positions to a new position, it is easy for critics of such negotiations to misapply arithmetical tests to such moves and find them wanting. It is correspondingly difficult for the negotiators to find the political courage, and vocabulary, to defend their actions to their own constituencies.

Fifth: while we are on the subject of Northern Ireland, consider forgiveness. Quite apart from moral imperatives, why is it so important for humans' psychological health to forgive and to be forgiven? Is it because forgiveness is (so to speak) a moral lump sum which, when placed in the right account by the right depositor, makes good a moral debt? No – though no doubt it is this false picture of what forgiveness involves that makes it seem such a problematic notion to so many people because, on this picture, the victim of the wrong has to give to the perpetrator as well as *vice versa*. Given the distinction between rational and arithmetical summing, we can offer a better explanation of why it is so humanly important to forgive. It's important because without forgiveness a rational sum remains incompleted. In a metaphor that may be getting familiar, not to forgive is to freeze a story. It is to prevent an incomplete process from having any significant further continuation, let alone any happy resolution. It is to fasten obsessively on one way of seeing a thought or experience, and to reject any opportunity for revising how you see it. This may help show why refusing to forgive, or not receiving forgiveness, can be such an emotionally stultifying experience.

Sixth: consider the familiar criticism of utilitarianism, that very often it can only make sense of certain reactive attitudes – blame, praise, regret, reactions to atrocities like murder – 'from the outside'. Thus, for example, Williams points out that Smart has a 'causal theory of moral comment'. That is, Smart holds the consistent utilitarian's view of moral comment, as an activity that matters only insofar as it is a means to influence outcomes – usually by bringing actions to be intentionally directed at those outcomes, but quite possibly by other causal routes as well.[13] One of the weaknesses that Williams identifies in the causal theory of moral comment is

> ... that it makes it very difficult to make sense of a man's view of his own conduct; particularly if he himself believes the causal theory, since then the lack of openness I have mentioned stands between the man and himself – it is hard to see how he can blame himself if he knows what he is doing in doing that. Now utilitarians in fact are not very keen on people blaming themselves, which they see as an unproductive activity: not to cry over spilt milk figures prominently among utilitarian proverbial injunctions (and carries the characteristically utilitarian thought that anything you

might want to cry over is, like milk, replaceable). (J. J. C. Smart and Bernard Williams, *Utilitarianism: for and against*, p. 124)

Why is it, Williams asks, that the utilitarian can only make sense of the reactive attitudes of blame and regret as inhibitors or stimulants of future intentional action? He points (not in this quotation) to the utilitarian's twin obsessions with causation and the future. He also points (in this quotation) to a third and allied element, the 'thought that anything you might want to cry over is . . . replaceable'. This third element makes explicit the connection between what Williams is saying, and my present thesis. The conception of the goods that underlies the utilitarian approach to the reactive attitudes turns out to entail the idea that goods are interchangeable and inter-replaceable; and this idea is just another form of the Aggregation Thesis. It also seems to be AT that makes it compelling to think that the reactive attitudes, one and all, cannot be understood from the inside, and are just irrational. How could it make sense to waste time regretting past losses, or my previous job as a concentration camp guard, when I could be spending the time in building up more units of good on my scoresheet instead? We need something like the distinction between the two sorts of summing which I have just made to answer that question. Such a distinction isn't available to the proponent of AT.

Seventh and last: if you are assessing the philosophical merits of (say) revolutionary socialism, it may well be nothing to the point to remark that there are four dozen arguments in favour of it and only one argument against.[14] What matters concerning arguments isn't how many of them on either side of a question we can head-count (on what principle of individuation, by the way?). What matters is whether any of these arguments is any good: that is, whether any of them is a rationally compelling argument, or failing that whether any of them is at least rationally persuasive. (It's also important to see if any of them cancels out any other arguments.) The rational/arithmetical contrast helps to show where the irrationality lies in taking literally the metaphor of weighing arguments, as for example, I'm told the Jesuits do or did.

So much for AT – the thesis that goods can be summed, and hence that the goodness of a life relates to the number of goods (or bads) in it in a simply additive manner. I turn next to the Taxonomical Thesis (TT): the view that the human goods that there are or appear to be together constitute no more and no less than a list. The criticism that I offer of this notion will also apply to AT.

The criticism is this. No taxonomy or list can be sufficient for an account of the good for humans: even though, as already argued in 1.2 to 2.3, some such taxonomy is necessary. There is at least one essential requirement for any account of the good for humans which no such list can include as a part of that list. This essential requirement is an answer to the question of how the goods in any such list can be co-ordinated with each other (to put it another way, an answer to the Problem of Reconciliation).

Consider the Aristotelian Completeness Test for proposed accounts of *eudaimonia* (human well-being). At *Nicomachean Ethics* 1097b7ff. Aristotle says: 'The most complete good, we take it, is self-sufficient . . . and what is self-sufficient, we suppose, is whatever is able *on its own* to make life choice-worthy, and lacking in no respect. This is what we believe *eudaimonia* to be like.'

As Irwin puts it: 'If we think some good G is to be identified with happiness, but then find that we can add some further good H to G so that the total of G + H is greater than G alone, then G cannot be identified with happiness' (Terence Irwin, *Classical Thought*, p. 134). This is the Completeness Test in action.

Suppose – plausibly – that the Completeness Test should be applied to any candidate account of human well-being. If so, then that alone is enough to show that TT is false. For consider the Pleasure Wizard:[15] that is, the person who has as much as they could conceivably want of every good in some plausible taxonomy of goods, but nothing else.

The Pleasure Wizard spends his early mornings poring over a menu of goods, picking out[16] which ones he happens to fancy experiencing today. He spends the day experiencing these, goes to bed for eight hours' dreamless sleep, and gets up tomorrow to do the same again.

The Pleasure Wizard never has any bad experiences, any experiences of desire frustration or of pain or of unhappiness. His good experiences need not be limited to (say) the satisfaction of preferences for what Mill called the 'lower pleasures'. They can include fulfilled preferences for some things like those on Parfit's lists, or on mine at 2.2. Again, the Pleasure Wizard freely chooses everything he experiences. We might even add that he lives for ever, or indefinitely. For all that, who would seriously and non-frivolously want to be a Pleasure Wizard rather than a normal human being?

Any day in a Pleasure Wizard's experience is, in an important way, just like any other.[17] Such a life seems to be going nowhere. However pleasant such a life may be, it seems impossibly bland, meaningless and boring; perhaps in the same way in which the experiences of the writer of *Ecclesiastes* were meaningless, or in the way in which Heaven, or eternal life, is often supposed to be boring.[18]

Of course, the Pleasure Wizard's life does not fail the Completeness Test for *eudaimonia* in exactly the way that Irwin describes. The problem with it is not that there is some good, from whatever list of goods we accept, which it lacks. By hypothesis, that isn't the case: whatever the list, there is no good from that list which isn't present in the Pleasure Wizard's life. Rather, it fails the Completeness Test because the goods in it have no overall structure.[19] There's no development, no progress, no shape to such a life.

But here's the problem with TT: according to TT, the Pleasure Wizard's life is as good as the best life there could be!

If the shapeless life of a Pleasure Wizard is the best that TT can offer us, then TT is an inadequate account of the human goods. For nothing in TT meets the requirement that a human life which displays *eudaimonia* should display structure.

Can't the defender of TT meet this problem simply by adding the requirement 'that one's life be structured' to the list of goods? No. Structuredness, properly understood, isn't just a good; it is also our way of pursuing the goods. Hence, if that requirement is put on the list, it can't itself be what co-ordinates all the requirements on the list into a structure. Structuredness will itself be one of the things which we are trying to structure into the life which displays *eudaimonia* – by some other means (what?). A requirement of structuredness which is itself on the list can't do the job of structuring choices between items on the list. What does that job is necessarily outside the list, just as the procedural presupposition that *modus ponens* is a valid form of argument is necessarily outside any axiomatic system consisting of inferences in *modus ponens*. (Cp. again Lewis Carroll (1895).) But if anything we need for *eudaimonia* is necessarily outside any taxonomy of the goods, then TT is false.

So, for example, I don't think Parfit can build structuredness into his version of the Taxonomical Thesis by talking as he does of 'the development of one's abilities' as an example of the kind of preference-fulfilment that we might want to have, and so which might be on the Objective List of goods. Certainly developing one's abilities is something that does (or could) have the sort of self-consciously imposed 'shape' or narrative structure that we are looking for. But consider a Pleasure Wizard who enjoys this sort of good among others. How does this good relate to the other goods he enjoys? Either as part of a larger structured whole still. Then we're on the right track – but not a track that an adherent of the Taxonomical Thesis seems able to take, because this notion of a larger structured whole has just appeared out of nowhere without being accounted for by TT. Or else this sort of good is an island of structuredness in a sea of one-thing-after-another days of enjoyment of goods. Then its presence is just another item in that mêlée, and can do little to give the rest of the mêlée any shape.[20]

Given the Completeness Test, the Pleasure Wizard is a counter-example to TT. According to TT, his life is as good a life as there could be. Yet it fails to satisfy the Completeness Test, because we can easily say what it lacks: structuredness in the way it pursues the different goods. The Pleasure Wizard is also a counter-example to AT. His case shows that further addition of simple quantities of goods, up to no matter how high a level, is on its own insufficient to ensure that the subject in question is enjoying complete *eudaimonia* – living as well as possible.[21]

So if it's right to apply the Completeness Test to proposed accounts of *eudaimonia*, then TT and AT are both false. And by now our third target – the Thesis of the Indifference of Ends (TIE) – has been hit as well. TIE is the view that

> (TIE) When compiling an account of the good for humans, it doesn't matter what you put into the list. For what the good is and how to get it are two separate matters.

It no longer looks at all likely to be true that, as TIE claims, 'what the good is and how to get it are two separate matters'. It's just emerged from our thoughts about the Pleasure Wizard that how we are to achieve the good-for-humans is necessarily by way of having a structure to our lives. But having a structure to one's life is also an essential part of what the good-for-humans is. Without structure, our lives could be no better than a Pleasure Wizard's. So 'what the good is' and 'how to get it' aren't two separate matters. They are constitutively interconnected.

The other two parts of LCG (the Aggregation and Taxonomical Theses) turned out to be false. We can now see that TIE is false as well. This comprehensively refutes LCG, because LCG is just the conjunction AT + TT + TIE. It also refutes, along with TIE, any instrumental account of rationality. Instrumental accounts of rationality too must presuppose that there's an obvious and intuitive distinction between *what the good is* and *how to get it*. But, leaving aside some special cases (for example, Wiggins's billiards players: see 'Deliberation and Practical Reason' in Wiggins (1987), p. 230), there is no such distinction.

5.2   THE NARRATIVE CONCEPTION OF THE GOOD

'Well, perhaps LCG is refuted in all three possible ways. Perhaps it's true that we shouldn't accept either TIE or AT or TT. But we haven't yet found any true alternative conception of the good. Anyway, perhaps our standards are too high. In particular, our rejection of TT on the grounds of the Completeness Test is all very well. But could *any* account of *eudaimonia* pass the Completeness Test? If the answer is No, why does the Test matter? If the answer is Yes, what is the account?'

I think there is a possible account of *eudaimonia* which passes the Completeness Test. This account will also – I hope – at least begin to show how to meet a need which Griffin notes: 'Philosophy has not yet provided a fully satisfactory explanation of how we bring system to our various ends' (*Well-Being* p. 35). This account, which I'll now offer for examination, is the Narrative Conception of the good (NCG). Examination of NCG will provide us with an alternative to LCG. It will also clarify my answers to two other important questions. These are the question raised in 4.3, 'What matters ethically concerning personal identity?' and the second part of the Problem of Reconciliation – the question of how to interrelate those pursuits of the good which are legitimated by the Threefold Schema.

What is the Narrative Conception of the Good? We can begin to get some idea by comparing Rawls's notion of a 'rational plan', or 'life-plan':

> The rather complex notion of a rational plan . . . is fundamental for the definition of good, since a rational plan of life establishes the basic point of view from which all judgements of value relating to a particular person are to be made and finally rendered consistent . . . we can think of a person as being happy when he is in the way of a successful execution (more or less) of a rational plan of life drawn up under (more or less) favourable conditions, and he is reasonably confident that his plan can be carried through. Someone is happy when his plans are going well, his more important aspirations being fulfilled, and he feels sure that his good fortune will endure. (John Rawls, *A Theory of Justice*, p. 409)

NCG is a conception of the human goods that says that they are necessarily experienced within 'a rational plan of life' which, as Rawls puts it, 'establishes the basic point of view from which all judgements of value relating to a particular person are to be made and finally rendered consistent'. (As we'll see when we consider the place of subjectivity within NCG, Rawls's words 'relating to a particular person' are of crucial importance to this formula.) We may explore NCG further by contrasting it with the three theses of LCG which caused us to reject that conception.

Adherents of NCG reject the Taxonomical Thesis and the Thesis of the Indifference of Ends. For NCG, our conception of *our relation to* our conception of the good is central to our conception of the good. The goods which we recognise aren't (just) items on a list. They can be seen as members of a taxonomy like the one in 2.2, but that isn't the central point about them. The central point about the human goods is their status as possible parts of the kind of *structure* of goods that we recognise as a good human life. This status also gives one major reason why, contrary to TIE, those things which we recognise as goods must matter vitally for everything else in ethics.

Aren't there many ways in which a life might have structure? Perhaps; but the kind of structure that I have in mind is *narrative* structure. This is the kind of structure that is characteristically displayed by a coherent narrative. The structure of a good life, as I use the phrase, just is the story of that life. Thus NCG says that a good life is structured by its pursuit of those goods which are such that the story of the agent's life's pursuit of them is the story of the agent's life.

But what do I mean by this use of 'pursuit'? The answer to this brings us to NCG's rejection of LCG's third thesis, the Aggregation Thesis. 'Pursuit' is being used here as it is also used in 3.1 to 3.2. As I pointed out there, it isn't being used to mean exactly what consequentialists mean by 'maximisation'. Goods aren't countable in the right way for it to make sense to talk of trying to maximise them. They are countable as units of meaning, not as simple quantities (5.1).

This claim about how to count or measure goods is both a rejection of AT, and a natural accompaniment to NCG's claim about what gives a life structure. One corollary of combining these claims (combining them, that is, in a rational sum!) is the

First Corollary: Two lives could have exactly the same amounts of good and evil in them, in simple quantitative terms, and yet one of them be a better life than the other.

This can be shown by comparing Structured's life, which is narratively structured, with Wizard's life, which isn't. Assume that in simple-quantitative terms, the values of the lives are the same. Then, despite the simple-quantitative equality, Structured's life will always be better than Wizard's on the other way of measuring the goodness of lives (the meaning-unit measure), and in fact better *simpliciter*[22] than Wizard's. For Structured's life has a feature that Wizard's life can't have: structure. This accords with our intuitions, which say that Structured's life <u>is</u> better than Wizard's life. This is another reason for thinking that we were right to reject AT, and use the meaning-unit measure of lives' goodness, not the simple-quantitative measure.

So our claims about how to count goods and about the structure of a good life have a

Second Corollary: Two lives, A and B, could differ in the amounts of good and evil in them, in simple quantitative terms. In those terms, A could have more good and less evil in it than B. We might also allow it to be true that B and A were both structured lives: that neither was merely the life of a Pleasure Wizard. For all that, *B could be a better life than A.*

Consider first an extreme case. Compare the lives of Oedipus and Vincent. Oedipus, a King of Thebes, has attained his eminent position by his own resourcefulness in self-defence and ingenuity in riddle-solving. He lives many delightful and contented years in a handsome palace in a spot with the pleasantest climate and oiliest olives in Greece, in the company of a bewitching Queen who perfectly satisfies Oedipus' predilection for the older dame. Unfortunately, at the end of his life it is discovered that this Queen is Oedipus' mother, and that Oedipus' early deeds in self-defence had included the deed of parricide.

By contrast Vincent, a painter, goes through seven kinds of psychiatric hell, is prone to abysmal depressions as well as wild elations, is frequently overwhelmed by his own suffering and that of those around him, and dies by his own hand, in penury and possibly insane. His pictures are so extraordinarily beautiful that, 100 years after his death, they are more talked about than ever before. But of course that wouldn't make Vincent's own life much easier even if he knew it, which he does not, because in his own time his work is completely unsaleable.

Take any pair of lives A and B such that A has far more goods than bads in it, whereas B has far more bads than goods in it. If AT is true, then it is perfectly obvious that A is better than B. But Oedipus' life is like A, and Vincent's life is like B. (The cost of denying this would surely have to be unhealthy amounts of cooking the books regarding what is to count as (how much of) a good.) So AT makes it perfectly obvious that Oedipus has a better or happier life than Vincent.

But this can't be right. Even if Oedipus' life is happier or better than Vincent's, it surely isn't, as AT makes out, *obviously* better. Perhaps it isn't better at all. Perhaps Vincent's life is happier, not Oedipus'.[23] (Who would you rather be?)

So the question of which life is better isn't a simple and clear-cut one, as the defenders of AT must say it is; and the reason why it isn't clear-cut is interesting. The reason is that we assess the goodness or badness of lives by assessing them as *stories*. We don't do it as AT recommends: by counting up the goods and bads in those lives. Any goods or bads there may be in the lives are important to our assessment. But they aren't important in the way that AT says – because, in a mechanically predictable way, they add or subtract from a simply quantitative sum of happiness. Rather, they're important because of what they mean. They're important because of the ways in which they affect the shape of the life's story so far.

Thus, Oedipus' discoveries that all along he has been married to his mother and usurping the throne of the father he murdered, aren't bad only because they make him suffer; after all, maybe they don't make him suffer as much pain as he has already enjoyed pleasure. Nor are they bad only because incest and parricide are terrible things to do, and deeds of these sorts are now to be added to the list of things that Oedipus has done. These discoveries are terrible because they transform the shape of the story of Oedipus' life. In a moment they turn his life-story from one of success, achievement, glory, wealth, and contentment, into one of humiliation and sacrilege.

Oedipus' life shows us that the contribution of particular goods to the overall goodness of a life isn't that of simple quantities to an arithmetical sum. It is that of units of meaning to a rational sum (though clearly in this case the rational sum isn't simply a syllogism: it is more like a story). Hence the well-known Greek view, reported by Aristotle, that we shouldn't say that anyone has hold of *eudaimonia*, until we know how the whole of their life's story goes.[24] It is always possible that some last-minute addition to that continuing process of rational summing may alter it in some catastrophic way – as happened to Oedipus.

More cheerfully, of course, the converse is also possible. A story that includes terrible suffering may nonetheless have a happy ending. I might struggle for years against squalor and penury, ducks on the wallpaper and deep depression, my next door neighbour's trombone-playing and editorial contempt, to complete my masterpiece. But one day, perhaps, it will be recognised. If it is, that success may make all the difference – perhaps even posthumously, as with Vincent van Gogh.

It may mean that my life turns out to have the shape of a happy story, not a sad one.

Another illustration of the First and Second Corollaries is this. With the shape of life narratives, compare the shapes of such narratives as Shakespearean dramas. What makes *The Winter's Tale* a 'comedy' (a happy play) and *Romeo and Juliet* a 'tragedy' (a sad play)? The answer isn't found simply by measuring, by some plausible yardstick, how much happiness and how much sadness occur in the two plays. Nor by counting (a) how many good things and (b) how many bad things happen to the principal characters of these plays, and subtracting (b) from (a), perhaps with some plausible weightings added to differentiate big good or bad experiences from little good or bad experiences. Perhaps Romeo and Juliet had such a wonderful time till things went wrong that they had 'a larger amount' of happiness than unhappiness. This wouldn't make it true that *Romeo and Juliet* was a happy play, nor that Romeo and Juliet were fortunate characters. Again, perhaps the eventual reunion of Leontes, Perdita and Hermione, joyful though it was, was not more joyful than their long separation was painful. Actually, this is a question that *The Winter's Tale* seems to leave deliberately unresolved. But even if it was resolved, no resolution of that question could make it true that *The Winter's Tale* was as unhappy a play as *Romeo and Juliet*.

These examples, I hope, show something about the way we assess the goodness or badness, happiness or sadness, of narratives. They show that normally the answer to the question 'What makes this play or story happy or sad?' has nothing to do with aggregative calculation. It has to do instead with how the narrative as a whole is to be taken or viewed. It has to do with how the good and bad experiences which occur within the narrative are to be made sense of as a story, by us and by those in the story; or, in the case of our own lives, by us as those in the story.[25]

Disasters are bad, and triumphs are good, no matter when they happen. Yet the degree to which they are bad or good can be relative to indefinitely many other factors: for there are indefinitely many other factors that could be part of what gives someone's story its shape.

For instance, events' goodness or badness can depend on <u>when they happen</u>. This is obviously true in a relatively uninteresting sense connected with aggregative measurement.[26] In that sense, for example, it is worse if the motorway bridge over the Manchester Ship Canal collapses at rush hour and when a packed ocean liner is directly underneath. Perhaps less obviously, it's also true in this second, and more interesting, non-aggregative sense: the badness of a disaster can depend on *when in my life* it happens. To be run over by a bus when I'm a retired philosopher of 105 is terrible, but it would be worse for me to be run over right now. This is true not just in the sense that, aggregatively, my being run over right now would (I expect) have more knock-on effects, just as the collapse of the bridge will have more knock-on effects if it happens at rush hour and when the *QE2* is directly underneath. It is also true in the non-aggregative sense that when I'm a retired philosopher of 105, I shall (I expect; but ask me again when I'm 104) already have done most of the things I really want to do with my life, such as writing this book. Whereas if I'm run over this evening, my story will have been cut short. I'll never finish writing this book, not even this chapter, never mind all the other books I'd like to write. Sudden death at thirty-two is obviously worse than sudden death at 105. This isn't just because agents who die 'before their time' lose a greater aggregate of possible goods. Nor is it just because it cuts off so much more of what – within the limits set by normally realistic human expectations, and by longevity – might have been my life-story. It is also because untimely death gives a very different, and far sadder, narrative shape to my life than death in old age does.[27]

Again, disasters can be worse depending on <u>to whom they happen</u>; and NCG can help us to see why. Consider dramatic irony. LCG can allow that it is worse if Thales is drowned than if I am drowned – but LCG can't explain why. A sophisticated form of LCG could have room for the bare fact that what Thales – the philosopher who claimed that all was made of water[28] – undergoes is in two ways a bad thing, not just one, as would be true if I drowned. But what no form of LCG can accommodate is an explanation of why drowning is, in the second and additional sense, a worse thing for Thales than for me. To explain that, we need to see how dying in this manner gives Thales' life, at least at its end, the shape of a tasteless joke made by fate at Thales' expense. To see this, we need NCG.

Another phenomenon that NCG has a better grip on than LCG is, in a way, equal and opposite to dramatic irony. This is the phenomenon of meaningless or absurd disaster or death.

Is this surprising, given NCG's emphasis on meaningfulness? Of course not; it's precisely because of its emphasis on meaningfulness, and of the difference between that and meaninglessness, that NCG is better able than LCG to explain what's peculiarly bad about, for instance, Aeschylus' death.[29] Aeschylus (the story is) died because he was bald, and because eagles have a habit of breaking turtle shells open as a thrush breaks a snail open – by dropping the captured turtle on to smooth shiny hard surfaces from a great height. This is a stupid way to die if anything is. But that means that it was a worse death for Aeschylus to die this way, than for him to die while fighting the Persians, or of old age while he was sitting writing. So why was death by turtle worse for Aeschylus? NCG offers us the answer: 'Because death by turtle was totally unfitting as an end to the narrative of Aeschylus' noble life. It isn't even a tasteless joke like Thales' death – or at least it's not specifically a joke against Aeschylus rather than any other (bald) human being. It's just a sick, unmeaning way to die.' If this is the right answer, that supports NCG.

Last, here's a simpler example of how the First and Second Corollaries can be put to work. Being born into poverty and failure is bad, even if you go on to become very happy and successful (like Charles Dickens). But it isn't as bad as dying in poverty and failure, after a life of phenomenal success (like Mozart).[30] This example shows another sense in which it's true that we don't just care about the quantity and/ or quality of goods in our lives, but about their distribution too. Quite apart from the amounts of goods and bads in our lives, we also want our lives to have a shape more like that of Dickens's life, and less like that of Mozart's. And we're pleased if this want is satisfied.

LCG naturally finds this preference of ours irrational or bad for us: possibly both. So Parfit argues (*RP* pp. 174–7) that it would be better for us to have *no* preferences about distribution within our lives, but instead to be like the man Parfit calls Timeless. Timeless is just as pleased by the memory of past pleasure as by the anticipation of future pleasure. The less Timeless has to look forward to, the more he has to look back to. So he needn't care even if all his pleasures are now over, and nothing remains to him but thirty years of pains or other ills, provided his life up to now has contained enough pleasure or other goods. But Timeless's story – and the very idea that we humans might be like him, or even might want to be – is a bizarre and foreign one.[31] That counts against LCG. It means that LCG is forced to reject as irrational what is central enough to human experience for the price of rejecting it to be very high. We can't imagine ourselves being divorced from any sense of the continuing narrative of our lives in the way that Timeless is. (In any case, it might be argued, no one could be like Timeless without also being a Pleasure Wizard.)

NCG, by contrast, seems able to explain why it wouldn't even make sense to try to be like Timeless. The reason is because the order of our pains and pleasures, our good and bad experiences, matters for narrative reasons. Never mind the much more complicated narrative considerations which I began to explore earlier: just take the very simplest narrative consideration of all, as last mentioned – that a life that begins badly but gets better is necessarily better than one that begins well but ends badly. That thought is, I take it, obviously a datum of ordinary moral thought. If LCG cannot make anything of this datum, so much the worse for LCG. If NCG can explain it, by showing how it needn't be irrational to think in this essential temporal way about our own experience of good and bad, so much the better for NCG.

In fact (we might even add), mightn't Dickens's destitute childhood be *part* of what made his life so good? This suggests a third corollary of combining NCG with the rejection of AT. The first and second corollaries depended on the point that the goodness or badness of a life overall is related to the goodness or badness of the contents of that life, not simply quantitatively, but by way of rational summing. The third corollary is a point in, so to speak, the opposite direction:

Third Corollary: Because the goodness of a life is the happiness of a life-story, the goods and bads in it are not only not aggregatively summable. They don't even have values aside from the structure of the life in which they occur. Instead, they depend upon the shape of that story for their value.

Oedipus' and Vincent's lives again provide dramatic examples of how this might be true. It could be said that in Oedipus' life, many items which we would normally expect to count as goods actually turn out to count as bads. Consider all the princely splendour and luxury, all the long years of serene contentment, which Oedipus enjoys. Not only does the positive value of these golden years fail to offset the negative value of the disaster that eventually falls on Oedipus. Those golden years actually make Oedipus' disaster *worse*. Because of the ending of Oedipus' life-story, they never were golden years. They were fool's-gold years.

Contrariwise, of Vincent's life it might be said that many items which we'd normally expect to count as bads turn out, in his case, to count as goods. Take all his depression and his mania, all his long years of (apparently) fruitless struggle. When these are rationally summed together with Vincent's eventual triumph, it seems possible to claim that they actually add something to that triumph. (Again, I skirt round the fact that van Gogh himself never knew of his own triumph, because that fact raises a difficulty that I needn't consider here.)

I reject the Third Corollary, however. The view that someone's penury or anguish could ever turn out to be simply and straight-forwardly a good for him because of the way his life turns out is a mistake. Penury and mental anguish are *bad*, and contentment and luxury are *good*. To abandon thoughts of that rather simple sort, on the grounds of more nuanced thoughts about the shapes that lives can have, would no doubt be a gain in potential for sophistication. Unfortunately, it would also be a gain in potential for sophistry. The danger is that such a move will lead us into the sort of twistiness of mind that one sometimes sees in theodicy – into the essentially dishonest view of Dr Pangloss that even the worst is always for the best.[32]

More fundamentally, to accept the Third Corollary as it stands would be to abandon the project of listing the goods altogether. There can be no chance of even beginning to constitute a stable taxonomy of goods if it's not stable whether *anything* counts as a good or not. To abandon that project of finding a taxonomy would be to lose our fundamental orientation in ethics. Orientation is, above all, what a taxonomy like that of 2.2 has to provide: an ethicist with no grasp of which the goods are is like a polar explorer who does not know where north is. If we give up the project of finding that taxonomy, we no longer have much idea even of the distinction between good and bad. If we have little idea of that relatively straightforward distinction, there won't be much hope of our grasping the much subtler distinction between right and wrong.

Still, something feels right about the Third Corollary. There is a true thesis somewhere in its vicinity which gives it its appeal – and gives it a grain of truth. (Cp. Note 26.) This is the

Fourth Corollary: The goods and bads in a life do have values aside from the structure of the life in which they occur. But their values aside from that structure aren't the same as their values within that structure.

The Fourth Corollary says that there are two ways of assessing the goodness or badness of things. One of them considers the relation of goods and bads to *any* life. The other considers the relation of goods and bads to *a particular* life. As I put it above: 'The central point about the goods is their status as possible parts of a good life which has structure.' A list or taxonomy of the goods like the one I offered at 2.2 tells us what 'possible parts' are available for such structuring. It tells us what has value in the first sense identified by the Fourth Corollary. Consideration of what the narrative of a good life might be like tells us what sort of shape can result from such structuring. It tells us what has value in the Fourth Corollary's second sense. Moreover, it tells us what mediates the transition from the first sort of value to the second sort. What mediates that transition is the agent's, and her observers', activity of structuring.

This shows us how to identify the grain of truth in the Third Corollary. The truth it hints at is this. Bad things in a life can be transcended by that life – made part of a pattern of good living – and so lose some, but probably not all, of their negative value. On the other hand, the good things in a life can be subverted by that life – made part of a pattern of bad living – and so lose some, but probably not all, of their positive value.

So Dickens's bitter sufferings in childhood were, and remained, genuinely sufferings, and so genuinely bad things. They were bad things in a general sense: they were bad things because they would have been bad, no matter to whom they had happened. Yet Dickens transcended them. This meant that, while remaining evils, the sufferings of his childhood really did become part of what made him great. As well as simply being evils, in the sense that they were things which would be bad no matter to whom they happened, they also came to be evils such that, within the structure of Dickens's life, their sting was drawn. Within his life, these evils were still evils. But they were not the evils they typically are. Their place in his life is a surprising one. Want and Squalor (like Lord Beveridge's other three giants, Ignorance, Idleness and Disease) have a very high potential for ruining a life, when we consider such things in themselves and apart from any particular life. Yet Dickens defeated that potential. This is a remarkable victory on his part. A cheering one, too: it can encourage the rest of us when we face adversities like his.[33]

These reflections clarify why we should accept the Fourth Corollary, but not the Third. As already pointed out, accepting the Third would mean that we no longer had a substantive conception of the human goods that could be formulated independently of our conception of a good life. But we need a substantive and independent conception of the goods; not only for the reasons already given, but also because, without it, our theory of the good is led straight into a theoretical dead end of a sort all too familiar in 'virtue ethics'. Goods will be just the sort of things that characterise good lives; and good lives will be just whatever they are said to be by 'the many and the wise' – by some Wittgensteinian consensus of horny handed Plain Men and lofty minded Gurus. There is, I believe, far less of interest down this easy obscurantist line than there is down the much riskier alternative line explored in chapter 2, which – right or wrong – at least tries to give an informative independent account of the goods.

Finally in this exposition of the Narrative Conception, consider the **Fifth Corollary**: things that are *per se* indifferent in their value, either positive or negative, for any life can have special value, positive or negative, within some particular life.

For an argument for the Fifth Corollary, consider Thales again. On his retirement from the Milesian Academy his colleagues present him, not with the usual carriage clock, but with a water clock.[34] There is – let's suppose – no difference as to cash value, accuracy, beauty, etc., between the water clock which Thales actually gets and the carriage clock which he might have got. It's a matter of indifference which is a better thing (or gift) *per se,* the water clock or the carriage clock. This indifference doesn't apply, however, to a choice between the water clock and the carriage clock *as a gift for Thales.* For a gift to Thales, and in view of his intellectual preoccupations, the carriage clock is a boring choice, whereas the water clock is a witty choice. Therefore what's of indifferent value in itself is better for Thales.

Offhand the Fifth Corollary looks attractive. This argument for it is questionable, however. It seems to run together two different claims: (1) that in normal cases the choice between the two clocks is a morally indifferent choice; and (2) that, again in normal cases, a choice of either is a choice of what is morally indifferent. The claim (1) is true, because the clocks are of equal value. The claim (2) is false, because the clocks are both of positive value. A choice of either is a choice of a good thing.

The argument for the Fifth Corollary can be defended against this counter-argument. It can be said that the argument at least succeeds in showing that the Fifth Corollary is true insofar as there are cases, like Thales' water clock, where there is a good in the offing which is person–relative. A choice of either clock captures the good of that clock itself. But the choice of the water clock captures a person–relative good predicated of one of the clocks and not the other, namely the good of appropriateness-to-Thales.

Consider a further complexity closely cognate with the person–relativity of some goods in the sense just explored. This is time-relativity. I said above that we'll be arguing in the wrong direction if we try to begin by defining the good life, and then define 'good things' as all and only those things which feature in a good life. But clearly, some goods are time-relative in the sense that they aren't goods at all unless they occur at the right stage in a life.[35] For example, marriage is (or can be) an instance of goods in the life of a twenty-six-year-old. But it is probably inappropriate for a sixteen-year-old, and it's not only inappropriate, but positively bad, for a six-year-old. This seems to imply that – at least in cases like marriage – we can't have a substantive conception of what count as good things which can be formulated independently of our conception of a good life after all.

There is a way out of this. First, most human goods aren't time-relative in this way. Health and pleasure and companionship and laughter and justice are as good (and necessary) for one-year-olds (or indeed nought-year-olds) as they are for 100-year-olds. So the problem's scope is strictly limited. Second, regarding the human goods that *are* in this way time-relative, like those present in marriage, we should concede that we can't have a substantive conception of how these goods count as good things which can be formulated independently of our conception of a good life. But we should make a distinction between two ways in which we might have a conception of a good life. And we should make a corresponding distinction between two sorts of time-relativity.

The two possible conceptions of the good life are the general and the specific. The specific conception of a good life is what I've been calling the life-story of this or that particular person. The general conception of a good life is the conception of the good life that applies to humans just as such. It is the conception of how, in general and abstracting from particular cases, the different sorts of goods that there are might be built up by some human agent into this or that specific structured life.

The distinction about time-relativity is between strong and weak time-relativity. Weakly time-relative goods are time-relative only to the general conception of the good life for humans. In this sense, for example, marriage is a weakly time-relative good: because marriage is something that can easily be seen as contributing to the goodness of anyone's life, provided it doesn't happen at an inappropriate stage of the anyone's life in question. Strongly time-relative goods, by contrast, are goods that are time-relative to a specific conception of the good life. For example, if it is an important part of my life-plan to marry only once I am forty, then it is a consequence of my conception (if correct) of what my life (though not necessarily anyone else's) must be like to be good that 'marriage once or shortly after I am forty' is a strongly time-relative good for me.

Now we can accept the claim that some goods are weakly time-relative (time-relative to the general conception) without having to accept the further claim that weakly time-relative goods can't be understood unless we assume that the weakly time-relative goods are a necessary part of any conception of the good life, general or specific. For there are specific conceptions of the good life of which at least some weakly time-relative goods aren't (an important) part: consider the relation of marriage to a celibate life. So it isn't true even of the weakly time-relative goods that our understanding of them wholly depends upon prior claims about the nature of the (any) good life. Still less is this true of the goods which are not time-relative at all.[36]

As for the strongly time-relative goods, these emerge as a result of particular choices between goods, and instantiations of goods, in particular lives. Such choice between goods is choice of what is to go into my story next. Such choices, if they are practically wise, will bear in mind the list of goods (and instantiations of goods) that are available to humans, and also the general conception of the good life for humans. But they won't just depend on these considerations. They will also reflect the unique shape of my story so far.

So there's no need to suppose of either strongly or weakly time-relative goods that we can't get a conception even of them (never mind of all the goods which aren't time-relative at all) which is independent of our conception of the good life. Because there are always at least two sorts of conception of the good life, the general and the specific, available to any agent, there's always going to be some useful conception of the good life of which an agent's conceptions even of the time-relative goods will be independent.

So strong time-relativity is very closely related to person-relativity. To take this discussion of these related notions further, we may now turn back to the claim about identity as integrity that we have worked out, which says that to think about *the shape of my story so far* is precisely to think about *who I am*. It is time to say more about that claim, in the course of considering some important objections to the Narrative Conceptions of goods, persons and rationality at which we have now arrived, in chapter 6.

NOTES

1. The 'theories about self-interest' stated at *RP* p. 4 are: the Hedonistic Theory ('what would be best for someone is what would give him most happiness'); the Desire-Fulfilment Theory ('what would be best for someone is what would best fulfil his desires throughout his life'); the Success Theory ('what would be best for someone is what would best fulfil his desires about his own life throughout his life'); and the Objective List Theory ('certain things are good or bad for us, even if we would not want to have the good things or avoid the bad things'). Parfit evidently thinks the last of these the most plausible: cp. his (1997).

2. This is Parfit's generic name for theories that try to answer the question 'What makes someone's life go best?' I prefer to call such theories theories of the good; partly because of my views about the egoism/altruism contrast (3.3), and partly also because I reject the idea that there's any deep divorce between the prudential and the moral (1.4, 2.4).

3. Hume, *Treatise* 2.3.3. No doubt few people will own up to holding TIE in quite as bald a form as I give it here. Subtler versions are available, but I see none that avoids the present criticisms of TIE. For one close approach to TIE, take Rawls's precarious attempts to put off considering the 'full theory of the good' as long as possible, on the grounds that 'in justice as fairness the concept of right is prior to that of the good'. Rawls concedes that 'to establish [the principles of right] it is necessary to rely on some notion of goodness, for we need assumptions about the parties' motives in the original position'. However, 'since these assumptions must not jeopardise the prior place of the concept of right, the theory of the good used in arguing for the principles of justice is restricted to the bare essentials' (*Theory of Justice* p. 396). In other words Rawls wants to start his theory with some moves, based on his famous thought-experiment, of a purely proceduralist kind – some moves which ignore all questions about what the list of goods contains. But then he finds himself compelled to admit that pure proceduralism would make any theory of action for the agents behind the veil of ignorance simply impossible. Instead of taking this as a refutation of (pure) proceduralism, as we might expect, Rawls tries instead to run a distinction between thin and full theories of the good.

4. See Parfit (1997) for a rejection of Hume's instrumentalism about motivation. It is of course possible to reject instrumentalism and accept TIE; e.g by thinking that, although there are external reasons, it's a matter of brute and logically isolated contingency which sorts of reasons admit of being external.

5. Despite Parfit's frequent use of quantitative language to talk about goods (as just illustrated), my claim that he accepts AT needs qualification. *RP* Appendix I distinguishes 'Summative' from 'Global' theories of self-interest (p. 496). The Preference-Hedonist and Success theories about self-interest are *Summative* 'if they appeal to all of someone's desires, actual and hypothetical, about either his states of mind, or his life. In deciding which alternative would produce the greatest total net sum of desire-fulfilment, we assign some positive number to each desire that is fulfilled, and some negative number to each desire that is not fulfilled . . . The total net sum of desire-fulfilment is the sum of the positive numbers minus the negative numbers.' Such theories are *Global* if they appeal 'only to *global* rather than *local* desires or preferences', where a preference is global 'if it is about some part of one's life considered as a whole, or is about one's whole life' (p. 497). Parfit says: 'The *Global* versions of these theories I consider to be more plausible' (p. 497). His reason is that 'There are countless cases' – e.g. drug addiction, or the desires of someone who is repeatedly relieved of great pain – 'in which it is true both (1) that, if someone's life went in one of two ways, this would produce a greater sum total of local desire-fulfilment, but (2) that the other alternative is what he would globally prefer, *whichever* way his actual life went' (p. 498). Again (p. 499): 'Suppose that I could either have fifty years of life of an extremely high quality, or an indefinite number of years that are barely worth living . . . On the Summative Theories, if the second life was long enough, it would be better for me . . . If we merely add together whatever is good for me, some number of these extra days would produce [a greater] total sum. [But] it is likely that . . . I would globally prefer the first . . . the Global Theories would then imply that the first alternative gives me a better life.'

   Parfit's preference for the Global versions of these theories about self-interest over the Summative versions is a step away from AT. As such I welcome it. The only trouble is to see how can anyone working within a consequentialist framework like Parfit's can be entitled to take it. Parfit virtually admits this when he observes (pp. 498–9) that his choice of the Global over the Summative theory is a one-life analogue of his rejection, in *RP* Part IV, of the many-lives case which he calls the Repugnant Conclusion. Parfit calls that Conclusion 'hard to accept', '*intrinsically* repugnant' (p. 390). Yet the Repugnant Conclusion isn't one that Parfit can disprove. It follows from premises to which he is deeply committed. (For some of these premises v. *RP* pp. 381ff.) Likewise, Parfit wants to reject Summative theories too – but his own presuppositions seem to commit him to them. On his consequentialist premises, he ought to accept, both in one- and many-life cases, that a simple summing of goods always yields more overall good. Parfit admits that he has no good explanation of why it might not. Such an explanation is offered here – but it's a non-consequentialist explanation.

6. The notion of a rational sum is a loose one at this stage. There is no harm in this looseness so long as we are conscious of it.
7. A third distinction is between two sorts of causal power: *quantitative* and *conceptual*. For example, the kind of causal power which makes me, by reflex, withdraw my hand from a burning-hot stove is quite different from the kind evident in the effect on me of the information (if given to me soon enough) that 'The stove is burning hot'. The causal powers of goods (and evils), as such, seem to be conceptual, not quantitative. This suggestion raises interesting problems. My first distinction has the corollary that simple quantities are countable on the scale of real numbers, but units of meaning only on the scale of natural numbers. But mechanics suggests that the idea of *any* causal power is the idea of a simple quantity (thus of something measurable in real numbers); whereas the idea of a concept is the idea of a unit of meaning (thus of something measurable in natural numbers). How then can there be such a thing as conceptual causal power? The dilemma looming here is a choice between Cartesian interactionism and Humean inertness.
8. One notable ancestor of my two distinctions is Aristotle's distinction between the idea of mixture on the one hand, and his doctrine of substantial composition on the other – his view that, where a new substance S2 is formed, what it is formed from (S1) doesn't remain present in S2, or at any rate doesn't remain present as S1: 'As regards that which is compounded out of something so that the whole is one – not like a heap, however, but like a syllable, – the syllable is not its elements, ba is not the same as b and a, nor is flesh fire and earth; for when they are dissolved the wholes, i.e. the flesh and the syllable, no longer exist, but the elements of the syllable exist, and so do fire and earth. The syllable, then, is something – not only its elements (the vowel and the consonant) but also something else.' (*Metaphysics* Z, 1041b11 ff, (tr.) Ackrill) Cp. 4.4 on the compositeness of substances.
9. For one engaging attempt to dispel AT's disagreeable features, v. Griffin, *Well-Being* p. 36, who compares our estimations of the value of different goods to a cook's calculations about the ingredients of a stew – 'we can measure the quantities of wine and beef and onions separately, but we can only measure their value to the dish by considering them in various combinations'. Griffin's moral is that we shouldn't think in simply aggregative terms; but he qualifies this by adding that 'there is a strong sense' in which his account retains aggregation, because it retains the notion of trade-offs, 'judgements of the form: this loss of value is less than that gain'. Despite Griffin's pains to deny the existence of a super-value (cp. 1.2), such remarks do prompt the question 'Less *what*?'.
10. Cp. Dworkin's distinction 'between what we value incrementally – what we want more of, no matter how much we already have – and what we value only once it already exists' *(Life's Dominion* p. 73). Dworkin instances knowledge on the one side of this distinction, and human life on the other. Isn't Dworkin running two distinctions together here? (1) What we want more of no matter how much we already have vs. what we want more of only up to a point; (2) what we value only once it already exists vs. what we would like to exist. Examples: (1) knowledge (?) vs. shag-pile carpets; (2) the natural world as it actually is, or some particular species in it, vs. another baby for me and my wife, or a new 'City Forest'. Perhaps not even knowledge is something that (sane) people always want more of no matter how much they already have: cp. my reasons for preferring 'pursue' to 'maximise' in chapter 3, Note 9. Again, it's clearly false that human life is always something we value only once it already exists – as my 'another baby' case shows.
11. That e.g. hatred and love of red hair are inconsistent attitudes wouldn't be a good reason for the decision, unless you are already engaged in rational summing not arithmetical. Intentions to visit Venice and Padua could also be inconsistent; and anyway, it is quite possible to hold inconsistent attitudes.
12. Aristotle makes almost the same point when, in discussing his own 'doctrine of the mean' (*Nicomachean Ethics* II.6), he distinguishes 'the mean of the object' (*to meson tou pragmatos* – cp. quantitative summing) from 'the mean relative to us' (*to meson pros hemas* – cp. rational summing).
13. It is easy to imagine cases where the outcome can be improved by causing actions that are intentionally directed *away* from that outcome: as, e.g., if I am influencing a consistently inefficient or self-defeating agent. Again, given a consistently counter-suggestible agent I can cause actions to be intentionally directed towards some outcome by appearing to try to cause them to be intentionally directed away from that outcome – at least till the counter-suggestible agent catches on.

14. I pass over the point that presumably a position will have at least some plausibility if as many as forty-eight considerations can be assembled which others can be persuaded to see as counting in its favour.

15. I believe the phrase is Amartya Sen's, though I have never succeeded in tracing its origins in print. The term doesn't quite fit my case, because pleasure is only one of the goods in any decent taxonomy; but it's irresistible for all that.

16. Presumably on the basis of mere preference. One can allow the Pleasure Wizard to be capable of ordering goods from a menu, without supposing that anything rationally structures his orders, or that there is any more systematic structuring to his life behind his day-by-day ability to compose such orders. Such a structuring as his pickings out could hardly count as an adequate structure for a life anyway, even if it was maintained over longer periods than single days. The reasons why will become clear from my exposition of the Narrative Conception.

17. In the recent film *Groundhog Day*, Bill Murray plays a man who gets stuck in a cycle of recurrences of a single rather banal and frustrating day of his life. This being a Hollywood film, the cycle is in the end broken by Lurve – but as long as the recurrences persist, Bill Murray's life in the film is clearly a life 'which is going nowhere because any day in it is just like any other'. The Narrative Conception of the good can explain something important – and otherwise inexplicable, or hard to explain – about what's so bad about being trapped in this cycle. Bill Murray obviously isn't a Pleasure Wizard, however. The single day he keeps reliving doesn't include whatever he wants it to, and isn't a maximally pleasurable one. It remains a banal and frustrating day – frustrating partly because Bill Murray is aware that he is trapped in his cycle, which a Pleasure Wizard might not be (perhaps, by stipulation, wouldn't be).

18. For example, by Bernard Williams in 'The Makropoulos Case'. Williams's and others' assumption that Heaven could be boring faces the obvious and fatal objection that, if Heaven was boring, then it wouldn't be *Heaven*.

19. With my thought experiment of the Pleasure Wizard, designed to illustrate the claim that a structureless life can't be a good life, cp. John Broome's ingenious explorations of the issue whether, on a utilitarian account, it would matter if the 'unifying relations' which hold between different parts of a person's life had independent 'axiological significance': Broome, *Weighing Goods* chapter 11. His tentative conclusion is that it would matter a lot. Clearly, I agree.

20. A parallel (if less schematised and simplified) argument to this one will apply regarding each of the many goods in my taxonomy which naturally bring some sort of structuredness with them: e.g. friendship and achievement. Just as structuredness as one good among others on the list can't itself structure the relations between all the goods on the list, so the structuredness which such goods bring isn't enough on its own to ensure the overall coherence of the life itself. So the dilemma I describe here will apply with these goods too: either having them will lead the agent's life in the direction of structure in a way which will falsify TT, or else these goods will tend to create competing structures, which will mean that the agent's life is less good than it could be even though it contains lots and lots of every good in the taxonomy. This also falsifies TT.

21. It is, of course, irrelevant to this discussion that no one does live a life of full *eudaimonia*, nor come to that the life of an out-and-out Pleasure Wizard – though no doubt some of us are closer than others to those states. *Eudaimonia* is an ideal; my concern is just to describe it. To be coherent, an ideal life in the sense that interests me has only to be describable as to all its components, and possible in this sense: each component must be achievable on its own, and significantly large subsets of the total set of components of the good life have to be achievable together. The ideal life doesn't have to be *actual* in any of these ways.

22. Not because, being as good by one measure and better by the other, Structured's life so to speak Pareto-dominates Wizard's; but because the measure which makes Structured's life the better one is the correct measure.

23. Perhaps, as Aeschylus is made to point out in Aristophanes' play *The Frogs*, Oedipus doesn't have a happy life at all. (See Aristophanes, *Frogs* 1182–87, referring to Euripides' lost *Antigone*'s opening lines.)

24. Aristotle, *Nicomachean Ethics* 1100a10ff. With this piece of Greek folk wisdom, to which I shall return, it is interesting to compare the Urdu idiom reported by Kipling (in *Kim*, Chapter 5) whereby 'my father has lived' = 'my father has died'.

25. Objection: 'But you could turn a happy story into an unhappy story just by adding more and more horrors or disasters to it. Suppose someone made a gore-and-splatter film of *Winnie the Pooh*. The more gore, the less happy the story. Why can't it be as simple as that?' Because, first, to add gore to what was originally a relatively innocent story is itself to make a disturbing alteration to the story that is being told: not merely an alteration to its contents, but also to its form. These alterations are alterations of the *feel* and genre of the story. (They're also part of a quite commonplace way of making sinister things more sinister – namely by juxtaposing them with what is, prima facie, least sinister.) Second, because it wouldn't even be a coherent horror movie to add just one gore-and-splatter sequence to *Winnie the Pooh*. You'd have to add at least several, and situate them strategically too. This shows that even the (effective) use of gore is dictated by narrative, and not simply by quantitative, constraints – which disposes of the original objection.

26. With this distinction between the two ways in which an untimely death might be a bad thing, cp. Broome's distinction (*Weighing Goods* pp. 234–5) between the claims (A) that the unifying relations within a life have a merely causal axiological significance, and the claim (B) that they have an independent axiological significance. In his terms, my claim is that both claims are true – not merely (A), as a utilitarian can hold, but (B) too, as a utilitarian (as Broome rightly suspects) can't hold.

    Broome denies (B) on the grounds of his 'magic' thought experiment (loc. cit.): 'Take a person and imagine what it would be like if the unifying relations between her stages did not hold, but the good and bad of each stage remained the same . . .'. 'Broome goes on to argue that it would make no difference to the value of her life. But as he himself notes, 'Whether or not one takes [the view that this thought experiment is not only causally but also metaphysically impossible] will depend on one's theory of what the good or bad of stages consists in'. NCG is a theory of 'what the good or bad of stages consists in' which implies that Broome's thought experiment is metaphysically impossible. NCG denies something crucial concerning the good or bad of 'stages' of any particular life (as opposed to stages of human life in general: for this distinction see my discussion of the Fifth Corollary below). It denies that that sort of good or bad can be assessed at all, independently of the good or bad of the whole of the particular life, in any more than a rough and provisional, *ceteris paribus* way. So on NCG, to 'imagine what it would be like if the unifying relations between a person's stages did not hold', while trying to imagine at the same time that 'the good and bad of each stage remained the same', is to entertain an incoherent supposition. Cp. the Third and Fourth Corollaries.

27. This sort of case shows how it can make perfectly good sense to talk of outcomes' being better or worse than one another even outside a consequentialist framework. But every question like this question whether it's better for me to die at thirty-two or at 105 is patently a question that doesn't even make sense unless it is asked as a *ceteris paribus* question. And even if we could find a way of putting it that wasn't *ceteris paribus*, it would still need to be shown that the basis of rational action was provided by nothing but the answers to questions like that one. Hence such talk has no tendency to generate consequentialism.

28. I am not interested here in the historical accuracy of these remarks about Thales (or Aeschylus). Even if the story of Thales' drowning is, as some authorities think, a tasteless joke on the part of his enemies rather than on the part of fate, it's still interesting to reflect (1) on what makes this joke feasible (and tasteless), and (2) on the fact that such jokes sometimes really are played by fate.

29. I'm sorry my examples keep on being so severely classical. They just happened that way. Never mind.

30. Interestingly, it's harder to think of examples for the latter shape of life than it is for the former shape. (What does that say about what matters to us in assessing lives, and about which life stories stick in our minds?) The historical Mozart (as opposed to the one in Peter Shaffer's *Amadeus*) wasn't *very* rich or successful, even at his acme. Still, on the whole, his life discernibly moves from triumph (as infant prodigy) to disaster (as out-of-fashion invalid) – more clearly than that of, say, Elvis Presley, who obviously ended his life in a bad way, but on the other hand began it that way too.

31. Part of what's odd about Timeless, no doubt, is his attitude to temporal indexicals. Cp. Prior (1959). Indeed it's not merely a matter of oddness. We might wonder whether Timeless's attitude to time is even a coherent one for a creature that lives in time.

32. Cp. J. L. Mackie, *The Miracle of Theism*, pp. 150–6.

33. Despite my rude remarks about Dr Pangloss in connection with the Third Corollary, there presumably is a moral for theodicy in the Fourth Corollary.
34. Patently, there is no pretension to historical exactitude about Thales here either.
35. Cp. Slote, *Goods and Virtues*, chapter 1.
36. With this distinction between the general good and the good of an individual cp. my remarks in 2.5 on the explanatory links between 'X is a good' and 'X is a good for A'.

The unfinished or indeterminate character of our ideals and value structure is constitutive both of human freedom and, for finite creatures who face an indefinite or infinite range of contingencies with only finite powers of prediction and imagination . . . of practical rationality itself.
David Wiggins, 'Deliberation and practical reason', in *Needs, Values, Truth*

Persons both are . . . fragmented and seek not to be, seek personal coherence and integrity. The influence of conflicting values on persons is such that they are not always certain what or who they are, or what or who they want to be. However, it is distinctive of persons to reflect on their own values and attitudes, and thus to arrive at judgements about what they should do . . . In thus seeking coherence they are seeking their very identities as persons, seeking to determine themselves out of the various subsystems responsive and responsible to various conflicting interests and values; in deliberating about what to do they are trying to determine who they really are . . . Personal coherence is not something that is given by experience or observation, even at a single point in time; it's something that must be achieved. Moreover, it is fragile . . .
Susan Hurley, *Natural Reasons*, p. 262

6

———— • ————

NARRATIVE CONCEPTIONS EXAMINED

Examination of the Problem of Reconciliation, and of the question of the ethical importance of personhood, has in effect led us (via critique of the List Conception of the good) to three main conclusions, which can now be presented like this:

> **The Narrative Conception of the good** (NCG): Goods are important, not merely as items on a list, but also – and more centrally – as possible components of a good human life. A good human life is one that is coherently structured by its (generally successful) pursuit of those real human goods which are such that the story of the agent's pursuit of them is the story of the agent's life.
>
> **The Narrative Conception of rationality** (NCR): For non-maximising choice between an irreducible plurality of goods to be rational, that choice should be guided, within the limits of the Threefold Schema, by the Narrative Conception of the good.
>
> **The Narrative Conception of the person** (NCP): For the purposes of personal identity conceived in the strict logical sense, persons are *substances* – living individual human animals. This sense of 'person' grounds one crucial way, correlative to the Three-fold Schema, in which persons and their identities matter (4.4). But for the purposes of personal identity conceived as integrity, persons are *narratives* – continuing narratives, in the case of persons who are still alive. This sense of 'person' grounds a second crucial way, correlative to the Narrative Conception of Rationality, in which persons and their identities matter.

In this chapter I consider sets of objections to all three of NCP, NCG and NCR (6.1 to 6.3). My answer to the objections to NCR will then involve me in a discussion of free will (6.4) with which the argument of this book will conclude.

6.1   THREE OBJECTIONS TO THE NARRATIVE CONCEPTION OF THE
PERSON

1 What is the relation to each other of the two parts of the Two-part
View? If 'persons' are both individual human substances and also self-
constituting narratives, how are we to understand the relation to each
other of these two claims?

This objection shows no reason why persons *can't* be individual
human substances *and* self-constituting narratives. As for the relation
between the two senses of 'person', my claim is that any human is
first of all, and fundamentally, an individual biological substance; and
secondarily that, within the constraints of our animal nature (which
are, so to speak, practical analogues of the ethical constraints of the
Threefold Schema), there's room for us to construct our own life-
narratives. Thus the best key to the interrelations of the two senses of
'person' is given by the parallel that I've drawn between the relation
of those two senses and the relation of the two parts of the ethical
theory offered in this book.[1]

2 How can anyone be a 'self-constituting narrative'? Doesn't the idea
involve us in a kind of bootstrapping – in the absurdity that this view
makes the person the writer of the narrative *and* a character within it?

The answer to this is simply that there is nothing absurd about this
sort of bootstrapping. As much as with any other narrative you might
write, you *can* be the writer of your own life's narrative, *and* also its
main character. There's no impossibility here.

3 But isn't there an undesirability about it? Isn't it rather self-
absorbed or self-indulgent or self-conscious to view one's ethical life
as being about choices concerning how one's life is to go on?

To this the answer is, first, that this isn't all one's ethical life is
about. My thesis is that ethical decisions are made by narratively
rational reflection *only within* the constraints of the Threefold Schema;
even there it is of course possible that the narrative reflection that
occurs may not be very self-conscious, or even explicit at all. Second,
such choices aren't only about your own life, but about the lives of
others, too, and also about the corporate lives of supra-personal units
with which you identify (nations or societies, for instance). Hence
reflection on ethical narratives is neither a solitary pastime (on the
contrary, it's one of the constitutive activities of any real community)
nor a self-indulgent one (on the contrary, it entails a very demanding
and searching kind of honesty about yourself). Third, the objection
seems to suggest that we should prefer to reflection on ethical narratives

a kind of unthinking, 'soldiering-on' approach to ethics that just tries to do its best in the face of oncoming ethical problems as and when they arise. This may have a bracing air of Kantian stoicism and quietist self-denial to it. But like most forms of stoicism and quietism, it also suggests an unintelligent, cramped, and reactive view of life. Chess players who have no strategy except to play, one at a time, the best single moves given the current state of the board usually lose. Agents who think of nothing but how to respond to the most immediate ethical pressures which they presently find themselves under tend not to get on very well either.

6.2 EIGHT OBJECTIONS TO THE NARRATIVE CONCEPTION OF THE GOOD

1 NCG may look more plausible than LCG for moderately good or bad lives. It may even look plausible for what would on LCG be extremely good lives, like the Pleasure Wizard's. But what about the opposite extreme from the Pleasure Wizard?

Consider the life of the *Pure Martyr*, who never experiences anything but agonising pain, mental and physical. Considerations about structuredness of life, or the lack of it, are quite irrelevant to him. All that matters in his case is the dreadful pain. But if so, then NCG is false. If there can be Pure Martyrs, then it's false that a life's goodness or badness is always settled by its narrative structure. On the contrary, a Pure Martyr's life is a bad one simply because it is nothing but pain – and not for any other reason.

This objection wouldn't be decisive even if it held water. NCG doesn't need the strong claim which (1) has just foisted on it, that a life's goodness or badness is *always* settled by its narrative structure. NCG would still be defensible if it were true only in the vast majority of cases, though not in exceptional cases like the Pure Martyr.

But, in fact, NCG can sustain the strong claim, so coming out true even of Pure Martyrs. We shouldn't say that a Pure Martyr's life is a bad one simply because it is nothing but pain. Instead we should say that a Pure Martyr's life is a bad one because it is simply nothing but pain. That is, his life isn't bad just because of the awful suffering it involves. It is also bad because there isn't anything else in it – and there ought to be. The Pure Martyr's awful suffering precludes any possibility that anything else might go on in his life. In particular it precludes the possibility of a narrative shaping of that life. A human whose life is nothing but continual pain – one thinks of some of the more harrowing and extreme cases of neural tube defects in infants –

isn't deprived merely of pleasure, or even merely of the absence of pain. Someone in that dreadful situation is also deprived of any chance of shaping their own life. That deprivation isn't irrelevant to their plight. It is part of it. So the Pure Martyr is no counter-example to NCG.

2 The objector could respond to this by insisting that even the life of a Pure Martyr *can* have a narrative to it, if we choose to see it that way. For just any concatenation of events *can* count as a narrative, if that's what we want to count it as. So NCG is vacuous.

Objection (2) misses the point of NCG. No doubt there are, or could be, indefinitely many possible narratives for any life. From this no doubt it follows that some narrative is applicable to almost any series of events, in a life or outside it. Again, it may well be that, to some series of events, almost any narrative is applicable. None of this shows that just any narrative has an equally good claim to be a coherent narrative – as a good life needs to be. (And what is coherence? See 6.3.) Nor does it follow that just any narrative – or even just any narrative that includes all and only the events in my life – has an equally good claim to be *the* narrative of my life.

There are, sadly enough, some human lives of which it is reasonable to say that really they never even begin to be narratives. Consider a child who dies in her mother's womb in the third trimester of gestation. There is a perfectly good sense in which we can say that that child's life was not a narrative. It wasn't a narrative *for her*. She never had a chance to contribute to her own story. In a sense her life was a narrative for others: her mother felt her kick, her parents saw her on an ultrasound scan and buried her. But this is an attenuated sense of 'having a narrative'. These events are more part of the parents' life-stories than of the child's. Because then senses of having a narrative can be attenuated or not attenuated, there need be nothing wrong with NCG's claim that some narratives are more genuinely narratives than others. The main usefulness of objection (2) is really just that it prepares us to think about a third, and more interesting, objection (or clutch of objections) concerning lives that we agree do have narratives.

3 (a) What *does* make some narrative truly *the* narrative of a life? And (b) what's the difference between *the* narrative of a life and any other narrative? And (c) which viewpoint on these matters is authoritative?[2]

We should answer (b) by claiming that there always is such a difference. Or at least, there is up to that vaguely defined point beyond which indefinitely many further increases in the accuracy or detailedness of the narrative are still possible, but not strictly necessary for a basically proper understanding of how the life went (or is going). Hence (c) should be answered by saying that there's always some correct viewpoint (or set of viewpoints) on what is the narrative of any life. We shouldn't, however, accept the word 'authoritative' from the questioner. Unless we want to bring God's viewpoint into the question (which we aren't positively obliged to do), there's no need to suppose that the correct viewpoint on what is the narrative of any life is going to be the same viewpoint every time. In particular, even though the person living the life has a special relationship – that of subject – to the way in which the life-story develops, it remains true that the correct viewpoint on what the real shape of a life-story is isn't always the first-personal one. (Remember Teiresias and Oedipus; and how difficult it is to acquire genuine self-knowledge, or to face up to it once acquired. More on this in a moment.)

Objection 3(a) still demands an answer. We're now in a position to say this. What makes some narrative truly *the* narrative of a life is that it reflects the story of that life as it really happened (or has happened up to now). So the true narrative of a life (i) falsifies nothing in the life, and (ii) includes all that life's important events, projects and intentions, and all the important relations between them, as they were also included in the life (or: as they are also included in the life so far).

And how's that? If we say that the true narrative of the life reflects the true story of the life as it happened, how much more does this addition tell us? Not much. But not much more is needed. Pre-philosophically, ordinary humans who aren't either mentally deficient or under the age of five or so, already know how to assess the story of someone's life from (the right sorts of) data about it. Anyone who's capable of following a soap opera is capable of the sort of assessment I'm talking about.

Still, it is a matter of moral sensitivity, and not of technical skill, to perform this kind of assessment (of yourself or of others) *well*. There are no rules about how to 'read off' the shape of a life from facts about it which are any more than rules of thumb.[3] The difference between a happy life-narrative and an unhappy one depends on the degree and the form of participation of the lives in question in such goods as are found in the taxonomy of 2.2. But (5.2) it doesn't depend on those goods in any arithmetical way. Good lives aren't arithmetical sums of the goods in them, but rational. This means that the contribution to the goodness of the life of any particular good which is a component of that life is strictly unpredictable because strictly (arithmetically) uncomputable. The difference between a good human life and a bad one can often be gross and palpable. (Compare the obvious differences between the stories of Oedipus and the Yorkshire Ripper and those of, say, Albert Einstein or Mahatma Gandhi or David Hume.) But even when the difference is obvious, it isn't always obvious for the obvious reason (or what must seem the obvious reason to consequentialists), namely because of the relative *quantities* of goods and bads in the lives being compared.

Here's one reason why this is so. Of a life story still in progress, it is always and obviously true that our assessments of the shape of a life are massively defeasible. All sorts of reassessments may yet be made necessary by further developments in my life story. Thus, even though there can always be a right view of my life so far, there is no conclusively right view of the shape of a whole life until it is over.

As observed in discussing objection (2), one reason why the first-person viewpoint on the shape of a life isn't always authoritative is that it can often take others, such as Teiresias, to tell us the most important truths about ourselves, and about what we are up to whether we know it or not. Another reason is implicit in Solon's advice, already quoted from Aristotle, to 'Call no man happy until he is dead'. There may even be a sense in which a true understanding of the whole of someone's life isn't even possible from the first-person viewpoint. (On all this cp. 5.2.)

Oedipus' tale shows the tension between the way a life truly is, and the way it's seen from the first-person viewpoint by the person who's living the life. So admittedly the first-person viewpoint on the shape of a life isn't always the authoritative one. But still, we might say, it is always the operative one (where it is present at all). After all, the first-person viewpoint on the life is the viewpoint of the subject and agent who is present in that life. So mustn't it be privileged at least to some degree?

Surprisingly perhaps, the answer to this too is No.[4] It's possible to be dominated by others to the degree that one's own viewpoint on one's own life is *not* really the 'operative' viewpoint. As Marxists have often rightly insisted, it's even possible to be dominated in this sort of way without realising it. I can be loud in my praise of a relationship in which I stand, and yet also a victim of economic or sexual or personal oppression which is mediated through that relationship, and which works by making me see myself in quite misleading terms.[5]

By definition such things happen only or principally to those whose life stories aren't going very well. But even if my life story is going well, and even if I'm not being oppressed in the sort of way just described, my own viewpoint on my life won't always be either the privileged (that is, specially accurate) or the operative viewpoint. No doubt it's part of a good life, for an adult who isn't mentally subnormal, that their own viewpoint on their lives should *mostly* be specially accurate and pre-eminently the operative one. But we don't live alone, and not all others are enemies. Those who teach me about myself, and those who provide the perceptions of how my life is going which make me act, needn't be my oppressors. They can be my friends. If I am a child, they will certainly be my parents. For a child, others' viewpoints on how his life is going are usually the dominant ones for years and years. Not only does this not do him any harm; it's essential for his well-being. Even once he is an adult, such sources of teaching can obviously still be influential and beneficial. It's hard for any human life to go well without such sources and influences.

(So what's the difference, in such cases, between oppressive and friendly influences? That's a big question, but at least the following three points must be relevant. A friend's interest in how my life is going differs from an oppressor's – even an unconscious oppressor's – in being (1) concerned for the truth about me, as such: (2) concerned for my well-being, as such; and (3) fully respectful of the fact that I am an autonomous person with interests and concerns of my own.)

That's enough on the third objection. I move on to the fourth and fifth.

4 What if the narrative structure of someone's life is that of an appalling tragedy? Why should we think it better that someone's life should have *this* structure than no structure (and so no tragedy)?

5 Connectedly, what if someone is actually better off not seeing their life as a structured narrative?

Asking (4) 'Which is the better life: one with a sad structure or one with no structure?' is a bit like asking 'Which is the better bicycle: one with no front wheel or one with no back wheel?' A life lacks one element essential to its being a good life if it has no structure. It lacks another essential element if it has a sad or bad structure. That's all I need say – for the moment. (More on the tension between 'good life-narrative' and 'coherent life-narrative' in 6.3.)

The same remark deals with (5). We can imagine people who would, in some imaginable sense of the words (which? That may vary from case to case), be 'better off' if they had no grasp of the narrative of their own life, or even a false grasp. If Oedipus had lost his mind at the crucial point, he might have lived out the rest of his days a contented couch potato, and never realised his parricide and incest. So if we were happy to take only the subjective states of Oedipus' mind as constitutive of his happiness or well-being, it might actually be true that he would have been better off as a couch potato with large-scale delusions. But we don't in fact pay attention only to subjective states of mind in deciding whether or not someone is happy or flourishing or living well. So for 'better off' we should read 'less badly off'. Oedipus the contented couch potato is – perhaps – in some sense – less badly off than he would be if he realised the truth. But this doesn't show the falsity of my claim that narrative structure is of crucial ethical import-ance. It shows the truth of a corollary of that claim. This is that if someone is better off not seeing their life as a structure, or not seeing it as the structure it truly is, then they're pretty badly off.

6 Can't you be a consequentialist and accept NCG?

Objection (6)'s invitation is tempting. After all, my claim (5.2) that there are two ways of summing items, arithmetical and rational, still leaves the door open for any proponent of summing as a technique of ethical assessment who doesn't mind if the sort of summing relevant to ethical assessment turns out not to be the arithmetical sort.

But when we try to run this idea as part of a distinctively consequen-tialist theory, it seems not to work. The rational-summing consequentialist will presumably want a prescriptive moral theory which can be summarised in something like this injunction:

(RSC) Act so as to promote the greatest overall rational sum of goodness within the narrative of a life.

The first problem with RSC is that it misses the whole point about rational sums, which is that they're not properly speaking quantitative (even if they are properly speaking sums, which in a sense isn't true either). As we saw in 5.2, 'Socrates is mortal' is obtainable by one sort of rational summing from 'All men are mortal' and 'Socrates is a man'. It doesn't follow that 'Socrates is mortal' and 'Socrates is a man' stand in any of the three relations 'same', 'less', or 'more' to each other. (Same, less, or more *what?*) Because rational sums aren't quantitative, talk about the 'greatest overall rational sum of goodness within the narrative of a life' is just senseless. It confuses that which is genuinely quantitative with that which isn't. Perhaps it is always possible to make any actual life more flourishing. But you don't necessarily make a life more flourishing by adding more of anything.

Still, we can imagine this not cutting much ice with a really resolute consequentialist; one, for instance, who isn't in the habit of being put off by mere senselessness. After all, it is (as we saw above) possible to say that lives are more or less happy, or flourishing, according to their narratives. So, the argument may go, it must be possible to rank lives for happiness, or else for preferability-to-well-disposed-agents – at least roughly. So it must also be possible to make sense of RSC's injunction to us to aim for the top of the ranking.

This suggestion misses the point that there are still indefinitely many ways of aiming at the top of the ranking – indefinitely many lives which it would be superlatively good to live because each of them is an unimpaired instantiation of human happiness. So this sort of whole-life maximising tells us either to stop ranking when we get to the superlatively good lives; or else it tells us to rank every one even of the superlative lives. But in the former case, the 'maximising' account simply tells us to aim at *eudaimonia* – which is no more and no less than the present non-maximising account tells us. And in the latter case the 'maximising' account moves illicitly from the possibility of a ranking to the acceptability of a ranking (cp. 1.2 on Griffin). To say that we *can* stipulate a complete ranking of individuals' or societies' lives for happiness or preferability doesn't yet show that theoretical considerations say we *should*. Nor does it show that such a ranking has any real meaning. (I could provide the reader with a ranking of the months for blueness: 'May is certainly the most blue, and August is clearly the least blue, while September . . .'. Would the fact that this ranking is possible, or even the fact that I might be able to persuade the reader to agree to some such ranking, show automatically that such a ranking is either literally meaningful, or (even) a useful metaphor?)

If you're a pluralist about the value of the basic goods, and hence about the value of the lives into which those goods can be woven, then you accept that there are many different possible rankings of the dif-ferent goods (or lives) – but deny that it's meaningful or plausible to suppose that any ranking has any authority over the others. The pluralist claim is that different complete rankings of the basic goods are possible, but that it makes no sense to accept 'any of these possible rankings as *the* ranking of the goods. To make that move is to treat the results of some agents' choices as if they were the causes and justifications of those choices. (To put it another way, it is to read a canon of salience back from a decision into the antecedents of that decision: 6.4.) If pluralism about the good is true, it isn't clear that anything, except the sort of consideration adduced by the Narrative Conceptions, need be the cause or justification of choices between basic goods which aren't constrained by the Threefold Schema. Hence no ranking of goods or lives need be a cause or justification of any agent's choices.

7 If my generous pluralism about the good is true (1.2), then there are indefinitely many goods. But if so, then aren't there too many goods for us to be able to choose intelligently or rationally between them?

Objection (7) suggests a limitation on the possible intelligence or rationality of practical choice. But that suggestion as it stands has no bite. Compare Wiggins's remarks in the epigraph to this chapter: for finite beings like us, of course there are limitations on the possible intelligence or rationality of practical choice. This is no surprise. However galling it is to admit that we aren't infinitely practically wise, creatures like us can't attain even finite practical wisdom without facing up to it.

For (7) to have any teeth at all, it needs to claim that, given generous pluralism and NCG, there will be too many goods for us to be able to choose between them in a way that is even minimally practically intelligent. The suggestion would have to be that our practical choices are often determined by the accidental matter of which goods happen to come in our way, and therefore can't be even minimally rational. But even if we know what 'minimally' means here, still the argument seems a *non sequitur*. All that is suggested by the fact that we can't control which goods come our way and which don't is the possibility of 'moral luck' in respect of one's ethical environment and nurture; some connected Aristotelian thoughts about the importance of good education; and a maxim of cultural tolerance which says that other societies may well have had the moral luck to have goods or instantiations of goods come their way of which our society is ignorant. (Cp. the discussion of objectivism and subjectivism in 2.4.) These points are true and important. But none of them threatens NCG.

Not much more threateningly, it might also be argued on this sort of basis that practical choice, given generous pluralism, is bound to mean choice in a finite time from among an indefinitely large range of alternative goods. But why must this sort of choice be problematic for NCG? Perhaps the idea is that practical choice, given NCG, must mean that the agent has to look at each alternative good in turn, one at a time, one after the other, and starting as it were from nowhere in particular. Hence, it can be argued, the agent won't have much time to look at any one of the goods properly.

NCG has no need of the bizarre picture of choice between goods which this objection needs. For one thing, choice between goods can, according to NCG, perfectly well involve considering simultaneously a large number of goods. (Not an indefinitely large number, true: but again, this only shows that we're finite, not that we're helpless.) For another, the idea that we start any procedure of ethical choice 'from nowhere in particular' is as false as the assumption made by the Autodidact, in Sartre's *Nausea*, that we should begin to acquire knowledge from the beginning of the alphabet. Both with knowledge and with character, we start not from just anywhere, but from where we are. Where we are depends on our moral luck; but I've already pointed out that moral luck is just a fact of life, not an objection to NCG.

8 NCG claims to be an account of what 'the good life' is. Does that mean the happy life, or the virtuous life? Or is there just an equivocation in NCG?

None of the above. 'The good life', as I use it, isn't an equivocating phrase – although it is deliberately chosen for its fruitful ambiguity between happiness and virtue. Cp. my remarks on egoism in 2.3.

6.3 EIGHT OBJECTIONS TO THE NARRATIVE CONCEPTION OF RATIONALITY

First, recall our statement of the Narrative Conception of rationality:

> (NCR) For non-maximising choice between an irreducible plurality of goods to be rational, it is at least a necessary condition that that choice should be guided by the Narrative Conception of the good.

1 Let's begin by clarifying 'guided by'. How, according to NCR, is the Narrative Conception of the good supposed to 'guide' practical rationality?

NCG held that

> [NCG (part)] . . . A good human life is one that is coherently structured by its (generally successful) pursuit of those real goods which are such that the story of the agent's pursuit of them is the story of the agent's life.

The broad idea of conjoining NCR and NCG in this way, so that NCG 'guides' NCR, is that narrative practical rationality confronts problems of choice within the framework of the Threefold Schema by asking, either explicitly or implicitly, consciously or unconsciously, these two questions of any proposed option O:

(a) Does O constitute a good way, in general, for a human life-story to go on?

(b) Would O constitute a good addition to and continuation of my life-story in particular?

Now we can test out NCR's specification of what it is to engage in narrative practical rationality by raising some further objections to it.

2 The next objection says that NCR is false. For as a matter of fact, not all practical rationality is narrative. Some, for example, is instrumental.

That not all practical rationality is narrative, and that some is (for example) instrumental, is perfectly true, but no disproof of NCR. Distinguish strategic practical rationality (SPR) from tactical practical rationality (TPR). TPR may not always be narratively rational in its overt structure. Sometimes it will at least seem to display other forms of rationality, notably instrumental rationality. But in any reflective and well-structured life, instrumental rationality will only appear in our TPR, so to speak, by permission of our SPR. The SPR is never instrumentally but always narratively rational. It has to be, for the SPR isn't concerned with how to get the goods on some list, but with what the goods are, and with what is a good human life. These are questions on which instrumental rationality is by definition unable to pronounce. (Cp. 5.2 on TT and TIE.)

The use of instrumental rationality is just one of the gambits available to a more fundamental non-instrumental rationality. The usual mistake about instrumental rationality is to take it to be uniquely rational and (therefore) fundamental to the practical reasoning of a rational human being. Both claims are mistaken. As Onora O'Neill writes (*Constructions of Reason*, p. 73):

> The favoured empiricist conception of practical rationality [that is, instrumental rationality] is not merely not the only one: *it is never found in isolation*. The only beings who can reason instrumentally are free agents. The rational choosers of empiricist accounts are not special cases: they are missing cases. Either human beings must lack even instrumental capacities to reason – they must be *arbitria bruta* – or they must have more than instrumental capacities to reason.

3 A third objection says that NCR is not so much false as vacuous. This for two reasons.

First, as I've admitted in response to the third objection to NCP,

practical rationality might in practice be only implicitly or unconsciously narrative. It's no part of NCR to claim that people actually
confronted by choices between incommensurable but equally available
goods always explicitly or consciously ask themselves questions (a) and
(b), or are asked these questions by others. But this – it could be
argued – is no better than saying that we can imagine (a) and (b) being
asked about just any choice; which is hardly an interesting truth.

I reply that NCR's claim is, so to speak, a grammatical one. A good
grammar of English will describe simultaneously how English is spoken,
and also how it ought to be spoken. It is futile to offer a description
of how English should be spoken which totally ignores how it actually
is spoken; on the other hand, a description of how English actually is
spoken which doesn't even try to tell us which of the usages it records
are linguistically correct and which aren't is missing out the whole
point of a language – effective communication. In a similar way, what
NCR proposes is both a normative and a descriptive model of how
some sorts of human practical reasoning work. So all I need is the
claim that NCR provides us with a recognisable and suggestive way of
seeing (at least some of) our own decision-making processes. This is
the sense in which my thesis, if correct, isn't obviously or trivially but
interestingly correct. Because this is my target, I don't need the claim
that narrative rationality as I describe it is used by everyone, all the
time, explicitly and self-consciously. That would be a bad claim to get
committed to, anyway. Like most of the over-strong claims about the
transparency of practical rationality to practical reasoners that are
sometimes made, such a claim would be implausible and theoretically
unnecessary. Like at least some of those strong claims, such as those
made by crude utilitarians and criticised by subtler utilitarians along
lines first laid down by Sidgwick, it might be self-defeating too.

The second reason for accusing NCR of vacuity is the allegation
that practical rationality, as construed by NCR, could be used to justify
just about any practical decision. One can imagine people who could
find some reason to answer 'Yes' to both questions (a) and (b) no matter
what they were choosing. Therefore, NCR provides no substantive
criterion for practical choice. Therefore it is vacuous.

Well, first, this is a *non sequitur*. One might as well argue that because
(say) a telephone directory can be used for all sorts of bizarre purposes,
claims about 'what a telephone directory is for' must always be vacuous.
In one sense of the word 'use', *misuses* are uses too. It doesn't follow
that – in a tighter sense of the word 'use' – we cannot make sense of
a distinction between use and abuse.

Second, I repeat that NCR's questions (a) and (b) above aren't supposed to give the whole story about practical rationality anyway. NCR's two questions apply to those cases of practical decision not otherwise settled by the Threefold Schema (3.2).[6] The overall conception of rationality of which the NCR is part isn't vacuous at all, even if – as we'll see in discussing objection (8) below – there are deliberately set limits to its determinacy.

Returning to the first point – the use/misuse distinction – it might still be said that, if such a distinction applies to NCR, it isn't yet clear how. For (4) what makes a life-story good? And (5) what makes a life-story coherent? And (6) what is the right balance between goodness and coherence in a life-story, since these desiderata can plainly be set at odds? And (7) what is the right balance between considerations drawn from question (a), 'Does O constitute a good way, in general, for a human life-story to go on?' and those drawn from question (b), 'Would O constitute a good addition to and continuation of my life-story in particular?' And (8), even when all this has been explained, won't it still appear that NCR's account of practical rationality is necessarily too indeterminate to do any useful work?

4 What makes a life-story good has already been explained, by NCG. The answer on offer is that a life-story is good when it consists in a coherent narrative of (not usually frustrated) pursuit of and participation in, or at the least respecting of, the goods in some taxonomy like that of 2.2.

5 What makes a life-story coherent (as already explained) is the same sort of thing as that which makes any sort of story coherent. Narrative coherence is a function of the overall degree of rational connectedness between the items in the narrative. If that which the story contains isn't arbitrary, meaningless, and shapeless, but purposeful, structured, and directed towards the possibility of meaning, then we have a coherent story.

6 But suppose that some agent works with NCR as thus far expounded. He seeks to live a good life, but he also seeks to live a coherent life. To date, he has been a (reasonably contented and happy) waiter in a Paris café. But now he is confronted by an opportunity to throw away his tea-towel, elope with Simone de Beauvoir, and become an existentialist philosopher. The waiter thinks that to elope would be better from the point of view of living well. He also thinks that it wouldn't be better from the point of view of living coherently. So, because he sets a high value on coherent living, he chooses to miss his opportunity.

This example seems to drive a wedge between NCG and NCR. It could be said that there's nothing wrong with NCG, if NCG is the thesis that we appropriate and enjoy goods not just as items on a list, but by drawing or weaving them into our own continuing stories. By contrast there's something very odd indeed about NCR, if NCR is the thesis that an agent should reject any sort of good whatever if it isn't coherent with the way his story is going. Surely, it will be said, the mere fact that a good is a good is sufficient reason for choosing it. It doesn't have to be in the least coherent with my 'story so far' to count as choiceworthy. On the contrary: if my story so far is a story of stultified conformity, or of miserable oppression, or of atrocious wickedness, then the less coherently that story continues, the better.

Here recall my 'bicycle wheels' point, from the discussion of objection (4) to NCG. With mutated mutanda this carries straight over to objection (6) to NCR: an agent's practical rationality lacks one essential element if it doesn't aim at a structured life, and lacks another if it doesn't aim at a good life. So we shouldn't rest content with structured but miserable, or wicked, or even vaguely unsatisfactory, lives like the waiter's – any more than we should rest content with unstructured but very happy lives like the Pleasure Wizard's. Why not? Because such lives don't fully measure up to the demands of NCG's account of the good and NCR's account of practical rationality.

Because its account of practical rationality and the good includes two essential elements, so that practical rationality is fatally impaired if it fails to aim at both, the Narrative Conception needn't demand that the waiter should pass up his opportunity for a radically new start in life – no more than it need demand that the loyal[7] Nazi should pass up his opportunity, when it comes, to stop murdering Jews and join the Resistance instead.

Part of the reason for this is to do with the answer to objection (7), about finding the right balance between considerations drawn from the question about good human lives in general, and those drawn from the question about a good human life which is mine in particular (cp. 5.2). Often the agent should look beyond his own ethical circumstances, and think about what human ethical circumstances in general are like, and what opportunities they typically offer. *Always* looking beyond his own life might mean that he possessed an 'over-moralised self' (Susan Wolf, 'Moral Saints', 1982), or was envious of other lives or restless, or had an inadequate sense of his own (at least potential) distinctiveness. But *never* looking beyond his own life would display a pitiful lack of ethical imagination or ambition. No doubt that's what's wrong with Sartre's waiter: he doesn't even see how he is deprived of human possibilities, or how stunted the narrative he is living is, compared with how humans can live.

Now usually there's not much to say about how to distinguish between a virtue and its two flanking vices, except that it's a question of degree (of something) and a question of judgement (of some sort). So here. In looking for a way to square considerations drawn from the question about good human lives in general with those drawn from the question about a good human life which is mine in particular, we are looking for a balance. It follows that there's no *formula* that answers objection (7). Finding the desired balance is a matter of moral flair, not of computation. It has to be learned from examples, not from some Look-It-Up Book of Practical Wisdom.

So we have seen some of the things that NCR does *not* demand of agents under the heading of coherence. In particular we've seen that it doesn't demand that, if my life is coherently miserable, then I can't rationally make a fresh start in life. What NCR does demand under the heading of coherence is that, on pain of not counting as having a good life, you shouldn't go on and on making fresh starts. It is vitally important to be on the track of the good life. But it is also vital to ensure that you are on the track of the coherent life; for without coherence, there will be no good life. If your life isn't coherently structured at least after 'repentance', then even if your life is no longer miserable or wicked, it will fail to achieve the status of a good life. At best it will be, not evil, but (perhaps) chaotic.

As for the question 'Should an agent ever reject any good whatever just because it isn't coherent with the way his story is going?', actually the answer is Yes. Of course there are cases where an agent should reject a good just because it isn't coherent with the way his story is going. There are so many different goods (and instantiations thereof) to choose between that we can't always (or indeed ever) choose them all. That was the point of my arguments against pluralist maximalism at 3.1 to 3.2, and that is the point that poses the Problem of Reconciliation (2.6, 3.7), and the seventh objection to NCG above. Because an agent can't pursue every good at every node of choice, agents who are practically rational must have some rationally defensible means of preferring one good to another which have nothing to do with the goodness of those goods in themselves. The mere fact that a good is a good is always sufficient prima-facie reason for choosing it. But if pluralism about the good is true, there has to be more to ethical choice than the prima facie. If pluralism is true, we'll need more than that which the Threefold Schema describes – agent-neutral goods that give us agent-neutral reasons. Supervening on the agent-neutral goods which we recognise, we'll also need agent-relative goods which, within the area of moral space delimited by our agent-neutral reasons, give us agent-relative reasons. (Cp. 5.2.)

As we saw in 3.1 to 3.2 and 5.2, it's this point that makes genuine pluralism about the good so difficult to sustain for consequentialists, who typically define what are to count as 'rationally defensible means of choice between goods' exclusively in terms of the goodness of the relevant goods in themselves. This is usually supposed to be a key merit of consequentialism. In fact, it is an elephant trap, and the whole point of NCR is to escape it. NCR shows us that it can be practically rational to determine otherwise-undetermined choices between goods not on the basis of any intrinsic features possessed by the goods at stake, but on the relational basis of how those goods 'fit into my story so far' (either insofar as that story is distinctively mine, or else insofar as it can be taken as a typical human life: cp. the questions (a) and (b) that were identified above as part of the implementing of NCR). If practical rationality can be like this – can be narrative in its form – then practical rationality can avoid the consequentialist dilemma of 3.2. We needn't face a choice between describing practical choice as a matter of commensurability, or else as a matter of arbitrariness. To choose a good (a) because of its goodness and (b) because of its contribution to the continuing development of my life narrative is to choose neither arbitrarily, nor by means of commensurating arithmetic. In other words, if my answer to objections (6) and (7) to NCR is correct, then the Problem of Reconciliation is finally solved.

8 Is it, though? Do we yet have a totally determinate account of practical rationality?

Recall that an answer to the problem of how to choose between otherwise equally eligible basic goods is only part of an answer to the full Problem of Reconciliation. Part of the answer to that problem was provided by chapter 3's Threefold Schema, which eliminates choices that are not between 'otherwise equally eligible goods'. Once that part of the answer is provided, what's left to be answered is the question of how rational agents are to choose between those instantiations of goods present to them, choices of which aren't ruled out by anything in the Threefold Schema, without choosing either arbitrarily (which would be irrational), or else by means of commensurating arithmetic (which would be maximalist and anti-pluralist).

I've argued that the answer to this question is given by NCR. When the Threefold Schema does not otherwise direct us, we can choose between goods on the basis of their different contributions to the continuing development of our own, or the typical human, life narrative.

To say this much is, I suggest, to provide a full answer to the Problem of Reconciliation. But that doesn't mean that we have provided a totally determinate account of practical rationality. There are, anyway, limits to how determinate such an account ought to be.

Why? For one thing, because the ideal of a moral theory that yields a complete decision procedure for moral reasoning is an obviously false ideal.[8] The notion that which option we ought to take could be determined, on every occasion where it makes any difference, by the simple application of rules has no plausibility or attractiveness.[9]

A second reason why our account of practical rationality had better not be totally determinate is because, if it is, there will be no room for human freedom of action. An explanation of this remark will occupy us for another section: the last in the book.

6.4   FREEDOM OF THE WILL

(a) *Against ethical determinism*

If the correct account of practical rationality were totally determinate, there would be no freedom of the will; ethical determinism would be true. But ethical determinism is false.

Ethical determinism is the thesis, familiar from Plato's *Protagoras*, that 'No one willingly goes wrong' – the thesis that no one can deliberately choose anything that they regard as less than the best choice available. To do so must necessarily be to exhibit some sort of failure of rationality, or of knowledge, or of spontaneity – and so of voluntariness. How could any sane and sensible person who was aware that he could do either of two courses A and B, and aware that A was better than B, deliberately choose to do B rather than A?

Ethical determinism is entailed by any maximising account of practical rationality – that is, by any account of practical rationality that presupposes that no choice which wasn't a choice to maximise the good could be a rational and a voluntary choice. Maximising accounts presuppose some sort of commensurability between all instantiations of the good. So this appears to mean that ethical determinism is also entailed by any such account that presupposes the commensurability of all instantiations of the good. In other words, it looks very much as if ethical determinism may well be straightforwardly entailed by monism about the good itself.

If we accept monism about the good, there will be a strong pressure also to accept the thesis that all goods are commensurable. (What else but the fact that monism about the good supports commensurability is supposed to make monism about the good attractive?) But if we accept monism and commensurability, then maximisation beckons too. (How can we seriously resist the injunction always to do the best thing available, once we accept the view that except in evaluational ties, there always is an unambiguously best thing available?) Finally, if we accept monism and commensurability and maximisation, then ethical determinism looms. (If rational agents really accept the injunction always to do the best thing available, then if they do any voluntary action at all, what could possibly explain their not obeying that injunction except incapacity or ignorance or irrationality)?[10]

So if we want to avoid ethical determinism, we had better eschew monism about the good too. But even if this slippery slope towards ethical determinism is not ineluctable, still pluralism about the good can avoid it more easily than monism – by refusing to step on to it in the first place. For the pluralist, there is in most cases of ethical choice no question of even trying to maximise, to take 'the best option available' – still less of being inexorably driven towards maximising simply by one's understanding of the demands of rationality. For the pluralist, in most cases of tactical ethical choice which aren't emergencies, and in all cases of strategic ethical choice,[11] there *is* no unambiguously best option available (although it follows from the Threefold Schema that there will typically be many options that are ethically unavailable). For the pluralist, ethical choices are very often choices between incommensurable goods or instantiations of goods. It follows that, for the agent making such choices, the phrase 'best option available' very often has no antecedently given meaning. The items we are choosing between in such cases don't, as LCG supposes, come ready weighed for deliberation. On the contrary, it is our deliberation that gives those items their (subjective) weights. In Robert Nozick's words:

> The reasons do not come with previously given precisely specified weights; the decision process is not one of discovering such weights but of assigning them ... This process of weighting may focus narrowly, or[12] involve considering or deciding what sort of person one wants to be, what sort of life one wishes to lead ... The

weights of reasons are inchoate until the decision. (Robert Nozick, *Philosophical Explanations*, pp. 294, 296)

Hence the phrase 'best option available', even when meaningless in advance, can and often does acquire a (subjective) meaning, because of the deliberation (and therefore after, or at any rate not before, that deliberation). That is, it comes to mean 'the option that I preferred in my deliberation'. But as already pointed out, this weighting is a subjective one. If you and I are presented with the exclusive options 'novelist' and 'philosopher', we may go through just the same sort of ethical deliberation, both deliberate well, and nonetheless come out with different choices. It will then be true enough to say, if anyone sees any point in saying it, that you 'have a different preference-schedule' from me. But only a monist about the good need think that that difference between us, if combined with objectivism about the good, must yield the result that, unless the two goods in question are exactly equally valuable, it follows that one or other of us has made the wrong choice.

Notice, here, what I'm *not* saying; what I *am* saying; and what I haven't yet said, and still need to say.

What I'm not saying is that goods have *only* subjective value-weightings. That would be a reversion to the nihilism about the good rejected at 1.2. What I'm also not saying is that goods are really all equally (un)important or valuable or choiceworthy, and can be ranked even roughly only in a subjective fashion. On the contrary: it is not subjectively, but objectively, the case that some goods are necessarily more central, or more basic, than others to a decent human life.[13] (For example, health and friendship are more basic to the good life than art.) These ethical facts follow from facts about what it is to be living not just this or that particular human life, but any human life.

But because of the dependence of such claims about the different goods on the general (and not the specific) notion of the humanly good life (5.2), there is no fully determinate relation of such objective rankings of goods to the subjective rankings of different goods that may be set up within some particular humanly good life. That is, these objective rankings may be determinate enough to make claims like (R) clearly true:

(R) Other things being equal, a life that subjectively prioritises the good of collecting postage stamps is a less good life than a life that subjectively prioritises the good of saving others' lives (because less responsive to objective facts about which of these sorts of goods is more central).

But they are certainly not determinate enough to make it clear that the stamp collector's life, or the life of the backgammon player of 3.6, is simply a wrong way to live, because inadequately responsive to the objective facts about what is (a) good.

What I am saying, however, is that goods only subjectively have fully determinate value-weightings. That isn't nihilism about the good. It is just a corollary of the rejection of LCG and the adoption of NCG. NCG entails that it is only as goods are chosen, pursued and appropriated within lives that they come to be grasped fully by humans as goods, and so completely determinate in their value. It follows from this that the sense of value in which goods become completely determinate is a life-relative (or, as it is often called, an agent-relative) one. And that means a subjective one – in the precise sense of 'subjective': agent-relative reasons are real enough, but they aren't reasons for anyone to whom they are not relative.

What I haven't yet said, and still need to say, is something to spell out the exact connection between NCR and the claim that pluralism about the good can accommodate the rejection of ethical determinism in a way that monism about the good can't. The sight of an account of freedom that goes straight from determinism to indeterminism is a drearily familiar one. But haven't we just done that? If we reject ethical determinism, along with the monism about the good which got us into that determinism, haven't we just lost any chance of explaining how choice between goods could be anything other than arbitrary?

But this question is just an indirect way of putting the Problem of Reconciliation – which we now know how to answer. NCR answers that problem in its straightforward form; NCR also facilitates answers to other forms of the same problem, like this one. NCR doesn't only provide a way for choice between goods to be rational without being arithmetically rational as commensurating rationality is. It also provides a way for choice between goods to avoid indeterminacy without being (ethically) determined.

Recall here my rejection of the thesis that the objects of choice 'come ready weighed for deliberation'. Given such antecedently determined weightings, we are already well on the way to ethical determinism. With the List Conception of the good, there goes a List Conception of rationality. This turns out to be a Weighing and Measuring Conception; and the evidence is everywhere that that conception is a deterministic one. By contrast, in the absence of such antecedently determined weightings, there's no reason to think that there is always some way in which any rational deliberation is bound to come out.

NCR makes it possible for choice between goods to be rational without being arithmetically rational. NCR says that, even when there is no otherwise compelling reason for me to choose one way or the other between two incommensurable goods G1 and G2, it can still be rational for me to choose (say) G1 rather than G2, because that choice represents a continuation of my life's narrative which I think is more coherent, or makes my story more better, or for some other narrative-related reason. This means that such choices can have (or can lack) a rationality – narrative rationality – which has nothing to do with arithmetical summing or commensurability.

It also means that such choices are not indeterminate, but not (ethically) determined either. Further additions to the shape of any narrative are (as I called them above) rational additions, not arithmetical additions. One thing that this means is that there is usually no single determinate answer to the question 'How would it be best for the narrative to go next?' Sometimes there is, but more often there is room for creativity, spontaneity, and surprise in the way in which the narrative may be added to.

To see this, consider a simple, perhaps flippant, example: the party games where one has to continue a narrative, usually of a joky sort. The game called 'Consequences' is such a game. But it would be more interesting to think about a game with less predictability built into it than 'Consequences' has.[14] So suppose that six or so people sit round in a pub, each adding a sentence at a time to the story they are telling between them.

Further additions to this narrative, especially if they are made with any skill or aptitude, will always be inherently unpredictable in advance. To add to the narrative in an apt, interesting and funny way is to add to what is already salient[15] or striking about that narrative. But there is no canon of the salient or striking. Often what makes the next addition apt will be straightforward enough. It might be apt just because it simply says 'what happens next', for example, what happens to the survivors of the shipwreck when they finally land on the desert island, in the most obvious way given what the story already makes salient. But it might also be that what makes some addition apt is the way in which it brings to our attention something that wasn't salient in the sense that we were already aware of it as an element in the story – and yet something that also was salient, in the sense that it was, at least potentially, there for us to be aware of. Thanks to the new addition we notice that our narrative's protagonists have, so far, all been men; or that none of them has noticed the possibility of escaping their plight by simply looking in Yellow Pages to find out if there is an airport on their desert island; or that, all along, a pun on the word 'desert' has been lurking, which someone could have made use of in developing the narrative; or . . .

Narrative development is skilfully performed if it goes according to what is salient and striking. But narrative development is itself only partially constitutive, and continually reconstitutive, of what counts as salient or striking:

> Continually reconstitutive, because every new (rationally summed) addition to the story gives the totality of the narrative a shape it didn't quite have before – possibly a radically new shape;

> Only partially constitutive, because there are always further criteria of the salient and the striking which lie outside anything that is in the story.

These criteria may be to do with facts about how we tell any story – about how, for example, we can introduce into our desert island narrative elements of parody of other desert island narratives or themes (Gulliver, Robinson Crusoe, *The Lord of the Flies*, *The Tempest*, *Philoctetes*, *Desert Island Discs* . . .); or facts about the language in which we tell it, such as the availability of the pun; or very general facts about what makes any story a happy one, or a sad one, or a funny one (5.2); or facts about what humans need in the most general sense, in or out of the narrative; or . . .

Telling good stories is a skill that depends on our having an eye for saliences; but no formula can capture with anything like predictive certainty, in advance of the telling of the actual story, what will count as a salience in it and why; and, although there sometimes seems to be just one obvious way to go on, normally there isn't; and even when there seems to be just one way to go on, this appearance is almost always no more than a defeasible truth.

I hope the analogy between these thoughts about a possible pub game, and the present thesis about what it is like ethically to be living a human life, is now more or less obvious. In Alasdair MacIntyre's words:

> Man is in his actions and practice, as well as in his fictions, essentially a story-telling animal . . . The narratives which we live out have both an unpredictable and a partially teleological character. If the narrative of our individual and social lives is to continue intelligibly – and either type of narrative may lapse into

unintelligibility – it is always both the case that there are constraints on how the story can continue *and* that within those
constraints there are indefinitely many ways that it can continue.
(Alasdair MacIntyre, *After Virtue*, p. 216; first sentence transposed
from a later position)

My objective in propounding my three Narrative Conceptions is
the spelling-out of MacIntyre's slogan that humans are 'story-telling
animals', and of his claim that 'it is always both the case that there are
constraints on how the story can continue *and* that within those constraints there are indefinitely many ways that it can continue'. I'm
spelling out the slogan by arguing, as MacIntyre himself does, that our
manner of participation in the human good is essentially narrative.
This is NCG. I'm spelling out the claim about constraints and their
absence by arguing that human practical rationality is determinately
constrained insofar as it responds to the demands of the Threefold
Schema; but that it is free from determinate constraint, though not
indeterminate, insofar as that within the framework of those demands
it attempts by narrative rationality to construct a good but not uniquely
good way of carrying on the story of the life in question. This is NCR.

Now because such continuations are additions to a rational sum,
they are strictly non-additive and non-computable. So they aren't made
in a way that even could be subject to ethical determinism. Ethical
determinism claims that it is only by some sort of involuntary spasm,
some malfunction or other, that humans can ever choose any option
that isn't a maximising option. But if NCG and NCR are true, it can
be shown, not only that this claim is false, but also – what is perhaps
a more compelling point – that there is a coherent way of thinking
about ethical choice that doesn't commit us to ethical determinism. If
this is right, then one important component of a general deterministic
outlook, ethical determinism, can be refuted.

(b) *Against causal determinism*

Not that this point will much shake hardened determinists even if they
accept it. Most modern determinists base their faith in determinism
not on considerations about practical reason and ethics,[16] but on quasi-
scientific considerations about causation. Nonetheless, as a case study
of Mill could quickly show,[17] the conceptual (and historical) connections
between ethical and causal determinism are strong. It seems to be a
consequence of those connections that there is an argument against

causal determinism which runs in close parallel to the argument just given against ethical determinism. Before concluding this chapter, it is worthwhile briefly to consider this second way of arguing against determinism.

To see the analogy between ethical and causal determinism, reflect that, if my arguments for NCG are right, we can explain how ethical determinism may have got its grip on us[18] in the first place. In all likelihood, it got that grip by inciting interpreters of action to 'read back', from decisions once taken by practical rationality, to a canon of salience which allegedly must have predetermined them. This inference is mistaken for two reasons.

First, the attempt to find such a canon at work, in cases of practical rationality, involves a misunderstanding of what's going on in those cases. As pointed out above, practical rationality isn't, in any sense except a very general and unspecific one, predetermined by the imprecise but objective weights of the various goods, the items between which it chooses in constructing its own version of human flourishing. On the contrary, practical rationality *gives* those items their precise but subjective weights. Thus, the decisions taken by practical rationality can't have been predetermined by the alleged canon of salience. For it's only after those decisions are made that what is taken by the ethical determinist to be the canon of salience is even set up.

Second, and connectedly: in the sense required by ethical determinism, there is no such thing as a canon of salience anyway. There is no uniquely determinate set of rules for deciding what counts as salient, and how much salience it counts for, which can be extracted out of any case (or set of cases) of practical rationality, and then applied to all cases of practical rationality as a predictive device.

These two points about ethical determinism have close analogues about causal determinism. In older versions, such as Laplace's, that modern determinists might think naive, and also in modern versions, such as Honderich's,[19] causal determinism depends upon a crucial presupposition. The presupposition is that we can know all the facts.

Given knowledge of all the facts, plus covering laws of nature, it is not too hard to see how we could arrive at a vast deductive system of causal explanation and prediction of everything. This system – call it the Total System – would be deterministic in two senses. First, our knowledge of what, according to it, was going to happen would be certain, provided our knowledge of the facts and of the covering laws was certain. Second, the Total System would give a complete explanation. If that system of causal explanations were correct, there wouldn't be room for any other sorts of causes – for example, the other sort of causes that reasons are sometimes held to be.

There is no prospect of the Total System's ever being achieved, however. This isn't because it's hard to get hold of 'all the facts'. It's because, outside the special sciences, nothing *counts* as 'knowing all the facts' anyway.[20]

This is not an epistemological point but a logical one. The point is that, like good lives (4.3), facts are densely spaced. 'Between' any two facts somehow individuated, there is a third fact which would appear on some other method of individuating facts. Fatally for the Total System, there's no such thing as the right way to count facts. To devise any way of counting them is to engage in stipulation. Such a stipulation can be very fruitful. For example, it can give us physics or chemistry or anthropology or the science of probability. But these science-founding stipulations remain just that – stipulations. They are ways of regimenting the inherently unmanageable into a variety of forms.

Something that looks like a non-total determinism may well be true of any or each of these forms of science or inquiry, within its own domain. Nothing here precludes the possibility that any special science can be deterministic (though some apparently aren't, or needn't be: the social sciences, for example.)[21] What I am precluding is the possibility that any science can be both deterministic and not special, but quite general. If it is deterministic, it won't be completely general; and vice versa.

To see this, consider what follows if the point about the uncountability of facts is taken to oblige the proponent of the Total System's deterministic science of complete generality to retreat. Instead of the presupposition that we can know all the facts, he may now base his argument for the Total System on the presupposition that we can know all the *relevant* facts. Will that do the trick?

No. The reason why not brings us closer to the analogy with the refutation of ethical determinism. What makes any sort of fact relevant to any sort of causal explanation? The answer is: that it plays (or is liable to play) a role in that explanation. But how can we know for sure which facts are going to (be liable to) play any role in a causal explanation, until we already know what event it is that is going to have to be causally explained?

The proponent of the Total System needs to find a canon of relevance – a way of saying, in advance of attempts to explain any particular events, what sort of factors are going to be relevant to explaining those events; how relevant they will be; and why. This means, in effect, that the proponent of the Total System can't construct the Total System until he has constructed the Total System. His project is impossible to begin without begging the question against non-determinist views.

The notion of relevance plays something like the same role in these arguments for causal determinism as the notion of salience played in the previous argument for ethical determinism. Thus, two further points apply to causal determinism of this sort, which are analogous to those made about ethical determinism.

First: the hunt for a general canon of causal relevance, of the sort that could be used to individuate facts so as to provide explanations of events within a Total System, involves a misunderstanding of the general notion of causal explanation (that is, the notion of causal explanation which isn't peculiar to any special science). Quite generally, it isn't predetermined what is going to be relevant to causal explanation. Causal explanation is *ex post facto*. The standing temptation, to which the determinist happily succumbs, is for interpreters of events to 'read back', from results once brought about by causal processes, to a canon of causal relevance which allegedly must have predetermined those events. But it wasn't until those causal processes had already occurred that the alleged canon of causal relevance was even set up.[22]

Second: there's no such thing as a general canon of causal relevance anyway. There is no uniquely determinate set of rules for deciding what counts as causally relevant which can be extracted out of any case (or set of cases) of causal processes, and then applied to all cases of causal process as a predictive device.

This last point (call it T) isn't an anti-scientific point – although it is an anti-scientistic one, because it clearly and designedly implies that 'science' (better, the sciences) can't explain everything. If the reader thinks T is an anti-scientific point, I ask her to reread T, which I accept, and compare it with the following claim F, which I reject. (What distinguishes F from T is in bold type.)

> (F) There is **no set of rules whatever** for deciding what counts as causally relevant **within any special science** which can be extracted out of any case (or set of cases) of **those causal processes with which that science is concerned**, and then applied to all cases of **those causal processes with which that science is concerned** as a predictive device.

The claim F clearly is anti-scientific. But F is also, as its name suggests, false. If F were true, it would be totally impossible even to begin doing science: but obviously, it isn't. The point of T isn't to show, as F purports to show, that sub-total deterministic systems are unattainable, for – so far as I can see – in principle at least, they aren't. Instead T shows that a Total System of causal determinism is unattainable. If this is true, it seems a sufficient disproof of causal determinism.

Two possible objections to this argument against causal determinism are as follows. The first denies that, for Total System determinism to be true, we need any such thing as a general canon of causal relevance. All we need is the different special sciences' special canons of causal relevance. Between them, these will cover every case.

But what is the meaning of 'cover every case'? Does it mean 'have something to say about every case of causation'? Or does it mean 'have something indefeasibly correct to say about every case of causation'? Perhaps the special sciences can without abuse be applied to almost every case in which causal explanation is needed. It doesn't follow that what any science says about such a case will happen, with no defeasibility.

As we've already seen, not all the special sciences are deterministic anyway; but, that aside, consider a simple example of defeasibility. Chemical laws predict an enormous explosion in some test-tube at about half-past twelve. But fortunately, at ten-past, the laboratory technician's cat knocks over the test-tube and breaks it harmlessly. In one sense, the laws of chemistry covered this case all right; they produced a law-based and intelligibly reliable prediction about what would happen. In another sense, they didn't cover it at all. For, because a defeating condition – the cat – wandered on to the scene, that which the laws of chemistry said would happen, didn't happen. Our prediction was good chemistry; but it was a wrong prediction.

The laws of chemistry concern the objects of chemistry: test-tubes full of noxious steaming solutions and so forth. The laws of chemistry don't cover the behaviour of laboratory technicians' cats. But then they don't have to to be perfectly good laws *qua* laws of chemistry. This explains why it's no objection to those laws to point out that on this occasion that which the laws predicted didn't happen.

It also explains two other things, which are equally important. First, it explains why the laws of chemistry could only intelligibly be called 'deterministic' (as they sometimes are) if we performed a certain sort of abstraction from cases where non-chemical causes interfere with chemical ones. That is, it explains how chemistry could be a deterministic science and also admit the defeasibility of its laws. For the defeaters are always non-chemical defeaters, such as cats, or refused research grants, or cracks in test-tubes, or power cuts, or punctures on chemists' bicycles.

Second, therefore, our example also explains how chemistry's deterministic nature – if chemistry *is* deterministic, which I won't try to pronounce on – would be a consequence precisely of its limited scope. It is only by excluding laboratory technicians' cats, etc., from consideration that we can stipulate what are to count as chemical facts clearly enough to get going our strictly chemical predictions.

Can't we get round this, as the original objection suggested we should, by factoring in some information from other deterministic special sciences: Newtonian physics for the breaking of the test-tube; animal psychology, perhaps, for the behaviour of the cat? Possibly we can. (If, at any rate, animal psychology turns out to be another deterministic science. The statistical sample of the cats I have known makes this seem most unlikely to me.) But even if all the special sciences involved in the equation which we want to 'factor across' are deterministic, still we're not yet heading towards a Total System of determinism. For all that these moves will give us is the result that we can explain all the consequences of the coincidence of application of these different systems of explanation. What we can't yet explain is the coincidence of application itself.[23] To explain that, we need to find a method of factoring across the different forms of explanation that are relevant to the situation. What such a method would have to be is a canon of causal relevance. But, as I've already pointed out, no such method is available.[24]

The second objection to my argument says, more radically, that causal determinism doesn't need to be a Total System. It needs nothing more than the notion of a cause, in which the very notion of causal determinism is already inherent. This is mistaken. In the first place, even in this revised form causal determinism still needs the premiss that every event has a cause. It isn't immediately obvious that this premiss is bound to be true.[25] In the second place, even if every event does have a cause, there are plenty of notions of causation available to philosophers which aren't deterministic but indeterministic.[26]

Witness quantum physics for one such notion. Or, for another example which is both simpler and closer to home, witness whatever notion of causation it is that we have in mind when we consider repeated throws of a fair die. Whatever notion of causation is at work must entail the rejection, in some senses at least, of Hume's principle that 'from similar effects we infer similar causes' (*Dialogues Concerning Natural Religion*, II; cp. *Enquiry* VIII). That principle is essential to nearly all forms of determinism. But in a perfectly straightforward sense the case of the fair die disproves it by counter-example. The whole point of throwing the die is to generate indeterminacies. That is, it is to produce, from one and the same cause, effects that are (in the respect that interests us) dissimilar. A determinist who responds to this example that there is always *something* that determines the fall of the die is either merely begging the question, or else he's telling us that there is something wrong with the die. If there is something that determines how the die falls, then the die isn't a fair die.

'Indeterminism requires the idea of events which have no sufficient cause, though it does not require the idea of events which have no cause':[27] to see that X caused Y, and infer from this that X had to cause Y, is to fall back into the determinist's erroneous assumption that there is always, antecedently, a general canon of causal relevance.

There's no reason, then, to think that every cause is a deterministic cause. Given that fact, we have, in Dennett's phrase, all the 'elbow room' we need for agents to be causes. Moreover, on this argument we don't end up in the familiar predicament of a choice between determinism and randomness for the action-descriptions which will apply to free agents. Nothing in the argument against causal determinism has prevented us from holding that which was suggested by the argument against ethical determinism – the conclusion that agents can act quite rationally according to NCR, without in any sense acting either deterministically or arbitrarily.

So I conclude that causal determinism can't survive the objections to it. In any case, to command our rational acceptance, any determinism would have to do more than just survive. The counter-intuitive nature of the thesis[28] is such that, before it could be rational to accept determinism, it would have to be the only possible theory. But it isn't even one of the possible theories.

6.5 CONCLUSION

This book has now completed its project: to develop an ethical theory that explains the relation of the different goods to motivation and rationality. This project has led us to propose, first, a provisional taxonomy of goods, and second, the broad framework of the Threefold Schema: a framework that delineates three possible attitudes to any good, and provides that two of the three possible attitudes (promoting and respecting any good) are always *ceteris paribus* permissible, while the third (violating any good) is always unqualifiedly impermissible.

This left open at least part of the Problem of Reconciliation. It left open the question of how an agent might rationally be related to the different incommensurable goods in any more specific way than by not violating them, and by respecting or promoting some or other of them. I've proposed an answer to the Problem of Reconciliation which rests upon a re-examination of our conceptions of the self and of what matters in how we conceive of selves, of what it is to engage with a good, and of rationality. I've suggested that part of the ethical importance of persons derives from the status of persons, in one sense, as individual human substances; and that the other part of their ethical importance derives from the status of persons, in another sense, as self-constituting narratives that seek good lives that get their integrity through narrative rationality. In this chapter I've reviewed some important objections to the three Narrative Conceptions proposed in chapters 4 and 5; and, finally, I have added that the Narrative Conception has the very important capacity to show us how determinism can be false without this implying that there is nothing left for humans' actions to be but helplessly subject to indeterminism. It remains for me only to offer some brief conclusions.

NOTES

1. The question how these senses of 'person' interrelate may not be an objection to anything said here; but it is a crucial issue for human self-understanding. As Hamlet, and Pope, knew; compare this book's first epigraph, and *Essay on Man* II.2–18:

   > Placed on this isthmus of a middle state,
   > a being darkly wise and rudely great;
   > with too much knowledge for the Sceptic side,
   > with too much weakness for the Stoic's pride,
   > he hangs between; in doubt to act or rest,
   > in doubt to deem himself a God or beast,
   > in doubt his mind or body to prefer;
   > born but to die, and reasoning but to err;
   > alike in ignorance, his reason such
   > whether he thinks too little or too much:
   > chaos of thought and passion, all confused;
   > still by himself abused, or disabused;
   > created half to rise and half to fall;
   > great lord of all things, yet a prey to all;
   > sole judge of truth, in endless error hurled:
   > the glory, jest and riddle of the world.

2. And (d) isn't Sartre right, in *Nausea*, to make Roquentin say that there is no correct narrative for any life – that the very idea of a life-narrative is the idea of a falsification? No. For two points against Sartre's view v. MacIntyre, *After Virtue* chapter 15, pp. 214ff. (paperback edition). For a third, Sartre's thesis seems to trade on what we may call the Map Fallacy: the Nietzschean mistake of thinking that just to represent is to falsify. Because language itself is a form of representation, such a view can presumably avoid self-refutation only so long as no one tries to assert it.

3. Cp. Dancy, *Moral Reasons* p. 113: 'To justify one's choice is to give the reasons one sees for making it, and to give those reasons is just to lay out how one sees the situation, starting in the right place and going on to display the various salient features in the right way; to do this is to fill in the moral horizon. In giving those reasons one is not *arguing* for one's way of seeing the situation. One is rather appealing to others to see it . . . the way one sees it oneself, and the appeal consists in laying out that way as persuasively as one can. The persuasiveness here is the persuasivenesss of narrative: an internal coherence in the account which compels assent. We succeed in our aim when our story sounds right. Moral justification is therefore not subsumptive in nature, but narrative.' What Dancy wants to say about assessing moral states of affairs in general, I want to say about assessing one particular sort of moral state of affairs: those having to do with the shape of a life.

4. Notice two consequences. I say (1) that persons (in the present sense) are narratives, (2) that practical choices within the framework of the Threefold Schema are typically made on the basis of a first-personal understanding of one's own narrative, and (3) that one can be mistaken about the real shape or direction of one's own narrative. Usefully, these claims together entail (4) that I can misunderstand *who I am*, and (5) that I can make important practical choices on the basis of such misunderstandings.

5. This point has been well put in Dr Denise Meyerson's unpublished paper 'Real selves'.

6. Again, the fact that the Narrative Conceptions operate only within the constraints of the Threefold Schema ought to be enough to show why they don't entail that, for example, Hitler's life was a good life (because after all it contained lots of exciting and interesting narrative structure, as Martin Hollis has insisted to me). A life premissed like Hitler's on flagrant violations of multiple basic goods doesn't even satisfy the preconditions for participation in the human good. (Cp. Conclusions.)

7. Cp. Royce's account in *The Philosophy of Loyalty* of how the virtue of loyalty might play a role in securing and furthering narrative coherence; also MacIntyre's discussion of Jane Austen's virtue of 'constancy', *After Virtue* pp. 182ff; and Williams's notion of 'integrity', *Moral Luck* pp. 40–53. It is already clear from my discussion, and from this example of the loyal Nazi, that loyalty or constancy is no more automatically a good thing than coherence or courage is.

8. As Bernard Williams has pointed out (*Moral Luck*, p. x) – though I think he overdoes the point. See Conclusions.

9. The notion that *nothing* is determined by rules is equally unattractive. Cp. my remarks on Nussbaum in 3.4, Note 33.

10. For these three (not two) conditions on voluntary action, and for the whole problem of ethical determinism, see my (1995).

11. Cp. my discussion of Objection (2) to NCR.

12. Cp. my distinction between tactical and strategic practical rationality, made in discussing the second objection to NCR.

13. For a 'sensible subjectivism' cp. 3.5. For the point about different goods having different places in human life cp. 3.6.

14. 'Consequences' directs successive players on what kind of addition to make to the story: venue, which two people met there, at what time, what each said, what the consequence was, and so on. These constraints lessen the analogy with narrative rationality. The party game I describe has much less limiting constraints – though like narrative rationality, it does have *some* constraints.

15. I assume the talk of 'salience' originates in the work of Gareth Evans and John McDowell: v. e.g. Evans, *Varieties of Reference* §9.2. For the ethical application of the notion cp. Dancy, *Moral Reasons* pp. 111ff. Dancy thinks that what determines moral decision is the seeing of saliences. I agree, but want to add (1) more detail, along lines suggested by NCG and NCR, about what sorts of things are salient and why; and (2) a rider referring us back to the Threefold Schema, which I think specifies the first and most important way of seeing saliences. Presumably Dancy will reject at least addition (2), because he will say (rightly) that it is 'generalist'.

16. Ethical determinism may be 'part of a general deterministic outlook'; but it doesn't entail causal determinism nor vice versa. It could be that everything I do is either fixed by a maximising conception of the (my) good or irrational, and that there was causal indeterminacy. Conversely it could be that there was more to practical rationality than maximising, and that causal determinism was true.

17. See, e.g., Mill's *System of Logic* Bk.VI, ch. 12.
18. In my use of 'us' here, and in the error theory I offer for ethical determinism, I am referring to moderns. I'm not committed to the claim that it was these sorts of moves that led Socrates into ethical determinism – although that claim has its attractions.
19. V. Ted Honderich, 'One Determinism', in Honderich and Burnyeat (eds), *Philosophy as it is*.
20. For this point cp. Cartwright (1994): 'There is a tendency to think that all facts must belong to one grand scheme, and moreover that this is a scheme in which the facts in the first category have a special and privileged status. The others must be made to conform to them. This is the kind of fundamentalist doctrine that I think we must resist. Biologists are already doing so on behalf of their own special items of knowledge. Reductionism has long been out of fashion in biology and now emergentism is once again a real possibility.'
21. It can be argued that even Newtonian mechanics – historically the holy of holies of deterministic science – can't be kept free from indeterminacies, even by stipulation. V. Laraudogoitia (1996).
22. Compare Anscombe, 'Causality and determination', p. 73 in Sosa (ed.), *Causation and Conditionals*: 'When we call a result determined we are implicitly relating it to an antecedent range of possibilities and saying that all except one of these are disallowed. What disallows them is not the result itself but something antecedent to the result . . . Then "each stage of the ball's path is determined" must mean "Upon any impact, there is only one path possible for the ball up to the next impact" . . . But what reason could one have for believing this, if one does not believe in some system of which it is a consequence?'
23. Cp. David Owens, *Causes and Coincidences*, for an argument that coincidences have no causes. (As Richard Sorabji has argued in his *Necessity Cause and Blame*, chapter 1, Aristotle maintains the same thesis in *Metaphysics* VI.3.)
24. For this result, 'the incommensurability of the special sciences' as we might call it, and its relation to the refutation of causal determinism, cp. an earlier result (1.2), the incommensurability of the goods, and the relation of that result to the refutation of ethical determinism which has just been offered.
25. As Hume (sometimes) argued, though perhaps not for the reasons he thought. V. *Treatise* 1.3.2, and Anscombe, 'Whatever has a beginning of existence must have a cause', in her *From Parmenides to Wittgenstein*.
26. For more on these see Mellor (1988).
27. David Sanford, 'Causation', in Sosa and Kim (eds), *Blackwell Companion to Metaphysics*.
28. On determinism's counter-intuitiveness v. Denyer, *Time, Action and Necessity* p. 60: 'Determinism entails the view that every detail of the future is fixed and necessary. This in turn entails that no detail of the future is within the scope of deliberation. Determinism therefore entails fatalism. Now whatever people may have thought about the compatibility of free will with determinism, no one to my knowledge has ever supposed that free will is compatible with fatalism . . .'

CONCLUSIONS

It seems to have been of crucial importance to the shape of the theory that I have developed in this book that I built in the deontological constraints expressed in the Threefold Schema <u>before</u> I let in the Narrative Conception. What would have happened if I had done this the other way round – or left out the Threefold Schema altogether? Wouldn't I have then got either a moderately, or else a strongly, consequentialist theory?

In neither case would I have got any sort of coherent moral theory at all – still less a consequentialist theory. As argued in 3.1 to 3.3, if pluralism about the good is correct, then there simply can't be a coherent moral theory without (something like) the Threefold Schema. Without the Schema, or something close to it, we just have no framework whatever for pluralist practical rationality. To see this, suppose that I am choosing between a genuine plurality of goods but don't have either of the notions central to and distinctive of the Threefold Schema – the notions of supererogation and of a material moral absolute. Without those two notions, I am presumably left only with the notion of maximisation or pursuit. But what on earth am I to do with that notion on its own? How can I ever be justified in the belief that anything I choose is rational – when what makes it rational in one way (that is, its maximal pursuit of some one of the plurality of goods) is also precisely what makes it irrational in some other way (that is, its failure to be a maximal pursuit of some other of the plurality of goods)?

Consequently my decision to put in the Threefold Schema first wasn't just dictated by a brute urge not to be a consequentialist (however strong *that* might be). It was dictated by what I take to be demands of logic and consistency. If we are pluralists about the good, it simply doesn't make sense to try reversing the order in which we build in a schema of constraints and permissions, and the notion of character-constituting choice within the guidelines of that schema. That reversal can make sense only if we're monists – or nihilists – about the good.[1]

What about the more radical idea of not just reversing the order in which the notions of schema and pursuit go into our theory, but eschewing the deontological framework altogether, and working only with a conception of narrative choice between goods? That idea might perhaps be pursued by consistent monists, if there were any. But what about the idea that any moral theorist who is also a pluralist could do without the deontological framework altogether?

That idea seems to lead to absurdity. Not only would such a theory, ridiculously, make every choice a tragic choice. Also, it could have nothing to say about the difference between a practically rational life and a practically irrational one, except that the practically rational life had some sort of narrative shape. But that's not enough. Without the Threefold Schema, *any* sort of narrative shape could constitute a practically rational life – including Hitler's or Lucrezia Borgia's life, or the life of some unhappy Camusian who wants only to commit suicide. Moreover, on that picture (plus pluralism) any sort of narrative shape could turn out to be just as good as any other. For every sort of narrative shape is, for all we can show in the absence of the Threefold Schema, equally open to the accusation that it rides roughshod over some good or other.

In short, choices about how to live are either informed by something like the Threefold Schema (and also by something like the Narrative Conception of Rationality, because the Threefold Schema is no more capable of giving us a complete moral theory on its own than is the Narrative Conception), or else such choices are simply arbitrary assertions of will. My conviction that the latter conclusion is an absurd one hasn't been lessened by anything I have read by Nietzsche or his followers. All Nietzschean absurdism proves is the imperative necessity of devising a better account than Nietzsche's of practical choice – and of how to live in general – if at all possible. That it is possible is precisely the point of my theory: if my theory works.

But does it work? Indeed can it, if we may reasonably doubt whether any moral theory works, or could work?

One famous source of general scepticism about moral theory is the writings of Bernard Williams. So, for example, in the Preface to *Moral Luck* (p. x), Williams infers the impossibility of any moral theory from the impossibility of 'a philosophical structure which, together with some degree of empirical fact, will yield a decision procedure for moral reasoning'.

These remarks are ambiguous. If Williams's 'decision procedure for moral reasoning' means '*complete* decision procedure', then his claim is true, but not very interesting, because only extreme utilitarians are after this sort of completeness anyway. (Cp. my reservations about giving an exhaustive account of what practical rationality demands: 6.3 to 6.4.) Whereas, if Williams's 'decision procedure for moral reasoning' means '*any* decision procedure', then his claim is interesting, but plainly false. There's no reason to doubt the obvious intuition that 'the simple application of rules' can at least sometimes give us a decision procedure for moral questions (for example rules about murder or theft, in straightforward cases of murder or theft) – even if it is equally obvious that it doesn't always. Just this intuition is, I hope, captured by the mixture of determinacy and indeterminacy evident in my own attempt at a moral theory.

A second source of doubt about the very idea of moral theory, which Williams pursues in a number of places, is one which he also raises in the same passage in *Moral Luck* when he writes that the undertaking of producing a moral theory

> has never succeeded, and could not succeed, in answering the question, *by what right* does it legislate to the moral sentiments? The abstract and schematic conceptions of 'rationality' which are usually deployed in this connection do not even look as though they were relevant to the question – so soon, at least, as morality is seen as something whose real existence must consist in personal experience and social institutions, not in sets of propositions.

Williams's question by what right morality legislates to the moral sentiments remains – as he himself almost says – a pressing one only so long as moral philosophy doesn't have a decent account of practical rationality. For example, suppose we are faced with conclusions to moral arguments such as Singer's or Tooley's conclusions about the rights of the senile, disabled, newly born, or unborn.[2] It's entirely pertinent to ask of Singer and Tooley two variants of Williams's question: 'If this really is where moral philosophy leads us, what makes you theorists think that people should prefer to jettison their moral intuitions in favour of your moral philosophy rather than the other way round? If moral philosophy means, and must mean, *your* sort of moral philosophy, then the non-expert verdict is going to be that your sort of moral philosophy makes us morally worse. What sort of evidence can you give us that the non-expert verdict is not simply correct?'

The only answer to this challenge that seems possible for Singer and

Tooley is for them to insist that their conclusions are dictated to us by Reason with a capital R. But that response, as Williams would point out, deals only with the first part of the challenge. We can still reply 'Then so much the worse for Reason'. We can still argue that if this is what we are brought to by 'following the argument wherever it leads', then following the argument wherever it leads is ethically irresponsible.

This gives us Williams's question by what right any moral theory – even a logically compelling one – could legislate to the moral sentiments. It will be appropriate to react to this challenge by protesting that a position like Williams's is defeatist or irrationalist or prone to arbitrariness only if it can be shown that moral theory can do better than Singer and Tooley have done. If all that can be offered by moral theory, or by any attempt to give practical rationality coherence, is their sort of turpitude, then so much the worse for theory and coherence.

This book is the evidence that I do believe that moral theory can do better than Singer and Tooley. In particular, I hope I have shown that moral philosophy can have, what Singer and Tooley as consequentialists necessarily do not have, a decent account of practical rationality. If a moral theory is to get a grip, the roots of its account of practical rationality must run deep into what Williams calls our moral sentiments – our ordinary beliefs about what is valuable or worth pursuing and why. One of my central concerns throughout this book has been to register this point and find ways of responding to it.

Whether my account is enough to satisfy Williams's wish for a credible account of practical rationality, I don't know. (My account does at any rate satisfy, or try to satisfy, another desideratum on moral or ethical thinking which Williams mentions in *ELP* (p. 117) – namely that it should call on as rich a variety as possible of ethical resources.) But if something like the present account of practical rationality is credible, then moral theory based on such an account of practical rationality can be credible. And if moral theory can be credible in that way, then it can – at least sometimes – have the authority that Singer and Tooley want (but fail) to give it: the authority that enables it to outweigh at least some of our original moral sentiments. For our choices will then be between admittedly confused pre-theoretical moral sentiments, and a theory based on those sentiments which makes sufficiently good sense of enough of them to have the authority even to reform them in some cases. And presumably even Williams would agree that our pre-theoretical confusion of moral sentiments isn't preferable to the possession of a *good* moral theory, if there is one: one that enables us to resolve the confusion of our sentiments in convincing ways which make for moral progress and enlightenment. Just such a theory is what I have been after in this book. How far, if at all, has my pursuit of such a theory succeeded? It's time for the reader to decide.

NOTES

1. It doesn't always make sense even on that condition. Utilitarians often claim that a strategy of maximising whatever it is we are supposed to maximise can dictate non-maximising tactics of a shape not unlike some schema of constraints and permissions. But there are familiar doubts about whether, if the non-maximising tactics truly follow from nothing but the maximising strategy, they can really be non-maximising tactics at all.
2. 'In thinking about this matter we should put aside feelings based on the small, helpless and (sometimes) cute appearance of human infants . . . If we can put aside these emotionally moving *but strictly irrelevant* aspects of the killing of a baby we can see that the grounds for not killing persons do not apply to newborn infants' (Singer, *Practical Ethics* pp. 170–1: emphasis added).

BIBLIOGRAPHY

Ackrill, J. L. (1980) A 'Aristotle on *eudaimonia*', in A. O. Rorty, (ed.) *Essays on Aristotle's Ethics*, London, University of California Press.

Ackrill, J. L. (1987) *A New Aristotle Reader*, Oxford, Clarendon Press.

Aitchison, Jean, *The Reith Lectures 1996* (BBC Radio 4).

Anscombe, G. E. M. (1957) *Intention*, Oxford, Blackwell.

Anscombe, G. E. M. (1958) 'Modern Moral Philosophy', *Philosophy*.

Anscombe, G. E. M. (1975) 'Causation and Determinism', in Sosa, (ed.) *Causation and Conditionals*, Oxford, OUP.

Anscombe, G. E. M. (1981) 'Whatever has a beginning of existence must have a cause', in her *From Parmenides to Wittgenstein*, Minneapolis, University of Minnesota Press.

Aquinas, St Thomas (1951) *Summa Theologiae*, Madrid, Biblioteca de Autores Cristianos.

Aristophanes (1983) *The Frogs*, (ed.) K. Dover, Oxford, Clarendon Press.

Aristotle (1884) *Eudemian Ethics*, (ed.) F. Susemihl, Leipzig, Teubner Library.

Aristotle (1894) *Nicomachean Ethics*, (ed.) Ingram Bywater, Oxford, Clarendon Press.

Aristotle (1924) *Metaphysics*, (ed.) W. D. Ross, Oxford, Clarendon Press.

Aristotle (1956) *de Anima*, (ed.) W. D. Ross, Oxford, Clarendon Press.

Aristotle (1957) *Politics*, (ed.) W. D. Ross, Oxford, Clarendon Press.

Bentham, Jeremy, Selections from *Introduction to the Principles of Morals and Legislation*, in Mary Warnock (1962) *Utilitarianism*, London, Fontana.

Blackburn, Simon, (1984) *Spreading the Word*, Oxford, Clarendon Press.

Broome, John, (1991) *Weighing Goods*, Oxford, Blackwell.

Byatt, A. S. (1990) *Possession: a Romance*, London, Vintage.

Carroll, Lewis (1895) 'What the Tortoise said to Achilles', *Mind*.

Cartwright, Nancy (1994) 'Fundamentalism versus the Patchwork of Laws', *Proceedings of the Aristotelian Society*.

Chappell, T. D. J. (1995) *Aristotle and Augustine on Freedom of Action*, London, Macmillan.

Chappell, T. D. J. (1996a) *The Plato Reader*, Edinburgh, Edinburgh University Press.

Chappell, T. D. J. (1996b) 'Why is faith a virtue?', *Religious Studies*.

Chappell, T. D. J. (1996c) 'In defence of speciesism' in Oderberg, D. and Laing, J. (eds) *Human Lives: critical essays on consequentialist bioethics*, Cambridge, Cambridge University Press 1997.

Chappell, T. D. J. (1997) 'How to base ethics on biology', in Chappell, (ed.) *Philosophy and the Environment*, Edinburgh, Edinburgh University Press.

Chappell, T. D. J. (1998) 'The Incompleat Projectivist', *The Philosophical Quarterly*.

Churchland, Paul (1995) *The Engine of Reason, The Seat of the Soul*, Cambridge, MA, Bradford Books.

Cottingham, John (1996) 'Medicine, Virtues, and Consequences', in Oderberg and Laing, (eds) *Human Lives*.

Crisp, Roger (1996) 'The Dualism of Practical Reason', *Proceedings of the Aristotelian Society*.

Dancy, Jonathan (1993) *Moral Reasons*, Oxford, Blackwell.

Davidson, Donald (1980) 'How is weakness of the will possible?', in Davidson, *Essays on Actions and Events*, Oxford, Oxford University Press.

Denyer, Nicholas (1981) *Time, Action and Necessity*, London, Duckworth.

Descartes, René, *Meditations*, in Cottingham J., Stoothoff R. and Murdoch D., (eds) *The Philosophical Writings of Descartes*, Vol. II, Cambridge, Cambridge University Press, 1985.

Dworkin, Ronald (1993) *Life's Dominion*, London, Harper Collins.

Evans, Gareth (1982) *The Varieties of Reference*, Oxford, Oxford University Press.

Finnis, J. M. (1980) *Natural Law and Natural Rights*, Oxford, Oxford University Press.

Finnis, J. M. (1983) *Fundamentals of Ethics*, Oxford, Oxford University Press.

Finnis, J. M. (1992) *Moral Absolutes*. Washington, Catholic University Press of America.

Foot, Philippa, (ed.) (1967) *Theories of Ethics*, Oxford, Oxford University Press.

Forbes, Graeme (1985) *The Metaphysics of Modality*, Oxford, Clarendon Press.

Frankfurt, Harry (1988) *The Importance of What We Care About*, Cambridge, Cambridge University Press.

Gauthier, David (1986) *Morals by Agreement*, Oxford, Clarendon Press.

Glover, Jonathan (1977) *Causing Deaths and Saving Lives*, London, Penguin.

Griffin, James (1986) *Well-Being*, Oxford, Clarendon Press.

Grisez, Germain (1983), *Christian Moral Principles*, Chicago, Franciscan Herald Press.

Grisez, Germain (1993) *Living a Christian Life*, Quincy, IL, Franciscan Press.

Grisez, Germain, Boyle, Joseph, and Finnis, John (1987) 'Practical Principles, Moral Truth, and Ultimate Ends', *American Journal of Jurisprudence*.

Harris, John (1985) *The Value of Life*, London, Routledge.

Hollis, J. M. (1977) *Models of Man*, Cambridge, Cambridge University Press.

Honderich, Ted (1977) 'One Determinism', in Honderich and Burnyeat, (eds) *Philosophy As It Is*, London, Penguin.

Hughes, Christopher (1997) 'Same-Kind Coincidence and the Ship of Theseus', *Mind*.

Hume, David (1975) *Enquiries concerning Human Understanding and concerning the Principles of Morals*, (ed.) P. Nidditch, Oxford, Clarendon Press.

Hume, David (1989) *Dialogues concerning Natural Religion*, (ed.) Martin Bell, London, Penguin.

Hume, David (1985) *A Treatise of Human Nature*, (ed.) E. Mossner, London, Penguin.

Hurley, Susan (1989) *Natural Reasons*, Oxford, Oxford University Press.

Irwin, Terence (1987) *Classical Thought*, Oxford, Oxford University Press.

Kagan, Shelly (1989) *The Limits of Morality*, Oxford, Clarendon Press.

Kant, Immanuel (1956) *Critique of Practical Reason*, (ed.) Lewis White Beck, London, Macmillan.

Kipling, Rudyard (1901) *Kim*, London, Penguin.

Kripke, Saul (1980) *Naming and Necessity*, Oxford, Blackwell.

Laraudogoitia, J. P. (1995) 'A Beautiful Supertask', *Mind*.

Lewis, C. S. (1938) *Out of the Silent Planet*, London, Pan.

Locke, John (1979) *Essay concerning Human Understanding*, (ed.) P. Nidditch, Oxford, Clarendon Press.

Loux, Michael (1978) *Substance and Attribute*, Dordrecht, Reidel.

Luscombe, D. (1982) 'Natural morality and natural law', in A. Kenny, N. Kretzmann, and J. Pinborg, (eds) *Cambridge History of Later Mediaeval Philosophy*, Cambridge, Cambridge University Press.

MacIntyre, Alasdair (1980) *After Virtue*, London, Duckworth.

Mackie, J. L. (1977) *Ethics: Inventing Right and Wrong*, London, Penguin.

Mackie, J. L. (1982) *The Miracle of Theism*, Oxford, Clarendon Press.

McNamara, Paul (1996) 'Making Room for Going beyond the Call', *Mind*.

Martin, Christopher (1994) 'Virtues, Motivation and the End of Life', in L. Gormally, (ed.) *Moral Truth and Moral Tradition: Essays in Honour of Peter Geach and Elizabeth Anscombe*, Dublin, Four Courts Press, 1994.

Mellor, D. H. (1973) 'In defence of dispositions', *Philosophical Review*.

Mellor, D H. (1988) 'On Raising the Chances of Effects', in his *Matters of Metaphysics*, Cambridge, Cambridge University Press, pp. 225–34.

Mellor, D. H. and Crane, Tim (1990) 'There is no question of physicalism', *Mind*.

Mellor, D. H. and Oliver, Alex (1997) (eds) *Properties*, Oxford, Oxford University Press.

Mill, J. S. (1962) *Utilitarianism*, in Warnock, Mary, *Utilitarianism*, London, Fontana.

Mill, J. S. (1973) *A System of Logic*, in *The Collected Works of J. S. Mill*, (ed.) J. M. Robson, London, Routledge.

Millikan, Ruth Garrett (1993) *White Queen Psychology and Other Essays for Alice*, Cambridge, MA, The MIT Press.

Moore, G. E. (1993) *Principia Ethica*, (ed.) Thomas Baldwin, Cambridge, Cambridge University Press.
Mulgan, Tim (1993) 'Slote's Satisficing Consequentialism', *Ratio*.
Murdoch, Iris (1970) *The Sovereignty of Good*, London, Routledge.
Nagel, Thomas (1986) *The View from Nowhere*, Oxford, Oxford University Press.
Nozick, Robert (1974) *Anarchy, State and Utopia*, Oxford, Blackwell.
Nozick, Robert (1981) *Philosophical Explanations*, Oxford, Oxford University Press.
Nussbaum, Martha Craven (1986) *The Fragility of Goodness*, Cambridge, Cambridge University Press.
Nussbaum, Martha Craven (1990) *Love's Knowledge*, Cambridge, Cambridge University Press.
Oderberg, D. and Laing, J. (1997) (eds) *Human Lives: Critical Essays on Consequentialist Bioethics*, London, Macmillan.
O'Neill, Onora (1989), *Constructions of Reason*, Cambridge, Cambridge University Press.
Owens, David (1992) *Causes and Coincidences*, Cambridge, Cambridge University Press.
Parfit, Derek (1973) 'Personal Identity', *The Philosophical Review*.
Parfit, Derek (1987) *Reasons and Persons*, Oxford, Clarendon Press.
Parfit, Derek (1997) 'Reason and Motivation', *Proceedings of the Aristotelian Society* (Supplement).
Peacocke, C. A. B. (1997) 'Metaphysical Necessity', *Mind*.
Plato, *Protagoras*, and Plato, *The Republic*, (1900–7) in *Platonis Opera*, (ed.) J. Burnet, Oxford, Clarendon Press.
Pope, Alexander (1956) *Essay on Man*, in Pope, *Poetical Works*, (ed.) A. D. Ward, London, Macmillan.
Prior, Arthur (1959) 'Thank goodness that's over', *Philosophy*.
Quine, W. V. O. (1953) *From a Logical Point of View*, Cambridge, MA., Harvard University Press.
Rachels, James (1986) *The End of Life*, Oxford, Oxford University Press.
Rawls, John (1973) *A Theory of Justice*, Oxford, Oxford University Press.
Raz, J. (ed.) (1978) *Practical Reasoning*, Oxford, Oxford University Press.
Raz, Joseph (1984) 'Right-based moralities', in Waldron, J. (ed.) *Theories of Rights*, Oxford, Oxford University Press.
Raz, Joseph (1986) *The Morality of Freedom*, Oxford, Clarendon Press.
Raz, Joseph (1997) 'The active and the passive', *Proceedings of the Aristotelian Society* (Supplement).
Rorty, Amélie (1992) 'The advantages of moral diversity', in Paul, Miller and Paul, (eds) *The Good Life and the Human Good*, Cambridge, Cambridge University Press.
Royce, Josiah (1908) *The Philosophy of Loyalty*, New York, Macmillan.
Ryle, Gilbert (1954) 'Pleasure', *Proceedings of the Aristotelian Society*.
Sanford, David (1995) 'Causation', in Sosa, E. and Kim, J. (eds) *Blackwell Companion to Metaphysics*, Oxford, Blackwell.
Sartre, J.-P. (1958) *Being and Nothingness*, (tr.) H. Barnes, London, Methuen.
Sartre, J.-P. (1965) *Nausea*, London, Penguin.
Shakespeare, William (1978) *The Complete Works*, (ed.) Peter Alexander, London, Collins.
Sidgwick, H. (1893) *The Methods of Ethics* (5th edn) London, Macmillan.
Singer, Peter (1993) *Practical Ethics*, Cambridge, Cambridge University Press.
Skorupski, John (1989) *John Stuart Mill*, London, Routledge.
Slote, Michael (1983) *Goods and Virtues*, Oxford, Clarendon Press.
Smart, J. J. C., and Williams, Bernard, (1993) *Utilitarianism: for and against*, Cambridge, Cambridge University Press.
Sophocles (1979) *Antigone*, ed. R. Dawe, Leipzig, Teubner.
Sorabji, R. (1980) *Necessity, Cause and Blame*, London, Duckworth.
Steiner, Hillel (1996) 'Duty-Free Zones', *Proceedings of the Aristotelian Society*.
Taylor, Charles (1989) *Sources of the Self*, Cambridge, Cambridge University Press.
Teichman, Jenny (1985) 'The Definition of Person', *Philosophy*.
Teichman, Jenny (1997) *Social Ethics*, Oxford, Blackwell.
Tooley, Michael (1972) 'Abortion and infanticide', *Philosophy and Public Affairs*.
Urmson, J. O. (1975) 'Intuitionism', *Proceedings of the Aristotelian Society*.
Warnock, Mary (1962) *Utilitarianism*, (includes selections from Bentham and Austin) London, Fontana.
Wiggins, David (1968) *Identity and Spatiotemporal Continuity*, Oxford, Blackwell.
Wiggins, David (1980) *Sameness and Substance*, Oxford, Blackwell.

Wiggins, David (1987) *Needs, Values, Truth*, Oxford, Blackwell.

Williams, Bernard (1965) 'Ethical Consistency', *Proceedings of the Aristotelian Society*.

Williams, Bernard (1966) 'Consistency and Realism', *Proceedings of the Aristotelian Society*.

Williams, Bernard (1973) 'The Makropoulos Case: Reflections on the Tedium of Immortality', in Williams, Bernard, *Problems of the Self*, Cambridge, Cambridge University Press.

Williams, Bernard (1981) *Moral Luck*, Cambridge, Cambridge University Press.

Williams, Bernard (1985) *Ethics and the Limits of Philosophy*, London, Fontana.

Williams, Bernard (1986) 'Hylomorphism', *Oxford Studies in Ancient Philosophy*.

Williams, Bernard (1995) 'Moral Incapacity', *Proceedings of the Aristotelian Society*.

Wilson, Edward O. (1992) *The Diversity of Life*, London, Penguin.

Wittgenstein, Ludwig (1958) *Philosophical Investigations*, Oxford, Blackwell.

Wittgenstein, Ludwig (1961) *Tractatus Logico-Philosophicus*, London, Routledge.

Wolf, Susan (1982) 'Moral Saints', *Journal of Philosophy*.

Yeats, William Butler (1955) *Collected Poems*, London, Macmillan.

Index